Diversity

Strength

Readers featured in the "Longman Topics" series include:

A Longman Topics Reader

Diversity

Strength and Struggle

JOSEPH CALABRESE

SUSAN TCHUDI
University of Nevada, Reno

PEARSON
Longman

New York   San Francisco   Boston
London   Toronto   Sydney   Tokyo   Singapore   Madrid
Mexico City   Munich   Paris   Cape Town   Hong Kong   Montreal

Acquisitions Editor: Brandon Hight
Marketing Manager: Alexandra Smith
Production Manager: Donna DeBenedictis
Project Coordination, Text Design, and Electronic Page Makeup:
    GGS Book Services
Cover Design Manager: John Callahan
Cover Photo: © Flip Schulke/CORBIS
Manufacturing Manager: Mary Fischer
Printer and Binder: RR Donnelley & Sons Company/Harrisonburg
Cover Printer: Coral Graphics Services

For permission to use copyrighted material, grateful acknowledgment is made to the copyright holders on pp. 225–227, which are hereby made part of this copyright page.

Library of Congress Cataloging-in-Publication Data

Calabrese, Joseph T.
    Diversity : strength and struggle / Joseph Calabrese, Susan Tchudi, [editors].
        p. cm. — (A Longman topics reader)
    ISBN 0-321-31731-9
        1. Pluralism (Social sciences)—United States. 2. United States—Race relations. 3. Ethnicity—United States. 4. Stereotype (Psychology)—United States. I. Tchudi, Susan. II. Title. III. Longman topics.

E184.A1C28 2005
305.8'00973—dc22

                                                    2005044358

Please visit our website at http://www.ablongman.com

ISBN 0-321-31731-9

2 3 4 5 6 7 8 9 10—DOH—08 07 06

This book is dedicated to the Southern Poverty Law Center, the NAACP, and all those people who are working toward that day when "justice rolls down like waters and righteousness like a mighty stream."

PREFACE

Diversity: Strength and Struggle, a collection of essays (and one play), encourages an examination of diversity in America, in order to understand what both enriches and threatens the country's core values "of liberty and justice for all." Americans, on the one hand, are proud of the strengths of the diverse cultures that make up the United States. On the other hand, however, that same diversity has created—and continues to create—struggle and division. The pieces included here provide opportunities for students to examine accounts of the impact of "racial" and "ethnic" identity on diverse groups, some of them challenging the notion of race as a meaningful category for thinking about human identity. Identity includes complex factors—superficial factors, such as the color of hair and skin or the shape of features, or more meaningful factors, such as a common culture, shared values, religious traditions. Although Americans strive to be a nation that values our diverse identities, we often find that attention to racial and ethnic difference leads not only to unflattering stereotypes but also to exclusion and injustice.

Authors included in this collection write about the personal and political aspects of racial and ethnic identity in a variety of ways: They describe experiences and feelings of exclusion; they satirize stereotyping; they analyze the sources of alienation; they demonstrate how injustice based on stereotyping occurs; they argue for changes that will ensure inclusion. We have included this range of arguments, analyses, experiences, and feelings on the assumption that understanding leads to improved relationships among people who—while they have different histories and cultures—share the value of an inclusive and democratic society.

Many writers are included here, among them young people and old people, men and women—Americans of African, Hispanic, Asian, Arab, Jewish, Western European, and American Indian ethnicities, some of them new immigrants, some of them from families who have lived in the United States for generations. These writers do not necessarily share the same opinions about issues of race and ethnicity in America, but all of them agree that a diverse

ix

country such as this one has the potential for division, but also for the achievement of central American values—inclusiveness, justice, and equality. All groups want to feel that they are safe, that they have access to education and prosperity, are treated equally under the law. All want the liberty to demonstrate who they are without being maligned or misrepresented by racial and ethnic stereotypes that have been shaped by inveterate prejudices or contemporary media and popular culture.

We have divided the book into five chapters that highlight the issues our country faces in creating a truly multicultural society. Chapter 1, "Americans' Complex Identities," focuses on the notion of a simplistic ethnic and racial identity. In fact, the United States is, in some ways, becoming the "melting pot" it has frequently claimed to be. As people marry outside their ethnic and racial groups, it is no longer possible to manufacture easy stereotypes that categorize people. Moreover, many racial and ethnic groups compromise the culture of their ethnic origins to assimilate more easily into American culture. Issues of identity become increasingly complex under these circumstances. Chapter 2, "Reflections and Distortions in the Media and Popular Culture," includes essays that demonstrate the difficulty of countering prevalent images reproduced in entertainment and media. Stereotypes of the violent street-smart African American man, the Asian American technological genius, the drunken American Indian have been used over and over again in American films and television, making it difficult for viewers to avoid absorbing these worn-out and cruel images. The writers in Chapter 3, "Confinement Within Stereotypes," describe the difficulty one has breaking down established stereotypes. They describe how—despite their efforts to the contrary—they continue to be limited by the views that others have of them. In Chapter 4, "The Reality of the Personal," authors tell stories—sometimes painful ones—about their own direct experience. These people find that it takes a strong sense of self to counter feelings of alienation produced by the insensitivity of prejudiced policies and people. In Chapter 5, "Enduring Discrimination: Miles to Go, Promises to Keep," we present discussions of the political realities of ongoing racism in the United States. It is not enough to acknowledge that racial and ethnic bias still occurs in our country, these essays argue; people must work to eliminate the injustice that confines and alienates those who are perceived as "different."

The following features of this book are designed to engage students in reading, discussing, writing, and researching further on the issues of race and ethnicity in America:

- Each chapter includes readings about contemporary issues in race and ethnicity that vary in length and difficulty. While some were written within the past 15 years, many have been written in the past two to three.
- The essays represent a range of views from men and women, young and old, and a wide range of races and ethnicities.
- Each chapter begins with quotations taken from the essays and a brief introduction to the issues discussed in the chapter.
- Each reading includes an introduction that situates the piece and a brief biographical summary, including other works by the author.
- Following each reading selection are three to six questions—"For discussion and writing"—that represent different levels of reading response: literal, interpretive, analytical, and personal analogies.
- Each chapter ends with a "Reading, Research, and Writing" section, a list of five or six ideas for further reading, research, and writing.

ACKNOWLEDGMENTS

We would like to thank Joseph Opiela for helping us define this project in a way that makes it, we believe, an interesting and useful text; Brandon Hight, who faithfully shepherded the book through production; and Eden Kram, who answered many, many questions throughout the process. We also acknowledge the reviewers: Anne Bliss, Colorado University-Boulder; Leigh H. Edwards, Florida State University; Melissa Fiesta, California State University, Long Beach; Carol Henderson, University of Delaware; Joyce Marie Miller, Collin County Community College; Jim Murphy, Southern Illinois University Edwardsville; Dolores Quiles, Ulster Country Community College; Rashidah Shakir, Los Angeles Trade Technical College; Frank X Walker, Eastern Kentucky University.

JOSEPH CALABRESE
SUSAN TCHUDI

What Is Race For?

The concept of race is anything but new, and it has characterized and plagued many cultures besides ours. In India, China,
and even ancient Egypt, people have sorted each other according
to physical differences. Notions of race have certainly been part
of America, right from the start. Colonists defined "Indians" as a
separate people, and from 1619 Africans in America were seen as
a different and, in fact, inferior race. Colonial and national laws
have from our earliest days sorted citizens and noncitizens by
race, with virtually no questions raised about the validity of the
concept of race.

In the 18th century, Carolus Linnaeus sorted humans into
four groups, and other scientists of the day soon expanded on his
simple scheme to place people into racial categories. Sometimes,
the sorting was done by physical features, the most obvious being
skin color, but scientists also used hair texture, eye color, head
shape, and other characteristics to arrive at groupings. Soon
enough, people began to describe the behavior and aptitude of
the various "color" groups. Yellow people were good imitators,
white people were innovators, brown people had markedly less
intellectual capacity, and so on. All this sorting wasn't just an academic exercise either. Our country's laws and customs handed out
privilege and also punishments based on racial identity. But was
the science behind the sorting valid?

It soon becomes apparent to even casual observers that experience immediately contradicts racial orderings. First, some of the
so-called inferior people proved superior in many ways, and the
"more talented" groups included plenty of nonstarters in the race
for success. Take the claims for the intellectual superiority of

white Europeans, and the related claims for the mental limitations of Africans. Frederick Douglass, William Wells Brown, and Olaudah Equiano all wrote and spoke so well that they were able to win large audiences and gain a living from their efforts. Former slaves, they were clear proof that Africans could compete with the most gifted whites intellectually, and they were only the most well-known examples. After emancipation, thousands of former slaves went on to study medicine, law, and the arts. Clearly, the "science" that determined their inferiority was mistaken. Second, the biological categories break down because of a simple fact: Groups intermingle. They always have. As long ago as the 19th century, the escaped slave Frederick Douglass called attention to a blurring of lines between blacks and whites: "Every year brings with it multitudes of this [interracial] class of slaves . . . for thousands are ushered into this world, annually, who, like myself, owe their existence to white fathers, and those fathers most frequently their own masters." Whatever else one might believe about racial categories, it is plain that biology recognizes no barrier at all between various human groups.

Intermarriage has complicated racial identity in ways that might even boggle Douglass. Consider the obstacles to simplistic racial sorting posed by such people as Tiger Woods, who once referred to himself as Cablinasian. As Gary Kamiya reports it (at http://www.salon.com),

> [W]hen he was asked if it bothered him to be called an African-American, "It does," he said. "Growing up, I came up with this name: I'm a 'Cablinasian.'" As in Caucasian-black-Indian-Asian. Woods has a black father (or to be precise, if I am interpreting Woods' reported ancestry correctly, a half-black, one-quarter American Indian, one-quarter white father) and a Thai mother (or, with the same caveat, a half-Thai, half-Chinese mother). "I'm just who I am," Woods told Oprah Winfrey, "whoever you see in front of you."

Woods insisted on breaking with traditional, brutally simplistic racial categories when identifying himself. Many people have objected to those old labels both because they connote negative traits assigned during our racially intolerant past and because they are simply inaccurate. Think of a hypothetical but plausible case. A woman might be descended from Thai and Korean parents, and then marry a man whose father was Native American and Irish. A simplistic label for their children would be nonwhite, as if to say that white is the measure of all identity. This is the solution, in fact, of many racist groups. The good people are Aryan, the rest aren't. Period. It is a simple claim that appeals to many people who crave certainty in life. But it is false in fundamental ways as Robert Carroll points out in these remarks quoted at http://www.skeptic.com:

> "There's about a 15 percent genetic variation between any two individuals," according to science writer Deborah Blum. "Less than half of that, about 6 percent, is accounted for by known racial groupings. . . . A randomly selected white person, therefore, can easily be genetically closer to an African than another white."

DNA undermines the racial schemes of neo-Nazis. It provides a glimpse into the amazing complexity of ancestral makeup. We live in a world of people with complex backgrounds and the old schemes of four races or of white/nonwhite identity simply don't reflect reality.

It may be helpful to set aside the term "race" and to think instead about ethnicity, a more comprehensive and less problematic term. "What determines one's identity?" "Who decides how individual people are to be identified?" We could just ignore such questions and not talk about the issues. Some people think that if we don't talk about race, it will eventually just not matter. But Americans are not silent on the question, as a brief reading of any city newspaper will show. We argue over affirmative action; some people insist on censoring books that refer to race; some people defend racial profiling, others condemn it. Politicians get voted out of office or out of positions of power for racist remarks. Web sites urge white unity, brown power, black nationalism. It is unrealistic to expect silence on matters of race any time soon. It seems, in fact, wise to consider the issues, to hear from people who have grappled with problems of identity and the politics of race, to think carefully about the practical and philosophical issues involved in race relations. The essays collected in this volume offer views on some pressing questions of diversity in America. The book is meant as an invitation to think and speak about what may well be the single most significant fact about America—its diversity.

CHAPTER 1

Americans' Complex Identities

We were to stay with our own—that was the code—though we mixed some in the lunch line, in a few classes, on the football field, and in gym. We segregated ourselves.

Garrett Hongo

Scientists who doubt the meaningfulness of race are not nihilists. They just prefer another way of capturing, and explaining, the great diversity of humankind.

Sharon Begley

In our culture there is a long tradition, as well as a continuing tendency, to categorize people by race, and usually this means sorting people by "color" into one of five groups: black, yellow, brown, white, and red. This simplistic color scheme persists despite the increasing complexity of Americans' racial and ethnic identities. Our awareness of this complexity and of the inadequacy of the old schemes is reflected in responses to the 2000 census in our country. Approximately 6.8 million respondents refused to be grouped singly, preferring to be identified with two or more of the form's five major groups.

The readings in this chapter emphasize such complexity and also underscore the illogic and hazards of the conventional color divisions. Sharon Begley argues that grouping people by "primary colors" is deeply misleading. Race may reside in something other than skin color. It is, she argues, just as easy to group people by other shared genetic features. "If you divide humankind by which of two forms of the [hemoglobin] gene each person has, then equatorial Africans, Italians and Greeks fall into the 'sickle-cell race'; Swedes and South Africa's Xhosas (Nelson Mandela's ethnic group) are in the healthy-hemoglobin race." But even if people insist that color is the all-defining characteristic, how are we to think sensibly about the many ethnic groups lumped together under "brown"? As soon as we think we have isolated a group, internal variations arise that make the category trivial. Moreover, the people we group roughly often claim a more complex identity than we see. In "Being an Other," Melissa Algranati reveals that "throughout my whole life, people have mistaken me for other ethnic backgrounds rather than for what I really am." Those backgrounds are Puerto Rican, Egyptian, and Jewish. Such complex heritage provokes hateful responses from extremists who regard it as "mongrelization." Each group must maintain its purity, these people argue, even though this notion of purity flies in the face of centuries of interracial and interethnic marriage.

It isn't only white supremacists and other extremist groups who try to police the boundaries of ethnic groups. As Garrett Hongo notes, when he began a romantic relation with a Portuguese girl in his high school, he kept it secret. "We couldn't be seen together." They went to Chicano dances, both of them "passing for Chicanos," at least for awhile. His Japanese schoolmates discovered that he had crossed boundaries and they beat him up. "I paid for my naiveté with a bashing I still feel today. . . . Separated societies police their own separations." Jeanne Wakatsuki Houston survived internment in Manzanar, one of a dozen or so federal "relocation" camps where Japanese Americans were imprisoned during World War II, solely because they were of Japanese ancestry, and despite the fact of their U.S. citizenship. After that experience, she tried to live in Caucasian society, and faced difficulties in both cultures, particularly after she married a "blond samurai," a Caucasian man, in 1957. Each culture has its expectations that, while they don't amount to an aggressive policing of boundaries, still cause her many difficulties. Her children live in a world that remains suspicious of biracial people, and she hopes "that they have inherited a strong will to survive, that essential trait ethnic minorities in this country have so sharply honed." Perhaps these skills will diminish in importance as our national makeup continues to diversify. Bharati Mukherjee describes her history as a young woman, from being an "exotic" student from Calcutta and the Bengali-Hindu tradition that "forbade intercaste, interlanguage, interethnic marriages" to becoming an American citizen married to a Canadian man. In making the transition from expatriate to immigrant, Mukherjee takes her position as an American citizen "very seriously." She argues that America and Americans must reject the notion of "cultural balkanization" and hyphenations such as "Asian-American" that categorize "the cultural landscape into a center and its peripheries." This position has proved controversial among ethnic Americans who wish to maintain their ethnic identities. The chapter's final reading, "Ethnicity and Identity: Creating a Sense of Self," by Claire S. Chow, raises the possibility that, in fact, people choose their identity for themselves. They inherit possibilities from their parents, and as they grow in a culture, they create a sense of self, sometimes in protest against the identity thrust on them by others.

According to U.S. government figures, by the year 2030 at least 25 percent of the population will be either Hispanic or Asian, and less than 60 percent Anglo. Already there are, according to official reports, 25 major American cities that fit this mix (http://usinfo. state.gov/journals/itsv/0699/ijse/frey.htm). Think of all the subheadings in the Hispanic and Asian groups. The first includes, among others, people from Central America, the Caribbean, Mexico, and South America. Within these groups there are centuries of diverse bondings. Asians, too, comprise many different ethnic groups. Thai and Korean peoples would not think to lump themselves in a single category, much less a color-coded "yellow" category that masks robust variety. As you read the essays here, try to imagine the struggles each writer attests to, and try to bring into focus the attitudes that they decry, which no longer fit the reality of life in our country.

Three Is Not Enough

SHARON BEGLEY

Sharon Begley, a senior science writer for Newsweek *since 1990, was named senior editor of that magazine in 1996. She has won numerous awards for her science stories including a Clarion Award from the Association for Women in Communications for "Your Child's Brain"; an Educational Press Association's Distinguished Achievement Award for "The Puzzle of Genius"; and the Aviation/Space Writers Association Premier for "Doomsday Science." In the following article, from a 1995* Newsweek *issue with a cover story asking "What Color Is Black?," Begley reviews scientific theories about the nature of race, concluding that many scientists "doubt the biological meaningfulness of race."*

———————— ✦ ————————

To most Americans race is as plain as the color of the nose on your face. Sure, some light-skinned blacks, in some neighborhoods, are taken for Italians, and some Turks are confused with Argentines. But even in the children of biracial couples, racial ancestry is writ large—in the hue of the skin and the shape of the lips, the size of the brow and the bridge of the nose. It is no harder to trace than it is to judge which basic colors in a box of Crayolas were combined to make tangerine or burnt umber. Even with racial mixing, the existence of primary races is as obvious as the existence of primary colors.

Or is it? C. Loring Brace has his own ideas about where race resides, and it isn't in skin color. If our eyes could perceive more than the superficial, we might find race in chromosome 11: there lies the gene for hemoglobin. If you divide humankind by which of two forms of the gene each person has, then equatorial Africans, Italians and Greeks fall into the "sickle-cell race"; Swedes and South Africa's Xhosas (Nelson Mandela's ethnic group) are in the healthy-hemoglobin race. Or do you prefer to group people by whether they have epicanthic eye folds, which produce the "Asian" eye? Then the !Kung San (Bushmen) belong with the Japanese and Chinese. Depending on which trait you choose to demarcate races, "you won't get anything that remotely tracks conventional [race] categories," says anthropologist Alan Goodman, dean of natural science at Hampshire College.

The notion of race is under withering attack for political and cultural reasons—not to mention practical ones like what to label the child of a Ghanaian and a Norwegian. But scientists got there first. Their doubts about the conventional racial categories—black, white, Asian—have nothing to do with a sappy "we are all the same" ideology. Just the reverse. "Human variation is very, very real," says Goodman. "But race, as a way of organizing [what we know about the variation], is incredibly simplified and bastardized." Worse, it does not come close to explaining the astounding diversity of humankind—not its origins, not its extent, not its meaning. "There is no organizing principle by which you could put 5 billion people into so few categories in a way that would tell you anything important about humankind's diversity," says Michigan's Brace, who will lay out the case against race at the annual meeting of the American Association for the Advancement of Science.

About 70 percent of cultural anthropologists, and half of physical anthropologists, reject race as a biological category, according to a 1989 survey by Central Michigan University anthropologist Leonard Liebermnan and colleagues. The truths of science are not decided by majority vote, of course. Empirical evidence, woven into a theoretical whole, is what matters. The threads of the argument against the standard racial categories:

5 • **Genes:** In 1972, population biologist Richard Lewontin of Harvard University laid out the genetic case against race. Analyzing 17 genetic markers in 168 populations such as Austrians, Thais and Apaches, he found that there is more genetic difference within one race than there is between that race and another. Only 6.3 percent of the genetic differences could be explained by the individuals' belonging to different races. That is, if you pick at random any two "blacks" walking along the street, and analyze their 23 pairs of chromosomes, you will probably find that their genes have less in common than do the genes of one of them with that of a random "white" person. Last year the Human Genome Diversity Project used 1990s genetics to extend Lewontin's analysis. Its conclusion: genetic variation from one individual to another of the same "race" swamps the average differences between racial groupings. The more we learn about humankind's genetic differences, says geneticist Luca Cavalli-Sforza of Stanford University, who chairs the committee that directs the biodiversity project, the more we see that they have almost nothing to do with what we call race.

• **Traits:** As sickle-cell "races" and epicanthic-fold "races" show, there are as many ways to group people as there are traits. That is because "racial" traits are what statisticians call non-concordant. Lack of concordance means that sorting people according to *these* traits produces different groupings than you get in sorting them by *those* (equally valid) traits. When biologist Jared Diamond of UCLA surveyed half a dozen traits for a recent issue of *Discover* magazine, he found that, depending on which traits you pick, you can form very surprising "races." Take the scooped-out shape of the back of the front teeth, a standard "Asian" trait. Native Americans and Swedes have these shovel-shaped incisors, too, and so would fall in the same race. Is biochemistry better? Norwegians, Arabians, north Indians and the Fulani of northern Nigeria, notes Diamond, fall into the "lactase race" (the lactase enzyme digests milk sugar). Everyone else—other Africans, Japanese, Native Americans—forms the "lactase-deprived race" (their ancestors did not drink milk from cows or goats and hence never evolved the lactase gene). How about blood types, the familiar A, B and O groups? Then Germans and New Guineans, populations that have the same percentages of each type, are in one race; Estonians and Japanese comprise a separate one for the same reason, notes anthropologist Jonathan Marks of Yale University. Depending on which traits are chosen, "we could place Swedes in the same race as either Xhosas, Fulani, the Ainu of Japan or Italians," writes Diamond.

- **Subjectivity:** If race is a valid biological concept, anyone in any culture should be able to look at any individual and say, Aha, you are a . . . It should not be the case, as French tennis star Yannick Noah said a few years ago, that "in Africa I am white, and in France I am black" (his mother is French and his father is from Cameroon). "While biological traits give the impression that race is a biological unit of nature," says anthropologist George Armelagos of Emory University, "it remains a cultural construct. The boundaries between races depends on the classifier's own cultural norms."
- **Evolution:** Scholars who believe in the biological validity of race argue that the groupings reflect human pre-history. That is, populations that evolved together, and separately from others constitute a race. This school of thought holds that blacks should all be in one race because they are descended from people who stayed on the continent where humanity began. Asians, epitomized by the Chinese, should be another race because they are the children of groups who walked north and east until they reached the Pacific. Whites of the pale, blond variety should be another because their ancestors filled Europe. Because of their appearance, these populations represent the extremes, the archetypes, of human diversity—the reds, blues and yellows from which you can make every other hue.

"But if you use these archetypes as your groups you have classified only a very tiny proportion of the world's people, which is
not very useful," says Marks, whose incisive new book "Human
Biodiversity" deconstructs race. "Also, as people walked out of
Africa, they were differentiating along the way. Equating 'extreme' with 'primordial' is not supported by history."

Often, shared traits are a sign of shared heritage—racial heritage. "Shared traits are not random," says Alice Brues, an anthropologist at the University of Colorado. "Within a continent, you of
course have a number of variants [on basic traits], but some are
characteristic of the larger area, too. So it's natural to look for
these major divisions. It simplifies your thinking." A wide distribution of traits, however, makes them suspect as evidence of a
shared heritage. The dark skin of Somalis and Ghanaians, for instance, indicates that they evolved under the same elective force (a
sunny climate). But that's all it shows. It does *not* show that they
are any more closely related, in the sense of sharing more genes,
than either is to Greeks. Calling Somalis and Ghanaians "black"
therefore sheds no further light on their evolutionary history and
implies—wrongly—that they are more closely related to each
other than either is to someone of a different "race." Similarly, the
long noses of North Africans and northern Europeans reveal that
they evolved in dry or cold climates (the nose moistens air before
the air reaches the lungs, and longer noses moisten more air). The
tall, thin bodies of Kenya's Masai evolved to dissipate heat; Eski-
mos evolved short, squat bodies to retain it. Calling these peoples
"different races" adds nothing to that understanding.

10   Where did the three standard racial divisions come from?
They entered the social, and scientific, consciousness during the
Age of Exploration. Loring Brace doesn't think it's a coincidence
that the standard races represent peoples who, as he puts it, "lived
at the end of the Europeans' trade routes"—in Africa and China—
in the days after Prince Henry the Navigator set sail. Before Europeans took to the seas, there was little perception of races. If
villagers began to look different to an Englishman riding a horse
from France to Italy and on to Greece, the change was too subtle
to inspire notions of races. But if the English sailor left Lisbon
Harbor and dropped anchor off the Kingdom of Niger, people
looked so different he felt compelled to invent a scheme to explain
the world—and, perhaps, distance himself from the Africans.

This habit of sorting the world's peoples into a small number of groups got its first scientific gloss from Swedish taxonomist Carolus Linnaeus. (Linnaeus is best known for his system of classifying living things by genus and species—*Escherichia coli, Homo sapiens* and the rest.) In 1758 he declared that humanity falls into four races: white (Europeans), red (Native Americans), dark (Asians), and black (Africans). Linnaeus said that Native Americans (who in the 1940s got grouped with Asians) were ruled by custom. Africans were indolent and negligent, and Europeans were inventive and gentle, said Linnaeus. Leave aside the racist undertones (not to mention the oddity of ascribing gentleness to the group that perpetrated the Crusades and Inquisition): that alone should not undermine its validity. More worrisome is that the notion and the specifics of race predate genetics, evolutionary biology and the science of human origins. With the revolutions in those fields, how is it that the 18th-century scheme of race retains its powerful hold? Consider these arguments:

- **If I parachute into Nairobi, I know I'm not in Oslo:** Colorado's Alice Brues uses this image to argue that denying the reality of race flies in the face of common sense. But the parachutists, if they were familiar with the great range of human diversity, could also tell that they were in Nairobi rather than Abidjan—east Africans don't look much like west Africans. They could also tell they were in Istanbul rather than Oslo, even though Turks and Norwegians are both called Caucasian.
- **DOA, male, 58119 . . . black:** When U.S. police call in a forensic anthropologist to identify the race of a skeleton, the scientist comes through 80 to 85 percent of the time. If race has no biological validity, how can the sleuths get it right so often? The forensic anthropologist could, with enough information about bone structure and genetic markers, identify the region from which the corpse came—south and west Africa, Southeast Asia and China, Northern and Western Europe. It just so happens that the police would call corpses from the first two countries black, from the middle two Asian, and the last pair white. But lumping these six distinct populations into three groups of two serves no biological purpose, only a social convention. The larger grouping may reflect how society views humankind's diversity, but does not explain it.

• **African-Americans have more hypertension:** If race is not
   real, how can researchers say that blacks have higher rates of
   infant mortality, lower rates of osteoporosis and a higher incidence of hypertension? Because a social construct can have
   biological effects, says epidemiologist Robert Hahn of the
   U.S. Centers for Disease Control and Prevention. Consider
   hypertension among African-Americans. Roughly 34 percent
   have high blood pressure, compared with about 16 percent of
   whites. But William Dressler finds the greatest incidence of
   hypertension among blacks who are upwardly mobile achievers. "That's probably because in mundane interactions, from
   the bank to the grocery store, they are treated in ways that do
   not coincide with their self-image as respectable achievers,"
   says Dressler, an anthropologist at the University of Alabama.
   "And the upwardly mobile are more likely to encounter discriminatory white culture." Lab studies show that stressful
   situations—like being followed in grocery stores as if you
   were a shoplifter—elevate blood pressure and lead to vascular
   changes that cause hypertension. "In this case, race captures
   social factors such as the experience of discrimination," says
   sociologist David Williams of the University of Michigan.
   Further evidence that hypertension has more to do with society than with biology: black Africans have among the lowest
   rates of hypertension in the world.

15   If race is not a biological explanation of hypertension, can it
offer a biological explanation of something as complex as intelligence? Psychologists are among the strongest proponents of retaining the three conventional racial categories. It organizes and
explains their data in the most parsimonious way, as Charles
Murray and Richard Herrnstein argue in "The Bell Curve." But
anthropologists say that such conclusions are built on a foundation of sand. If nothing else, argues Brace, every ethnic group
evolved under conditions where intelligence was a requirement
for survival. If there are intelligence "genes," they must be in all
ethnic groups equally: differences in intelligence must be a cultural and social artifact.

Scientists who doubt the biological meaningfulness of race are
not nihilists. They just prefer another way of capturing, and explaining, the great diversity of humankind. Even today most of the

world's peoples marry within their own group. Intramarriage pre-
serves features—fleshy lips, small ears, wide-set eyes—that arose
by a chance genetic mutation long ago. Grouping people by geographic origins—better known as ethnicity—"is more correct both
in a statistical sense and in understanding the history of human
variation," says Hampshire's Goodman. Ethnicity also serves as a
proxy for differences—from diet to a history of discrimination—
that can have real biological and behavioral effects.

In a 1942 book, anthropologist Ashley Montagu called race
"Man's Most Dangerous Myth." If it is, then our most ingenuous
myth must be that we sort humankind into groups in order to understand the meaning and origin of humankind's diversity. That
isn't the reason at all; a greater number of smaller groupings, like
ethnicities, does a better job. The obsession with broad categories
is so powerful as to seem a neurological imperative. Changing our
thinking about race will require a revolution in thought as profound, and profoundly unsettling, as anything science has ever
demanded. What these researchers are talking about is changing
the way in which we see the world—and each other. But before
that can happen, we must do more than understand the biologist's suspicions about race. We must ask science, also, why it is
that we are so intent on sorting humanity into so few groups—us
and Other—in the first place.

For Discussion and Writing

1. What distinction does Begley make between race and ethnicity in this article? Why does she think ethnic grouping is superior to racial grouping in ac-
   counting for people's similarities and differences? How does this square
   with scientists' views of grouping?
2. What are some of the complications that occur when cataloguers try to slot
   people into particular groups? Develop a new system for categorizing people. What traits, histories, habits, and so on might you use to create your
   categories? Using your system, try categorizing the students in your class.
   What are the strengths and weaknesses of your system of categories?
3. Describe your own racial and ethnic background. What qualities do you have
   that you believe are attributable to racial influences? To ethnic or cultural
   influences? How might your family's history influence your physical attributes? What else might influence your biological makeup?
4. If scientists are right, that biological definitions of race are meaningless,
   why do you suppose there is so much stereotyping on the basis of race and

sometimes ethnicity? Account for the ease with which people make generalizations on the basis of race. How might Begley respond to these generalizations?

5. Begley's strategy is to list major arguments supporting the concept of race. How well does she do in refuting these? Discuss other arguments you have heard that seek to support the validity of the concept of race.

Being an Other

MELISSA ALGRANATI

Melissa Algranati's essay is taken from a collection of essays— Becoming American, Becoming Ethnic—*written by college students exploring their historical roots. Identifying herself as an "inter-ethnic" child, Algranati describes being faced with a standardized exam asking her who she is, feeling "lost in a world of classification," and having to become "the other."*

───────── ✦ ─────────

Throughout my whole life, people have mistaken me for other ethnic backgrounds rather than for what I really am. I learned at a young age that there are not too many Puerto Rican, Egyptian Jews out there. For most of my life I have been living in two worlds, and at the same time I have been living in neither. When I was young I did not realize that I was unique, because my family brought me up with a healthy balance of Puerto Rican and Sephardic customs. It was not until I took the standardized PSAT exam that I was confronted with the question: "Who am I?" I remember the feeling of confusion as I struggled to find the right answer. I was faced with a bad multiple-choice question in which there was only supposed to be one right answer, but more than one answer seemed to be correct. I did not understand how a country built on the concept of diversity could forget about its most diverse group, inter-ethnic children. I felt lost in a world of classification. The only way for me to take pride in who I am was to proclaim myself as an other, yet that leaves out so much. As a product of a marriage only a country like America could create, I would now try to help people understand what it is like to be a member of the most underrepresented group in the country, the "others."

My father, Jacques Algranati, was born in Alexandria, Egypt. As a Sephardic Jew, my father was a minority in a predominantly Arab world. Although in the minority, socially my father was a member of the upper middle class and lived a very comfortable life. As a result of strong French influence in the Middle Eastern Jewish world, my father attended a French private school. Since Arabic was the language of the lower class, the Algranati family spoke French as their first language. My whole family is polyglot, speaking languages from the traditional Sephardic tongue of Ladino to Turkish and Greek. My grandfather spoke seven languages. Basically, my father grew up in a close-knit Sephardic community surrounded by family and friends.

However, in 1960 my father's world came to a halt when he was faced with persecution on an institutional level. As a result of the Egyptian-Israeli conflict, in 1956 an edict was issued forcing all foreign-born citizens and Jews out of Egypt. Although my father was a native-born citizen of the country, because of a very strong anti-Jewish sentiment, his citizenship meant nothing. So in 1960 when my family got their exit visas, as Jews had done since the time of the Inquisition, they packed up and left the country as one large family group.

Unable to take many possessions or much money with them, my father's family, like many Egyptian Jews, immigrated to France. They proceeded to France because they had family who were able to sponsor them. Also, once in France my family hoped to be able to receive a visa to America much sooner, since French immigration quotas to the United States were much higher than those in Egypt. Once in France my family relied on the generosity of a Jewish organization, the United Jewish Appeal. For nine months my father lived in a hotel sponsored by the United Jewish Appeal and attended French school until the family was granted a visa to the United States.

Since my father's oldest brother came to the United States first with his wife, they were able to sponsor the rest of the family's passage over. The Algranati family eventually settled in Forest Hills, Queens. Like most immigrants, my family settled in a neighborhood filled with immigrants of the same background. Once in the United States, my father rejoined many of his old friends from Egypt, since most Egyptian Jewish refugees followed a similar immigration path. At the age of fourteen my father and his group of friends were once again forced to adjust to life in a new country, but this time they had to learn a new language in order to survive. Like many of his friends, my father was forced to leave the comforts and luxuries of his world for the hardships of a new world. But as he eloquently puts it, once his family and friends were forced to leave, there was really nothing to stay for.

Like my father, my mother is also an immigrant; however my parents come from very different parts of the world. Born in Maniti, Puerto Rico, my mom spent the first five years of her life in a small town outside of San Juan. Since my grandfather had attended private school in the United States when he was younger, he was relatively proficient in English. Like many immigrants, my grandfather came to the United States first, in order to help establish the family. After securing a job and an apartment, he sent for my grandmother, and three weeks later my mother and her fourteen-year-old sister came.

Puerto Ricans are different from many other people who come to this country, in the sense that legally they are not considered immigrants. Because Puerto Rico is a commonwealth of the United States, Puerto Ricans are granted automatic U.S. citizenship. So unlike most, from the day my mother and her family stepped on U.S. soil they were considered citizens. The only problem was that the difference in language and social status led "real" Americans not to consider them citizens.

As a result of this unique status, my mother faced many hardships in this new country. From the day my mother entered first grade, her process of Americanization had begun. Her identity was transformed. She went from being Maria Louisa Pinto to becoming Mary L. Pinto. Not only was my mother given a new name when she began school, but a new language was forced upon her as well. Confronted by an Irish teacher, Mrs. Walsh, who was determined to Americanize her, my mother began her uphill battle with the English language. Even until this day my mother recalls her traumatic experience when she learned how to pronounce the word "run":

"Repeat after me, run."

10   "Rrrrrrrrrun."

"No. Mary, run."

"Rrrrrrrrrun."

No matter how hard my mother tried she could not stop rolling her "r's." After several similar exchanges Mrs. Walsh, with a look of anger on her face, grabbed my mother's cheeks in her hand and squeezed as she repeated in a stern voice, "RUN!" Suffice it to say my mother learned how to speak English without a Spanish accent. It was because of these experiences that my mother made sure the only language spoken in the house or to me and my sister was English. My parents never wanted their children to experience the pain my mother went through just to learn how to say the word "run."

My mother was confronted with discrimination not only from American society but also from her community. While in the United States, my mother lived in a predominantly Spanish community. On first coming to this country her family lived in a tenement in the Bronx. At the age of twelve my mother was once more uprooted and moved to the projects on the Lower East Side. As one of the first families in a predominantly Jewish building, it was a step up for her family.

It was not her environment that posed the biggest conflict for her; it was her appearance. My mother is what people call a "white Hispanic." With her blond hair and blue eyes my mother was taken for everything but a Puerto Rican. Once my mother perfected her English, no one suspected her ethnicity unless she told them. Since she was raised to be above the ghetto, never picking up typical "Hispanic mannerisms," she was able to exist in American society with very little difficulty. Because of a very strong and protective mother and the positive influence and assistance received from the Henry Street Settlement, my mother was able to escape the ghetto. As a result of organizations like Henry Street, my mother was given opportunities such as fresh air camps and jobs in good areas of the city, where she was able to rise above the drugs, alcohol, and violence that consumed so many of her peers.

As a result of her appearance and her upbringing, my mother left her people and the ghetto to enter American society. It was here as an attractive "white" female that my mother and father's two very different worlds merged. My parents, both working on Wall Street at the time, were introduced by a mutual friend. Since both had developed a rather liberal view, the differences in their backgrounds did not seem to be a major factor. After a year of dating my parents decided to get engaged.

Although they were from two different worlds, their engagement seemed to bring them together. Growing up in the midst of

15

the Jewish community of the Lower East Side, my mother was constantly influenced by the beauty of Judaism. Therefore, since my mother never had much connection with Catholicism and had never been baptized, she decided to convert to Judaism and raise her children as Jews. The beauty of the conversion was that no one in my father's family forced her to convert; they accepted her whether she converted or not. As for my mother's family, they too had no real objections to the wedding or conversion. To them the only thing that mattered was that my father was a nice guy who made my mom happy. The most amusing part of the union of these two different families came when they tried to communicate. My father's family is descended from Spanish Jewry where many of them spoke an old Castilian-style Spanish, while my mother's family spoke a very modern Caribbean-style Spanish. To watch them try to communicate in any language other than English was like watching a session of the United Nations.

It was this new world, that of Puerto Rican Jewry, my parents created for me and my sister, Danielle. Resembling both my parents, having my mother's coloring with my father's features, I have often been mistaken for various ethnicities. Possessing light hair and blue eyes, I am generally perceived as the "all-American" girl. Occasionally I have been mistaken for Italian since my last name, Algranati, although Sephardic, has a very Italian flair to it. I have basically lived a chameleon-like existence for most of my life.

As a result of my "otherness," I have gained "acceptance" in many different crowds. From this acceptance I have learned the harsh reality behind my "otherness." I will never forget the time I learned about how the parents of one of my Asian friends perceived me. From very early on, I gained acceptance with the parents of one of my Korean friends. Not only did they respect me as a person and a student, but her father even went so far as to consider me like "one of his daughters." I will always remember how I felt when I heard they made one of their daughters cancel a party because she had invited Hispanics. Even when my friend pointed out that I, the one they loved, was Hispanic they refused to accept it. Even today to them, I will always be Jewish and not Puerto Rican because to them it is unacceptable to "love" a Puerto Rican.

20   Regardless of community, Jewish or Puerto Rican, I am always confronted by bigots. Often I am forced to sit in silence

while friends utter in ignorance stereotypical responses like: "It was probably some spic who stole it," or "You're just like a Jew, always cheap."

For the past three years I have worked on the Lower East Side of Manhattan at the Henry Street Settlement. Basically my mother wanted me to support the organization that helped her get out of the ghetto. Unlike when my mother was there, the population is mostly black and Hispanic. So one day during work I had one of my fellow workers say to me "that is such a collegian white thing to say." I responded by saying that his assumption was only partially correct and asked him if he considered Puerto Rican to be white. Of course he doubted I was any part Hispanic until he met my cousin who "looks" Puerto Rican. At times like these I really feel for my mother, because I know how it feels not to be recognized by society for who you are.

Throughout my life I do not think I have really felt completely a part of any group. I have gone through phases of hanging out with different crowds trying in a sense to find myself. Basically, I have kept my life diverse by attending both Catholic-sponsored camps and Hebrew school at the same time. Similar to my parents, my main goal is to live within American society. I choose my battles carefully. By being diverse I have learned that in a society that is obsessed with classification the only way I will find my place is within myself. Unfortunately, society has not come to terms with a fast-growing population, the "others." Therefore when asked the infamous question: "Who are you?" I respond with a smile, "a Puerto Rican Egyptian Jew." Contrary to what society may think, I know that I am somebody.

For Discussion and Writing

1. Algranati's essay hints at some of the elements that make interethnic relationships easy and—by implication—what make them difficult. Drawing on Algranati's experience and your own understanding, describe why people resist interethnic relationships.

2. Algranati admits that "throughout my life I do not think I have really felt completely a part of any group." Describe the "groups" you observe in your own environment. How are they constituted? Analyze the ways in which issues of racial identity, ethnic identity, or class identity seem to affect the makeup of the groups. Talk to people to assess their awareness of how these factors influence their "group."

3. Explore your own ethnic background. What various "components" create your ethnic or racial identity? What conflicts have you experienced as a result of your complex identity, if any? In what ways has your family had to "compromise" in uniting various ethnic traditions or practices? Write a brief memoir-style essay that captures your earliest awareness of your family's identity.

Fraternity

GARRETT HONGO

Garrett Hongo was born in Hawaii in 1951. He is the author of two books of poetry: The River of Heaven *(1988), which was the Lamont Poetry Selection of the Academy of American Poets and a finalist for the Pulitzer Prize, and* Yellow Light *(1982). His honors include fellowships from the Guggenheim Foundation, the National Endowment for the Arts, and the Rockefeller Foundation. He is currently professor of creative writing at the University of Oregon at Eugene, where he directed the program in creative writing from 1989 to 1993. His ironically entitled essay recalls scarring difficulties he faced as a young man who crossed invisible but violently policed boundaries. He and his girlfriend were ultimately separated "by our own peoples . . . taking our bodies from us."*

------------------ ✦ ------------------

It was high school in Gardena. I was in classes mostly with Japanese American kids—*kotonks.* Mainland Japanese, their ethnic pet name originated, during the war, with derisive Hawaiian GIs who thought of the sound of a coconut being hit with a hammer. Sansei *kotonks* were sons and daughters of the Nisei *kotonks* who had been sent off to the concentration camps during World War II. School was tepid, boring. We wanted cars, we wanted clothes, we wanted everything whites and blacks wanted to know about sex but were afraid to tell us. We "bee-essed" with the black kids in the school parking lot full of coastal fog before classes. We beat the white kids in math, in science, in typing. We ran track and elected cheerleaders. We *ruled,* we said. We were dumb, teeming with attitude and prejudice.

Bored, I took a creative writing class with an "academically mixed" bunch of students. There were Chicanos, whites, a black woman, and a troika of Japanese women who sat together on the other side of the room from me. They said nothing—*ever*—and wrote naturalistically correct *haiku*. Suddenly among boisterous non-Japanese, I enjoyed the gabbing, the bright foam of free talk that the teacher encouraged. An aging man in baggy pants that he wore with suspenders, he announced he was retiring at the end of the year and that he wanted no trouble, that he was going to read "Eee-bee White" during our hour of class every day, that we were welcome to read whatever we wanted so long as we gave him a list ahead of time, and that we could talk as much as we wanted so long as we left him alone. We could read, we could write, we could jive each other all class long. It was freedom. And I took advantage.

I sat next to a Chicano my age named Pacheco and behind a white girl a class younger than me named Regina. Behind us was a curly-headed white guy who played saxophone in the marching band. He'd been in academic classes with me, the only Caucasian among Japanese, a Korean, and a few Chinese. He was a joker, and I liked him, but usually stayed away—we didn't fraternize much across the races, though our school was supposed to be an experiment in integration.

Gardena H.S. wasn't so much a mix or blend as a mosaic. Along with a few whites and blacks, Japanese were in the tough, college-prep, "advanced placement" scholastic track. Most whites and blacks were in the regular curriculum of shop, business skills, and a minimum of academic courses. The "dumb Japs" were in there with them. And the Chicanos filled up what were called the *remedial* classes, all taught imperiously only in English, with no provision for language acquisition. We were a student body of about three thousand, and we walked edgily around each other, swaggering when we could, sliding the steel taps on our big black shoes along the concrete outdoor walkways when we wanted to attract a little attention, making a jest of our strut, a music in the rhythm of our walking. Blacks were bused in from Compton; the whites, Japanese, and Chicanos came from around the town. Girls seemed to me an ethnic group of their own too, giggling and forming social clubs, sponsoring dances, teaching some of us the steps.

Crazes of dress moved through our populations—for Chicanos: woolen Pendletons over thin undershirts and a crucifix; big low-top oxfords; khaki work trousers, starched and pressed; for the *bloods:* rayon and satin shirts in metallic "fly-ass" colors; pegged gabardine slacks; cheap moccasin-toed shoes from downtown shops in L.A.; and for us *Buddhas:* high-collar Kensingtons of pastel cloths, A tapered "Racer" slacks, and the same moccasin shoes as the bloods, who were our brothers. It was crazy. And *inviolable.* Dress and social behavior were a code one did not break for fear of ostracism and reprisal. Bad dressers were ridiculed. Offending speakers were beaten, tripped walking into the john, and set upon by gangs. They *wailed* on you if you fucked up. A girl was nothing except pride, an ornament of some guy's crude power and expertise in negotiating the intricacies of this inner-city semiotic of cultural display and hidden violence. I did not know girls.

I talked to Regina, saying "white girl" one time. She told me not to call her that, that she was *Portuguese* if anything, that I better *know* that white people were *always* something too. From vague memories of Hawaii, I reached for the few words in *Portuguese* that I knew, I asked her about the sweet bread her mother baked, about heavy donuts fried in oil and rolled in sugar. I said *bon dea* for "good day" to her. I read the books she talked about—Steinbeck, Kesey, Salinger, and Baldwin. Her mother brought paperbacks home from the salon she worked in, putting up other women's hair—*rich* women's. We made up our reading list from books her mother knew. I wanted desperately to impress her, so I began to write poetry too, imitating some melancholy rock and country-and-western lyrics. She invited me to her house after school. I was on the way, so I walked her home. It became a practice.

Her father was a big, diabetic man from Texas. With his shirt off, he showed me how he shot himself with insulin, poking the needle under the hairy red skin on his stomach, working it over the bulge of fat around his belly. He laughed a lot and shared his beer. There were other guys over too—white guys from the football team, a Filipino, and one other Japanese guy who played left tackle. They were tough, raucous, and talked easily, excitedly. I stood alone in the front yard one day, holding a soft drink in my hand, the barbecue party going on around me. Regina and her mother were baking bread inside. No one knew exactly what was going on, and I was still trying to pretend all was casual.

I took photographs of her. We had a picnic on the coast by the lighthouse near Marineland, on the bluffs over the Pacific. It was foggy, mist upon us and the tall, droopy grasses in the field we walked through, but we made do. She wrapped herself in the blanket she'd brought for us to sit on. We were in the tall grasses of the headlands far from the coast road. She posed. I changed lenses, dropping film canisters, other things. She waved to me, unbuttoning the blouse she was wearing, her body full of a fragrance. The warm, yeasty scent of her skin smelled like bread under bronze silk. We couldn't be seen together—not at the private, car-club-sponsored Japanese dances out in the Crenshaw District, not at the whites-dominated dances after school in the high school gym. Whites did not see Buddhas, and Buddhas did not see bloods. We were to stay with our own—*that* was the code—though we mixed some in the lunch line, in a few classes, on the football field, and in gym. We segregated ourselves.

Regina and I went to the Chicano dances in El Monte.   10
Pacheco introduced us to them. Regina, tanned Portuguese, passed for Chicana, so long as she kept her mouth shut and her lashes long. Pacheco showed her what skirts to wear, his quick hands fluttering through the crinolines and taffetas in her closet at home. He advised me to grow a mustache and let my black hair go long in the back, to slick it down with pomade and to fluff it up in front, then seal it all in hair spray. I bought brown Pendletons and blue navy-surplus bell-bottoms. I bought hard, steel-toed shoes, We learned trots and tangos. We learned *cuecas* and polkas. We *passed, ese,* and had a good time for a couple of months.

One day, Regina got hurt. She was stopped by one of the football players at the beach. She was stepping onto a bus when he came up behind her and grabbed her arm. She tried to twist away, and the arm snapped. She crumpled. Everyone ran. She rode in a friend's car to the hospital that day and had the arm set. She didn't call me.

I heard about it after school the next day, crossing the street against the light. It was summer, and I was taking classes while Regina spent her days at the beach. I'd see her weekdays, stopping at her house on the way home. I was going to her when, just outside the gates of our school, a guy I knew taunted me with the news. He was Japanese, and it was strange to hear him say anything about Regina. I hadn't realized anyone from my crowd knew about us.

I wanted to run the rest of the way to her house. I crossed over a rise of bare earth, then down to a bedded railway—a strip line so that scrap steel and aluminum could be shipped from the switching stations and railyards downtown to steel and aeronautical factories near our school. Brown hummocks rose above eye level and masked the track of crossties, steel rails, and the long bed of gravel. I was set upon there by a troop of Japanese boys. A crowd of them encircled me, taunting, then a single gangly fellow I recognized from gym class executed most of the blows. They beat me, grinding my face in the gravel, shouting epithets like *inu* ("dog"), *cow-fucker,* and *paddy-lover.*

I've seen hand-sized reef fish, in a ritual of spawning, leave their singular lairs, gathering in smallish, excitable schools—a critical mass—and, electrified by their circling assembly, suddenly burst the cluster apart with sequences of soloing, males alternating, pouncing above the finning group, clouding the crystalline waters above the circle with a roll of milt.

15   All spring and summer, I'd been immune, unaware of the enmity of the crowd. I hadn't realized that, in society, humiliation is a force more powerful than love. Love does not exist in society, but only between two, or among a family. A kid from Hawaii, I'd undergone no real initiation in shame or social victimization yet and maintained an arrogant season out of bounds, imagining I was exempt. It was humiliating to have been sent to Camp. The Japanese American community understood their public disgrace and lived modestly, with deep prohibitions. I was acting outside of this history. I could cross boundaries, I thought. But I was not yet initiated into the knowledge that we Japanese were *not* like anyone else, that we lived in a community of violent shame. I paid for my naïveté with a bashing I still feel today, with cuts that healed with scars I can still run my fingers along. I can still taste the blood, remember the split skin under the mustache on my upper lip, and feel the depth of an anger that must have been *historical, tribal,* arising from fears of dissolution and diaspora.

Separated societies police their own separations. I was hated one day, and with an intensity I could not have foreseen. I was lifted by my clothes, the hands of my schoolmates at the nape of my shirt collar and the back of the waistband of my trousers, and I was hurled against the scrawny trunk of a little jacaranda tree and beaten there, fists cracking against my arms as I tried to cover my face, thumping along my sides and back, booted feet flailing at my legs. I squirmed, crawled, cried out. And I wept. Out of fear and humiliation and a psychic wounding I understand only now. I was *hated.* I was high and needed lowering. My acts were canceled. Regina was canceled. Both by our own peoples, enacting parallel vengeances of their own, taking our bodies from us.

Our trystings were over, and, later that summer, Regina simply moved away. Her father was retiring, she said, and had found a nice trailer park up by Morro Bay. She wouldn't see me before she left. I had to surprise her at a Laundromat one Saturday. She gave me a paperback book. She laughed, made light of everything, but there was a complete *fear* of me that I felt from her, deeply, one I had not felt before—at least, it had never registered. *Race.* It is an exclusion, a punishment, imposed by the group. I've felt it often since. It is a fear of *fraternity.* A fraternity that is forbidden. I wept, but let her go.

For Discussion and Writing

1. According to Hongo, where did the identifying term *kotonk* come from? Compare the way this term functions to other ethnic terms you may have heard for groups you are aware of. How are these similar in effect?

2. What are some of the details in Hongo's opening remarks that make him seem the same as young students everywhere? In what ways does Hongo's group feel superior? When did Hongo discover that he was "dumb, teeming with attitude and prejudice"? In your view, what sort of experiences lead to such self-discovery?

3. Hongo characterizes life in Gardena High School as more of a mosaic than a blend. What differs between these two? What are some of the groups Hongo mentions? How well do they get along generally? In what ways are stereotypes reflected in day-to-day life in the school? How does this mix compare to the "student body" from your own high school?

4. What is it about being called "white" that disturbs Regina? What does she mean when she says that white people are always something too? Jeanne Wakatsuki Houston remarks in "Living in Two Cultures," the next reading, that Asian women fascinate Caucasian men. Do you think Hongo was fascinated by Regina or her ethnic background? Find a passage or two that reveal his feelings for her and discuss it.

5. What does Hongo mean when he says, "we *passed, ese*"? What "adaptations" in clothing and looks do they make in order to appear Chicano? In your view, what do their attackers fear about Hongo and Regina as a couple? What do you make of the term *inu*, or "dog," that Garrett's attackers shout at him?

Living in Two Cultures
JEANNE WAKATSUKI HOUSTON

In 1973 Jeanne Wakatsuki Houston's book Farewell to Manzanar, *a recreation of her experiences in a Japanese American relocation camp during World War II, was published. In 1984 she wrote* Don't

Cry, It's Only Thunder *with Paul G. Hensler. She published* Beyond Manzanar and Other Views of Asian-American Womanhood *in 1985, from which the following piece is excerpted. Houston was born in California in 1934 and attended the University of San Jose. During her college years Jeanne met her husband James D. Houston. The couple married in 1957.*

─────────── ✦ ───────────

The memories surrounding my awareness of being female fall into two categories: those of the period before World War II, when the family made up my life, and those after the war, when I entered puberty and my world expanded to include the ways and values of my Caucasian peers. I did not think about my Asian-ness and how it influenced my self-image as a female until I married.

In remembering myself as a small child, I find it hard to separate myself from the entity of the family. I was too young to be given "duties" according to my sex, and I was unaware that this was the organizational basis for operating the family. I took it for granted that everyone just did what had to be done to keep things running smoothly. My five older sisters helped my mother with domestic duties. My four older brothers helped my father in the fishing business. What I vaguely recall about the sensibility surrounding our sex differences was that my sisters and I all liked to please our brothers. More so, we tried to attract positive attention from Papa. A smile or affectionate pat from him was like a gift from heaven. Somehow, we never felt this way about Mama. We took her love for granted. But there was something special about Papa.

I never identified this specialness as being one of the blessings of maleness. After all, I played with my brother Kiyo, two years older than myself, and I never felt there was anything special about him. I could even make him cry. My older brothers were fun-loving, boisterous and very kind to me, especially when I made them laugh with my imitations of Carmen Miranda dancing or of Bonnie Baker singing "Oh, Johnny." But Papa was different. His specialness came not from being male, but from being the authority.

After the war and the closing of the camps, my world drastically changed. The family had disintegrated; my father was no longer godlike, despite my mother's attempt to sustain that pre-war image of him. I was spending most of my time with my new Caucasian friends and learning new values that clashed with those of my parents. It was also time that I assumed the duties girls were supposed to do, like cooking, cleaning the house, washing and ironing clothes. I remember washing and ironing my brothers' shirts, being careful to press the collars correctly, trying not to displease them. I cannot ever remember my brothers performing domestic chores while I lived at home. Yet, even though they may not have been working "out there," as the men were supposed to do, I did not resent it. It would have embarrassed me to see my brothers doing the dishes. Their reciprocation came in a different way. They were very protective of me and made me feel good and important for being a female. If my brother Ray had extra money, he would sometimes buy me a sexy sweater like my Caucasian friends wore, which Mama wouldn't buy for me. My brothers taught me to ride a bicycle and to drive a car, took me to my first dance, and proudly introduced me to their friends.

Although the family had changed, my identity as a female   5 within it did not differ much from my older sisters who grew up before the war. The males and females supported each other but for different reasons. No longer was the survival of the family as a group our primary objective; we cooperated to help each other survive "out there" in the complicated world that had weakened Papa.

We were living in Long Beach then. My brothers encouraged me to run for school office, to try out for majorette and song leader, and to run for queen of various festivities. They were proud that I was breaking social barriers still closed to them. It was acceptable for an Oriental male to excel academically and in sports. But to gain recognition socially in a society that had been fed the stereotyped model of the Asian male as cook, houseboy or crazed kamikaze pilot was almost impossible. The more alluring myth of mystery and exotica that surrounds the Oriental female made it easier, though no less inwardly painful, for me.

Whenever I succeeded in the *Hakujin* world, my brothers were supportive, whereas Papa would be disdainful, undermined by my obvious capitulation to the ways of the West. I wanted to be like my Caucasian friends. Not only did I want to look like them, I wanted to act like them. I tried hard to be outgoing and socially aggressive and to act confidently, like my girlfriends. At home I was careful not to show these personality traits to my father. For him it was bad enough that I did not even look very Japanese: I was too big, and I walked too assertively. My breasts were large, and besides that I showed them off with those sweaters the *Hakujin* girls wore! My behavior at home was never calm and serene, but around my father I still tried to be as Japanese as I could.

As I passed puberty and grew more interested in boys, I soon became aware that an Oriental female evoked a certain kind of interest from males. I was still too young to understand how or why an Oriental female fascinated Caucasian men, and of course, far too young to see then that it was a form of "not seeing." My brothers would warn me, "Don't trust the *Hakujin* boys. They only want one thing. They'll treat you like a servant and expect you to wait on them hand and foot. They don't know how to be nice to you." My brothers never dated Caucasian girls. In fact, I never really dated Caucasian boys until I went to college. In high school, I used to sneak out to dances and parties where I would meet them. I wouldn't even dare to think what Papa would do if he knew.

What my brothers were saying was that I should not act toward Caucasian males as I did toward them. I must not "wait on them" or allow them to think I would, because they wouldn't understand. In other words, be a Japanese female around Japanese men and act *Hakujin* around Caucasian men. This double identity within a "double standard" resulted not only in a confusion for me of my role or roles as female, but also in who or what I was racially. With the admonitions of my brothers lurking deep in my consciousness, I would try to be aggressive, assertive and "come on strong" toward Caucasian men. I mustn't let them think I was submissive, passive and all-giving like Madame Butterfly. With Asian males I would tone down my natural enthusiasm and settle into patterns instilled in me through the models of my mother and my sisters. I was not comfortable in either role.

10   Although I was attracted to males who looked like someone in a Coca-Cola ad, I yearned for the expressions of their potency to be like that of Japanese men, like that of my father: unpredictable, dominant, and brilliant—yet sensitive and poetic. I wanted a blond samurai.

When I met my blond samurai, during those college years in San Jose, I was surprised to see how readily my mother accepted the idea of our getting married. My father had passed away, but I was still concerned about her reaction. All of my married brothers and sisters had married Japanese-American mates. I would be the first to marry a Caucasian. "He's a strong man and will protect you. I'm all for it," she said. Her main concern for me was survival. Knowing that my world was the world of the *Hakujin*, she wanted me to be protected, even if it meant marriage to one of them. It was 1957, and interracial couples were a rare sight to see. She felt that my husband-to-be was strong because he was acting against the norms of his culture, perhaps even against his parents' wishes. From her vantage point, where family and group opinion outweighed the individual's, this willingness to oppose them was truly a show of strength.

When we first married I wondered if I should lay out his socks and underwear every morning like my mother used to do for my father. But my brothers' warning would float up from the past: don't be subservient to Caucasian men or they will take advantage. So I compromised and laid them out sporadically, whenever I thought to do it . . . which grew less and less often as the years passed. (Now my husband is lucky if he can even find a clean pair of socks in the house!) His first reaction to this wifely gesture was to be uncomfortably pleased. Then he was puzzled by its sporadic occurrence, which did not seem to coincide as an act of apology or because I wanted something. On the days when I felt I should be a good Japanese wife, I did it. On other days, when I felt American and assertive, I did not.

When my mother visited us, as she often did when she was alive, I had to be on good behavior, much to my husband's pleasure and surprise. I would jump up from the table to fill his empty water glass (if she hadn't beat me to it) or butter his roll. If I didn't notice that his plate needed refilling, she would kick me under the table and reprimand me with a disapproving look. Needless to say, we never had mother-in-law problems. He would often ask, with hope in his voice, "when is your mother coming to visit?"

My mother had dutifully served my father throughout their marriage, but I never felt she resented it. I served my brothers and father and did not resent it. I was made to feel not only important for performing duties of my role, but absolutely integral for the functioning of the family. I realized a very basic difference in attitude between Japanese and American cultures toward serving another. In my family, to serve another could be uplifting, a gracious gesture that elevated oneself. For many white Americans, it seems that serving another is degrading, an indication of dependency or weakness in character, or a low place in the social ladder. To be ardently considerate is to be "self-effacing" or apologetic.

15   My father used to say, "Serving humanity is the greatest virtue. Giving service of yourself is more worthy than selling the service or goods of another." He would prefer that we be maids in someone's home, serving someone well, than be salesgirls where our function would be to exchange someone else's goods, handling money. Perhaps it was his way of rationalizing and giving pride to the occupations open to us as Orientals. Nevertheless, his words have stayed with me, giving me spiritual sustenance at times when I perceived that my willingness to give was misconstrued as a need to be liked or an act of manipulation to get something.

My husband and I often joke that the reason we have stayed married for so long is that we continually mystify each other with responses and attitudes that are plainly due to our different backgrounds. For years I frustrated him with unpredictable silences and accusing looks. I felt a great reluctance to tell him what I wanted or what needed to be done in the home. I was inwardly furious that I was being put into the position of having to *tell* him what to do. I felt my femaleness, in the Japanese sense, was being degraded. I did not want to be the authority. That would be humiliating for him and for me. He, on the other hand, considering the home to be under my dominion, in the American sense, did not dare to impose on me what he thought I wanted. He wanted me to tell him or make a list, like his parents did in his home.

Entertaining socially was also confusing. Up to recent times, I still hesitated to sit at one head of our rectangular dining table when my husband sat at the other end. It seemed right to be seated next to him, helping him serve the food. Sometimes I did it anyway, but only with our close friends, who didn't misread my physical placement as psychological subservience.

At dinner parties I always served the men first, until I noticed the women glaring at me. I became self-conscious about it and would try to remember to serve the women first. Sometimes I would forget and automatically turn to a man. I would catch myself abruptly, dropping a bowl of soup all over him. Then I would have to serve him first anyway, as a gesture of apology. My unconscious Japanese instinct still managed to get what it wanted.

Now I just entertain according to how I feel that day. If my Japanese sensibility is stronger, I act accordingly and feel comfortable. If I feel like going all-American, I can do that, too, and feel comfortable. I have come to accept the cultural hybridness of my personality, to recognize it as a strength and not weakness.

Because I am culturally neither pure Japanese nor pure American does not mean I am less of a person. It means I have been enriched with the heritage of both.

How my present attitudes will affect my children in later 20 years remains to be seen. My world is radically different from my mother's world, and all indications point to an even wider difference between our world and our children's. Whereas my family's and part of my struggle was racially based, I do not foresee a similar struggle for our children. Their biracialism is, indeed, a factor in their identity and self-image, but I feel their struggle will be more to sustain human dignity in a world rapidly dehumanizing itself with mechanization and technology. My hope is they have inherited a strong will to survive, that essential trait ethnic minorities in this country have so sharply honed.

For Discussion and Writing

1. Gender is a significant part of Wakatsuki Houston's identity. Analyze the various ways her gender affected her experience. How did the intersection of gender and race shape Wakatsuki Houston's identity and behavior as a child and an adolescent? What conflicting expectations did she confront, and how did she respond to them?

2. Wakatsuki Houston states that after the closing of the relocation camp, her family "had disintegrated" and that her "father was no longer godlike, despite my mother's attempt to sustain that pre-war image of him." Speculate about how the father in the family lost his "godlike" role and how that affected the family. Why did Wakatsuki Houston try "to be as Japanese as I could" around her father?

3. Drawing on Wakatsuki Houston's essay, analyze the differences between Caucasian culture and Japanese culture in terms of gender roles. What expectations for men and women exist in the two cultures? In what ways do these roles enter into racialized stereotypes?

4. Wakatsuki Houston makes this comment about a difference between Japanese culture and American culture: "In my family, to serve another could be uplifting, a gracious gesture that elevated oneself. For many white Americans, it seems that serving another is degrading, an indication of dependency or weakness in character, or a low place in the social ladder." Discuss the validity of this distinction. What experiences or observations have you had that might support the validity of this claim? To what extent might these observations be based on stereotypes and to what extent are they validated by evidence?

5. At the end of the essay, Wakatsuki Houston says that she does not foresee a "racially based" struggle for her biracial children, but a struggle "to sustain human dignity in a world rapidly dehumanizing itself with mechanization and technology." She hopes they "have inherited a strong will to survive, that essential trait ethnic minorities in this country have so sharply honed." Why does she see a strong will to survive as an "essential trait" minorities "have so sharply honed"? How might biracial children be especially capable of sustaining a humane world? What arguments that support or challenge this assertion can you make?

American Dreamer
BHARATI MUKHERJEE

Bharati Mukherjee resists the "hyphenated" identity of the American citizen with immigrant roots, although many of the themes and characters in her work focus on Bengali-Hindu culture. Born in 1940 and educated at an undergraduate school in Calcutta, Mukherjee received her M.A. in English and ancient Indian culture in India before coming to the United States to attend the Writers' Workshop at the University of Iowa in 1961. She received both an M.F.A. and a Ph.D. at the University of Iowa. Mukherjee lived for 14 years in Canada before moving to the United States and becoming a naturalized citizen. She currently teaches at the University of California at Berkeley. Her novels include The Tiger's Daughter *(1971),* Wife *(1975),* Jasmine *(1989),* The Holder of the World *(1993), and* Desirable Daughters *(2002). Her short story collections are* Darkness *(1985) and* The Middleman and Other Stories *(1988).*

✦

The United States exists as a sovereign nation; "America," in contrast, exists as a myth of democracy and equal opportunity to live by, or as an ideal goal to reach.

I am a naturalized U.S. citizen, which means that, unlike native-born citizens, I had to prove to the U.S. government that I merited citizenship. What I didn't have to disclose was that I desired "America," which to me is the stage for the drama of self-transformation.

I was born in Calcutta and first came to the United States—to Iowa City, to be precise—on a summer evening in 1961. I flew into a small airport surrounded by cornfields and pastures, ready to carry out the two commands my father had written out for me the night before I left Calcutta: Spend two years studying creative writing at the Iowa Writers' Workshop, then come back home and marry the bridegroom he selected for me from our caste and class. In traditional Hindu families like ours, men provided and women were provided for. My father was a patriarch and I a pliant daughter. The neighborhood I'd grown up in was homogeneously Hindu, Bengali-speaking, and middle-class. I didn't expect myself to ever disobey or disappoint my father by setting my own goals and taking charge of my future.

When I landed in Iowa 35 years ago, I found myself in a society in which almost everyone was Christian, white, and moderately well-off. In the women's dormitory I lived in my first year, apart from six international graduate students (all of us were from Asia and considered "exotic"), the only non-Christian was Jewish, and the only nonwhite an African-American from Georgia. I didn't anticipate then, that over the next 35 years, the Iowa population would become so diverse that it would have 6,931 children from non-English-speaking homes registered as students in its schools, nor that Iowans would be in the grip of a cultural crisis in which resentment against immigrants, particularly refugees from Vietnam, Sudan, and Bosnia, as well as unskilled Spanish-speaking workers, would become politicized enough to cause the Immigration and Naturalization Service to open an "enforcement" office in Cedar Rapids in October for the tracking and deporting of undocumented aliens.

In Calcutta in the '50s, I heard no talk of "identity crisis"— communal or individual. The concept itself—of a person not knowing who he or she is—was unimaginable in our hierarchical, classification-obsessed society. One's identity was fixed, derived from religion, caste, patrimony, and mother tongue. A Hindu Indian's last name announced his or her forefathers' caste and place of origin. A Mukherjee could *only* be a Brahmin from Bengal. Hindu tradition forbade intercaste, interlanguage, interethnic marriages. Bengali tradition even discouraged emigration: To remove oneself from Bengal was to dilute true culture.

Until the age of 8, I lived in a house crowded with 40 or 50 relatives. My identity was viscerally connected with ancestral soil

5

and genealogy. I was who I was because I was Dr. Sudhir Lal Mukherjee's daughter, because I was a Hindu Brahmin, because I was Bengali-speaking, and because my *desh*—the Bengali word for homeland—was an East Bengal village called Faridpur.

The University of Iowa classroom was my first experience of coeducation. And after not too long, I fell in love with a fellow student named Clark Blaise, an American of Canadian origin, and impulsively married him during a lunch break in a lawyer's office above a coffee shop.

That act cut me off forever from the rules and ways of upper-middle-class life in Bengal, and hurled me into a New World life of scary improvisations and heady explorations. Until my lunch-break wedding, I had seen myself as an Indian foreign student who intended to return to India to live. The five-minute ceremony in the lawyer's office suddenly changed me into a transient with conflicting loyalties to two very different cultures.

10 The first 10 years into marriage, years spent mostly in my husband's native Canada, I thought of myself as an expatriate Bengali permanently stranded in North America because of destiny or desire. My first novel, *The Tiger's Daughter*, embodies the loneliness I felt but could not acknowledge, even to myself, as I negotiated the no-man's land between the country of my past and the continent of my present. Shaped by memory, textured with nostalgia for a class and culture I had abandoned, this novel quite naturally became an expression of the expatriate consciousness.

It took me a decade of painful introspection to put nostalgia in perspective and to make the transition from expatriate to immigrant. After a 14-year stay in Canada, I forced my husband and our two sons to relocate to the United States. But the transition from foreign student to U.S. citizen, from detached onlooker to committed immigrant, has not been easy.

The years in Canada were particularly harsh. Canada is a country that officially, and proudly, resists cultural fusion. For all its rhetoric about a cultural "mosaic," Canada refuses to renovate its national self-image to include its changing complexion. It is a New World country with Old World concepts of a fixed, exclusivist national identity. Canadian official rhetoric designated me as one of the "visible minority" who, even though I spoke the Canadian languages of English and French, was straining "the absorptive capacity" of Canada. Canadians of color were routinely treated as "not real" Canadians. One example: In 1985 a terrorist bomb, planted in an Air-India jet on Canadian soil, blew up after leaving Montreal, killing 329 passengers, most of whom were Canadians of Indian origin. The prime minister of Canada at the time, Brian Mulroney, phoned the prime minister of India to offer Canada's condolences for India's loss.

Those years of race-related harassments in Canada politicized me and deepened my love of the ideals embedded in the American Bill of Rights. I don't forget that the architects of the Constitution and the Bill of Rights were white males and slaveholders. But through their declaration, they provided us with the enthusiasm for human rights, and the initial framework from which other empowerments could be conceived and enfranchised communities expanded.

I am a naturalized U.S. citizen and I take my American citizenship very seriously. I am not an economic refugee, nor am I a seeker of political asylum. I am a voluntary immigrant. I became a citizen by choice, not by simple accident of birth.

Yet these days, questions such as who is an American and   15
what is American culture are being posed with belligerence, and being answered with violence. Scapegoating of immigrants has once again become the politicians' easy remedy for all that ails the nation. Hate speeches fill auditoriums for demagogues willing to profit from stirring up racial animosity. An April Gallup poll indicated that half of Americans would like to bar almost all legal immigration for the next five years.

The United States, like every sovereign nation, has a right to formulate its immigration policies. But in this decade of continual, large-scale diasporas, it is imperative that we come to some agreement about who "we" are, and what our goals are for the nation, now that our community includes people of many races, ethnicities, languages, and religions.

The debate about American culture and American identity has to date been monopolized largely by Eurocentrists and ethnocentrists whose rhetoric has been flamboyantly divisive, pitting a phantom "us" against a demonized "them."

All countries view themselves by their ideals. Indians idealize the cultural continuum, the inherent value system of India, and are properly incensed when foreigners see nothing but poverty, intolerance, strife, and injustice. Americans see themselves as the embodiments of liberty, openness, and individualism, even as the world judges them for drugs, crime, violence, bigotry, militarism, and homelessness. I was in Singapore in 1994 when the American teenager Michael Fay was sentenced to caning for having spray-painted some cars. While I saw Fay's actions as those of an individual, and his sentence as too harsh, the overwhelming local sentiment was that vandalism was an "American" crime, and that flogging Fay would deter Singapore youths from becoming "Americanized."

Conversely, in 1994, in Tavares, Florida, the Lake County School Board announced its policy (since overturned) requiring middle school teachers to instruct their students that American culture, by which the board meant European-American culture, is inherently "superior to other foreign or historic cultures." The policy's misguided implication was that culture in the United States has not been affected by the American Indian, African-American, Latin-American, and Asian-American segments of the population. The sinister implication was that our national identity is so fragile that it can absorb diverse and immigrant cultures only by recontextualizing them as deficient.

20   Our nation is unique in human history in that the founding idea of "America" was in opposition to the tenet that a nation is a collection of like-looking, like-speaking, like-worshiping people. The primary criterion for nationhood in Europe is homogeneity of culture, race, and religion—which has contributed to blood-soaked balkanization in the former Yugoslavia and the former Soviet Union.

America's pioneering European ancestors gave up the easy homogeneity of their native countries for a new version of utopia. Now, in the 1990s, we have the exciting chance to follow that tradition and assist in the making of a new American culture that differs from both the enforced assimilation of a "melting pot" and the Canadian model of a multicultural "mosaic."

The multicultural mosaic implies a contiguity of fixed, self-sufficient, utterly distinct cultures. Multiculturalism, as it has been practiced in the United States in the past 10 years, implies the existence of a central culture, ringed by peripheral cultures. The fallout of official multiculturalism is the establishment of one culture as the norm and the rest as aberrations. At the same time, the multiculturalist emphasis on race- and ethnicity-based group identity leads to a lack of respect for individual differences within each group, and to vilification of those individuals who place the good of the nation above the interests of their particular racial or ethnic communities. We must be alert to the dangers of an "us" vs. "them" mentality. In California, this mentality is manifesting itself as increased violence between minority, ethnic communities. The attack on Korean-American merchants in South Central Los Angeles in the wake of the Rodney King beating trial is only one recent example of the tragic side effects of this mentality. On the national level, the politicization of ethnic identities has encouraged the scapegoating of legal immigrants, who are blamed for economic and social problems brought about by flawed domestic and foreign policies. We need to discourage the retention of cultural memory if the aim of that retention is cultural balkanization. We must think of American culture and nationhood as a constantly reforming, transmogrifying "we."

In this age of diasporas, one's biological identity may not be   25
one's only identity. Erosions and accretions come with the act of emigration. The experience of cutting myself off from a biological homeland and settling in an adopted homeland that is not always welcoming to its dark-complexioned citizens has tested me as a person, and made me the writer I am today.

I choose to describe myself on my own terms, as an American rather than as an Asian-American. Why is it that hyphenation is imposed only on nonwhite Americans? Rejecting hyphenation is my refusal to categorize the cultural landscape into a center and its peripheries; it is to demand that the American nation deliver the promises of its dream and its Constitution to all its citizens equally.

My rejection of hyphenation has been misrepresented as race treachery by some India-born academics on U.S. campuses who have appointed themselves guardians of the "purity" of ethnic cultures. Many of them, though they reside permanently in the United States and participate in its economy, consistently denounce American ideals and institutions. They direct their rage at me because, by becoming a U.S. citizen and exercising my voting rights, I have invested in the present and not the past; because I have committed myself to help shape the future of my adopted homeland; and because I celebrate racial and cultural mongrelization.

What excites me is that as a nation we have not only the chance to retain those values we treasure from our original cultures but also the chance to acknowledge that the outer forms of those values are likely to change. Among Indian immigrants, I see a great deal of guilt about the inability to hang on to what they commonly term "pure culture." Parents express rage or despair at their U.S.-born children's forgetting of, or indifference to, some aspects of Indian culture. Of those parents I would ask: What is it we have lost if our children are acculturating into the culture in which we are living? Is it so terrible that our children are discovering or are inventing homelands for themselves?

Some first-generation Indo-Americans, embittered by racism and by unofficial "glass ceilings," construct a phantom identity, more-Indian-than-Indians-in-India, as a defense against marginalization. I ask: Why don't you get actively involved in fighting discrimination? Make your voice heard. Choose the forum most appropriate for you. If you are a citizen, let your vote count. Reinvest your energy and resources into revitalizing your city's disadvantaged residents and neighborhoods. Know your constitutional rights, and when they are violated, use the agencies of redress the Constitution makes available to you. Expect change, and when it comes, deal with it!

30   As a writer, my literary agenda begins by acknowledging that America has transformed me. It does not end until I show that I (along with the hundreds of thousands of immigrants like me) am minute by minute transforming America. The transformation is a two-way process: It affects both the individual and the national-cultural identity.

Others who write stories of migration often talk of arrival at a new place as a loss, the loss of communal memory and the erosion of an original culture. I want to talk of arrival as gain.

For Discussion and Writing

1. What prompted Mukherjee to leave Canada and move to the United States? How does Mukherjee compare Canada and the United States?
2. What metaphors does Mukherjee employ to characterize Canada's and the United States's relationship to their immigrants? What other metaphors do you think might be appropriate?
3. Mukherjee describes American multiculturalism as "the establishment of one culture as the norm and the rest as aberrations." What are the dangers in this sort of multiculturalism? What alternative ways of thinking does Mukherjee suggest? What are some alternative models you might suggest?

4. Mukherjee describes her decision not to hyphenate her name and identify herself—in part—through her national ethnic origin. Why is this decision controversial? Describe the arguments you think are compelling that go into such a decision.

Ethnicity and Identity: Creating a Sense of Self
CLAIRE S. CHOW

Claire S. Chow, a licensed marriage, family, and child counselor, is interested in the ways Asian Americans struggle with their identities living in an American culture with an Asian heritage. The following piece, excerpted from Leaving Deep Water: Asian-American Women at the Crossroads of Two Cultures, *is based on the personal narratives of women with Chinese, Japanese, Korean, and other Asian identities. Chow is an adjunct professor at the John F. Kennedy University's Graduate School of Professional Psychology and a member of the Asian-American Psychological Association. This excerpt explores the struggle to develop an ethnic identity when one lives between two cultures.*

———————————— ✦ ————————————

Who can say how ethnic identity is formed? Is it nurtured like the seed in the soil by parents who cultivate ways of thinking, values, preferences? Does it develop in response to the external world, a reaction to the stereotypes and perceptions promulgated "out there"? Is the simple fact of distinctive physical appearance enough to form the core of an identity, around which other influences solidify, the grain of sand that eventually becomes the pearl?

This is not a question that can be answered with certainty. But I believe there are a number of factors that influence the extent to which a person identifies with one or both cultures. First are the demographic characteristics: age, generational status, date of personal or family immigration. Also significant is the availability of extended family and ethnic community (especially as a child), peer influences, relationships with parents, sociopolitical events such as the internment, and exposure to political ideology, for example, the movement to ensure civil rights for Asian Americans. But perhaps the single most important factor is simply individual preference, which itself is based on life experience and temperament. Thus, two children growing up in the same house could come to maturity with different ideas about their ethnicity.

I believe that by the time an Asian American woman reaches adulthood, she chooses how to identify herself. That choice may be largely unconscious, but it is still a manifestation of individual will. After all, isn't this the grand and glorious thing about the American experience: the opportunity to define yourself, to forge your own image? Living here, the notion of the frontier, with its promise of transformation, beckons to us all.

In this [essay] are stories of women who have worked, sometimes against tremendous odds, to resolve this question of ethnicity and identity.

5   Doreen, who lives in a small town in North Carolina, talks about her struggle to hold on to the Asian half of her heritage.

"Today began as all others with a quick shower and a look in the mirror asking myself, 'Who am I?' Then, off to work I went. It is early fall and my skin is beginning to fade back to a natural yellow-ivory color. This is one of those minor features of mine that always provokes a question in the minds of curious people. In the course of this day, a coworker placed his arm next to mine and asked, 'Are you one of *those*?' 'Yes,' I answered quietly. 'My father was Chinese.'

"Ever since I can remember, I have felt different, I have had this sense inside that I was not like the people who surrounded me. Everyone in my family is tall, red-haired, green-eyed. I'm short and on the stocky side. Doing good at five five and a half. No legs. Eyes slanted just a little too much. Face just a little too round. In the fourth grade, the teacher had us project our profiles on an overhead. My nose was so flat, the kids all started laughing. And when my beautiful tall white mother, who is of Welsh-Scottish descent, got mad at me, which she did frequently, she'd scream, 'You have such a *fat, flat, ugly* nose.'

"My mother put her maiden name on my birth certificate. No father. Virgin birth, of course. When I was twelve, she admitted that the man she was married to was not my father. But she refused to tell me who my real father was. One Christmas she asked what I wanted. 'The name of my father,' I said, not missing a beat. No answer. So I continued to feel different, to look at myself in the mirror and try to figure it out. I used to cut that long blond hair off my Barbies; it made me mad that I was never given a doll who looked like me. For a long time, I was bitter about the Miss America pageant, never a dark-skinned or dark-haired beauty queen.

"Two years ago, I got my hair cut very short, almost a bob. I had a picture taken of myself and gave a copy to my mother. She was furious. She hated that photograph. Finally, my husband said to me, 'You've got to pursue this. You need to confront her.' So I did. And in her anger, my mother told me the one true thing, one of the very few things I could ever believe. She told me that my father was Chinese. That statement helped put things in place, gave me an explanation that made sense. But at a deeper level, I didn't really need to hear her say those words out loud, because I *knew* it was true. I have always known, it has just never been articulated before.

"Learning about my parentage explains a lot. Like why, as a   10 small child, I always treasured Oriental things. Like why I feel more comfortable around Chinese people than whites. Not even Japanese so much, but Chinese. Like why, at eighteen years of age, I left the South, took a bus to New York City determined to live in Chinatown. I remember arriving at Port Authority, sitting in a coffee shop for a few hours and then telling myself, 'OK, this is why you came here, to live among Chinese people. Now go do it!' I had a wonderful experience. The Chinese would confirm stuff about me. Look behind my glasses at my eyes. They knew. I learned to speak Cantonese, a little Mandarin. They didn't treat me like a whole Chinese, but that's OK because I didn't expect them to. But at least they didn't treat me like I was white. I've never really felt white.

"Perhaps if my mother hadn't treated me the way she did, my need to know my father wouldn't be so great. Perhaps if I didn't have this feeling that I made my mother uncomfortable, that she doesn't like to look at me, doesn't want to be reminded of my Chinese father, I might not have quite this drive to pursue my heritage. But that's not what has happened.

"My husband and I now live in North Carolina. I'd love to be somewhere where there are more Chinese people. For example, Hong Kong. I'd love to have been there in '97, watching the clock tick off the minutes until the country reverted back to China. But we're here now because of my husband's job. When we bought our house a few years ago, one of the neighbors stopped in to say hello. She also asked, 'What is your nationality?' When I told her, she said, 'I knew you weren't pure white.' Now I want to ask you, what the heck is 'pure white'? *Who* is 'pure white'? All these white people came here from somewhere else. So I call myself a mutt.

"I would like to know more about my father. But I'm afraid that I may never be able to trace him. The only thing I have to go on is what a relative once told me, that a Chinese doctor from Manchuria brought over a group of his friends to live here when the Japanese were invading. Perhaps my father is one of those men. But my mom will not give me his name or his identity. In the meantime, it just helps to be able to look in the mirror and have a better sense of who that person really is. What I want is this: More than anything else, I want my Chinese heritage."

The adoption of an Asian child by white parents adds another level of complexity to the question of developing an ethnic identity. Renée is thirty-two years old, lives in Oregon, and works with battered women.

15 "A few years ago, I hired a good attorney, got a restraining order, and after eight years of marriage, left my abusive husband. Now, maybe for the first time in my life, I feel free to find out who I really am: as a woman, as a Korean American, as a person worthy of dignity and respect.

"My Korean mother abandoned me as an infant. I was adopted by white parents through an agency when I was twenty-four months old and moved to Salem, Oregon. I'm not too keen on the agency these days. Their philosophy, at least back then, was that the little Korean children should be grateful to be raised by white Christian families. I still have a letter from the woman who ran the agency saying that 'since an orphan has no place in Korean society, you were a nobody and now you are a person.'

"My mother is religious in a Bible-beating sort of way, and she also bought these notions of gratitude and Christian service, which she has tried to impose on me. She wanted me to go to a Bible college, but when I went to an academic school instead and majored in social science, she was convinced I would be doomed. Now I have this nice purple candle in my living room. It has a sun, star, and a moon on it, sits in a simple brass holder. She asks me what I need that for. I tell my mom that it's my way to honor witches and lesbians. My ex-husband also thought I should be grateful. He loved to introduce me as his Korean wife who should be 'serving him,' and frequently pointed out that if I had stayed back in Korea, I would be 'eating dogs and worms.'

"I grew up thinking I was white. After all, I was raised in an all-American family, with all-white relatives, on hamburgers. In fact, sometimes I blame all those cow hormones for my overdeveloped bust, which was a source of constant discomfort for me as a teenager. I used to think, 'If these things keep growing, one of these days I'm just going to fall over and die.' My uncle and aunt, whom I call the 'King and Queen of the Right Wing,' also would treat me as if I was white. In their eyes, I *was* white. So the fact that I'm a woman of color, that I do oppression training in my work, completely eludes them. They love to talk about how the Mexicans in our town are always the ones getting picked up for DUIs, etc., right in front of me. Usually, I just let it go, but once in a while if I do decide to speak up, I feel like one of my relatives is thinking, 'We better cool it, the race police is here.'

"I was never pushed to excel academically, but I became an over-achiever all on my own. I worked hard for good grades, joined all kinds of clubs, etc. I even got elected to be on the homecoming court. But even so, I always felt unattractive. In high school, I got into this big thing about eye surgery. My mother had a cousin who was a plastic surgeon and I went to see him when I was fifteen. He refused to do the surgery and tried to convince me that my eyes were in fact pretty. That didn't stop me from trying to curl my lashes with one of those curler things, which always caught my eyelid instead of my lashes anyhow. And my nose was too flat. So flat, in fact, that at the time of the *Roots* thing, kids were calling me Kunta Kinte. And my breasts were too large, especially for an Asian, who should be petite. And my hair was wrong too. It was black, not blond. My hair stylist had to break the news to me that my hair just would not feather like Farrah Fawcett's.

"After high school, I suddenly started getting asked out a lot. 20 There was this whole 'all Asian women are beautiful and sexy' thing going on. White guys would come up to me and start gibbering, then tell me, 'In Cantonese, that means you're beautiful.' I bought it. I was only attracted to white men and there were plenty available, so that was a period of my life marked by a lot of oversexualized behavior. I also used to go to the library and check out books in the Asian section and look up the chapters on women's roles. I read about geishas, I learned that we should be compliant and passive along with being sexually enticing. In fact, I have to admit that I used my 'Asianness' to attract my ex-husband. The stereotypes allowed me to project an image of myself that was exciting to me, one that made me stand out a little from the crowd. Besides, at that period of my life, I was screwed up in so many ways that this gave me at least *some* kind of an identity.

"The main reason I was screwed up is that I hadn't resolved the sexual abuse I suffered as a child. When I was nine years old, a Chinese pastor came to live with us. He was married to this nutso woman whom my mother had fostered. One day, when I was eleven, I was asked to pour him some tea at dinner. I was so mad that I deliberately spilled hot tea on his leg. My mother asked me why, and I started screaming, told her that he had been touching me for two years and I wanted him *out* of the house. What really got to me was that no one said anything after that. They just wanted to get on with dinner. Later, I repeated my message to my mother. She tried to tell me that he was a pastor, sometimes men do something they're sorry about, etc., etc. But finally, she did kick him out. After that, I never wanted anything to do with Asian men again. I was afraid they'd all be like this guy, who preyed on me because of my ethnicity. Who was also, I realize now, the perfect pedophile in the most insidious way.

"Marrying a white guy unfortunately did not spare me further abuse. During those terrible years of marriage—the name-calling, threats, the jokes about taking nude pictures of me to send to Asian porno magazines, and the rape (my ex claimed there was no such thing since he 'owned me')—my mother's only response was to 'pray about it.' Well, I don't know about prayer, but I do know that divorce has made a fundamental difference in my life. At my divorce party (where I gave away wedding presents from his family, who hated me anyhow for being Korean, as door prizes), I realized I had all these friends who really supported me. They clapped and cheered for me and I knew that this was my real family, the place where I could really be myself. A Korean American woman and proud of it!"

Sarah, like Renée, was adopted by white parents. Unlike Renée, however, Sarah was encouraged by her family to pursue her cultural roots. But even with this support, she describes a lifetime of grappling with the question, "What makes me Asian?"

"When I was twenty-five, I went to Hawaii to meet my birth mother for the first time in my life. The day before I was due to leave was very hard. I cried a lot and she held me. As I curled up in her arms, I could hear her heart beat and I said to myself, I *know* this. I can't describe the feeling any better. It was amazing to see her, to touch her, to know it was her. I look a lot like my birth mother and I realized that for the first time in my life, I had a *match*.

"All my life, I have been searching for my Asian heritage. I was adopted by white parents who tried hard to give my sister (also adopted, and Filipina) and me a connection to our culture. My mother took lessons in Chinese cooking, brought us along to her Asian studies classes, bought us books about Asian women. But still, somehow, it wasn't enough. I'm not sure I could say what exactly I needed, all I know is that something was missing.

"In third grade I decided to try to copy my Asian friends' behavior. They were quiet, reserved, polite: They knew how to make themselves invisible. I learned to imitate them, but it never felt right. Rubbed against the grain. Still, to this day, I sometimes fall back on that behavior. I'm quieter in groups, more polite than a lot of people I know. I'm sure what I felt was that if I could be more Asian, I could find my identity. And if I could be more Asian, I could be more like my birth mother.

"At the same time that I was trying to figure out what it meant to be Asian, my teachers would take one look at me and know what it meant to *them*. It was naturally assumed that I should be in the gifted and talented program even though my test scores didn't quite justify it. Also, I could do no wrong. I looked so innocent. Who would suspect that I was the one responsible for those paper airplanes sailing across the classroom? I loved it! I played it for all it was worth. And yet, I always had the sense that 'I'm Asian, but I'm not.' I had a lot of Asian friends, but my home life wasn't nearly as restrictive as theirs. Unlike them, I had the freedom to follow my heart's desires. And I'm grateful for that.

"My grandmother also treated me on the basis of how I looked. I used to get so mad because she could never tell me and my sister apart. We don't look that much alike aside from both being Asian. She'd ask, 'Now, which one are you?' and every year would give us identical presents. Two red sweaters. Two white bears. As a result of all this, I felt that I didn't really fit in

25

anywhere. I had a bunch of friends, but I floated from group to group. A true chameleon.

"I had another chance to experiment with my ethnic identity in college. I went to Humboldt State, where I was one of a very few Asians. I cultivated the 'long-haired exotic Polynesian' look and dated anyone I set my sights on. I got what I wanted. In this guise, I could get away with things my friends wouldn't dare to try. For example, I was able to date three different men and one woman at the same time, be perfectly open about it, and not have to justify my behavior to anyone. That's 'just Sarah,' my friends would say. A package deal.

30   Then, I cut my hair very short. My whole life changed. I was no longer the enticing Asian. No one asked me out. I was now the 'dyke,' even if I was dating men. I knew when I cut my hair this might happen, but it was still disappointing. Two and a half feet of hair does not a person make. I wished they could see beyond that. The whole question of my identity was up for grabs again.

"I also had the experience, at Humboldt, of feeling for the first time in my life that I wished I was not Asian. One evening, my friends and I went out to a bar. Somewhere along the line, I noticed this scruffy-looking guy in the corner just staring at me. He gave me the creeps. But it was more than just being a woman and feeling vulnerable to the power of a man. I had this sense that he was one of those white supremacist types who wanted to hurt me because I was Asian, and I was reminded of nightmares where men in white hoods would hunt me down, of hanging from a tree. I realized that, in this town, I had *nowhere to hide*. I could not blend in, I would always be identifiable.

"Today, I call myself an Asian woman. I don't like the term 'American,' because to me, American means 'white male.' I still may not know exactly who I am, but at least I know who I'm *not*."

For Discussion and Writing

1. At the beginning of the piece, Chow asks some important and unanswerable questions—or at least questions that have multiple answers. On the basis of your reading in this chapter, your observations, and your experiences, discuss your ideas and tentative answers to her questions: "Who can say how ethnic identity is formed? Is it nurtured like the seed in the soil by parents who cultivate ways of thinking, values, preferences? Does it develop in response to the external world, a reaction to the stereotypes and perceptions

promulgated 'out there'? Is the simple fact of distinctive physical appearance enough to form the core of an identity, around which other influences solidify, the grain of sand that eventually becomes the pearl?"

2. How do the women interviewed by Chow view their color and appearance? What physical qualities do they attend to? How has appearance shaped their identities and their relationships with other people? Compare and contrast the attention they give to appearance, as well as the feelings they have and the actions they take as a result.

3. Both Wakatsuki Houston, in the previous essay, and Chow's interviewee Renée comment on white men's attraction to Asian women. Sarah touches on it when she talks about cultivating "the 'long-haired exotic Polynesian' look." How do the women account for men's attraction to Asian women? How do their responses to that notion differ?

4. Chow's interviewee asks the question: "What makes me Asian?" Compare and contrast the different ways the women in this piece might respond to that question. In what ways do they recognize and conform to the stereotype of the Asian woman? In what ways do they reject the sterotype? Characterize the way each of them—even tentatively—forges an identity.

Reading, Research, and Writing

1. Consider the term "miscegenation" and the assumptions that lie beneath it. At different times in our country's history, laws were enacted to prevent interracial marriages and interracial sexual relations. Do a little research into some of these laws. You might start by looking up the case of *Loving v. Virginia*, a famous case readily available on the Internet. A Google search based on "law" and "miscegenation" will also yield quite a lot. Write a paper that analyzes the prohibitions on interracial relations, looking into the assumptions, underlying fears, and goals of such laws. Draw on the readings from this chapter in support of your own ideas.

2. Bharati Mukherjee objects to the use of hyphenated labels for ethnic groups in America. Investigate the history of labels for ethnic identities in this country. Have all immigrants always hyphenated their identities with names such as "German-American," "African-American," and "Hispanic-Americans"? What differences do you find among ethnic groups in who maintains the hyphen and who does not? What sorts of transitions and changes in labels have occurred? Look, for example, at the various labels African Americans have preferred over the years. What arguments can you find about labels for ethnic groups?

3. Explore the ethnic diversity of your campus. Try to get data from your school's office of admissions or other campus resources about the ethnic makeup of the student population. To further your research, you might carefully design a questionnaire that probes the attitudes and perceptions of a good sampling of students about the school's ethnic makeup, mixed ethnicity, and interracial relations. Would people want to see more diversity? Do they object to the presence or exclusion of some groups? Do their perceptions fit with the data you've found? Write an essay based on your most provocative findings.

4. One way to approach identity is to look closely into several families' experiences, to talk about their sense of identity, about what has shaped this. Include very concrete examples, like family recipes, religious affiliation, the celebration of holidays, and so on. Most families have diverse backgrounds. Why do some of these families identify with one group rather than another? Do all the siblings agree on their ethnic identity? Do children begin to alter their attachment to ethnicity when they marry? You might begin with your own family and extend the research to other families that seem interesting to you.

5. America celebrates its diversity, but as Garrett Hongo reveals, crossing boundaries within our society can be a dangerous and painful experience, one often doomed to failure. What are the consequences of ignoring boundaries and social barriers? Have you ever crossed such boundaries? Do you have a friend who has? What happened? Would you, or your friends, characterize the experience as happy? Revealing? Disastrous? What did it teach you? Write a paper, perhaps in the style of a memoir, that focuses on some such crossing of boundaries. Include in your memoir references to the experiences of the writers in this chapter.

CHAPTER 2

Reflections and Distortions in the Media and Popular Culture

The good news at the movies obscures the bad news in the streets. . . . The movies reflect the larger dynamic of wish and dream.

Benjamin DeMott

Since 1925, Hollywood has released more than 2,000 films, many of them rerun frequently on television, portraying Indians as strange, perverted, ridiculous, and often dangerous things of the past.

Ward Churchill

Popular culture refers to things that we often dismiss as trivial or so short-lived that they aren't worth serious attention. So what if a ball team has an ethnic mascot? Who really notices? If a company decides to sell its junk food with the help of a stereotype like the Frito Bandito, what's the worry? Bandits, savages, and other such relics, like Sambo's restaurants and Aunt Jemima pancakes, belong in museums along with Amos 'N Andy and Al Jolson's blackface performances. Hasn't their effect long since faded from our lives? And what harm did simplistic images and stereotypes do? It isn't as if such things have shaped the experiences of minorities in America. But, in fact, they have. A brief look back in American history will reveal many examples.

Consider the fate of Chinese immigrants who arrived here in the 19th century. In his brief, thorough study, *The Yellow Peril*, William F. Wu considers the relation between popular stereotypes of Chinese and anti-Asian discrimination in our past. "When the Chinese immigrants first arrived in the United States, they came into a society that already viewed them with hostility and condescension." This hostility was quickly reflected and expanded in the media of the day. Novelists and politicians portrayed the Chinese as dirty, vice-ridden, clannish, and irredeemably alien to the American way of life. Newspapers repeated these stereotypes. Witnesses in congressional hearings repeated the characterizations already widespread in our culture, and Chinese immigrants became the targets of murderous mobs in the West. Some were slaughtered, many were driven from their homes, or imprisoned without the benefit of rights granted to citizens. American industry had invited Chinese laborers to our shores, and depended on the workers for many services, most famously for the dangerous and difficult labor of building railroads that connected our coasts. But the work of the 1860s gave way in only a few years to the 1882 Exclusion Act that outlawed further Chinese immigration, a ban left in place for over 60 years.

Was the change in the treatment of the Chinese the result of prejudices fed by media lies and distortions? It's a question of degree. Who can claim that the widespread and repeated misrepresentation of people has no influence on how others see them? That would be dangerously naïve. Mark Twain said the difference "between a cat and a lie is that a cat has only nine lives." As was the case with the Chinese in America, if we see the media distortions of an ethnic group as part of a stream running through American life, we might understand the cumulative effect of such distortions. The images and claims become so familiar that we hardly notice their influence over us until that influence crystallizes in some overt act like a hate crime or a false arrest, or the passage of a law that restricts the basic rights of an entire group of Americans.

Many white Americans who have had virtually no actual contact with African American males admit to mistrust and fear of these men. If that fear is not based on experience, what is its source? We all see, hear, and absorb media images, and sometimes we act as much on these distortions as on actual facts. In a *Los Angeles Times* article, Robin Yaesha Deane notes that white

Americans "are afraid of us because they don't know us. They don't know our capabilities, our achievements, our versatility. They don't know about our integrity, our self-determination, our entrepreneurships and quest for higher education. They don't know we have assets, inventions, investments and we do more than hip-hop, dunk, rap and commit crimes."

The readings in this chapter examine the links between media distortions and social injustice. As Benjamin DeMott notes in his essay, "Put On a Happy Face: Masking the Differences Between Blacks and Whites," Hollywood gives us a view of harmony and equity between blacks and whites, but the facts are far different. Film fantasy won't overcome injustices either. Tiana Thi Thanh Nga asserts that Hollywood has for many decades portrayed Asians in a stereotypical manner, and kept Chinese actors out of leading roles. Nga argues that the "long march" is far from over. Like Nga, Julie Chapa notes that the pace of change, the dying out of stereotypes, is very slow. Her essay "The Don Juan Syndrome" considers how stereotypes have limited both the roles available to Hispanic actors and the public's acceptance of Hispanics in general. She relates the frustrations of Fred Estrada, an actor and attorney who has suffered in both his professions because of the caricatures of stereotypes. Estrada explains how the image of the "'Latin playboy' [has] haunted him throughout his legal career." In "Crimes Against Humanity," Ward Churchill lists numerous injustices suffered by Native Americans, from land confiscation to genocidal policies, and argues that one important "reason for public acquiescence before the ongoing holocaust in Native North America has been a continuation" of media distortions on the nature of Native Americans that present them as "strange, perverted, ridiculous, and often dangerous things of the past." Such distortions take their toll as the Arab American film critic Jack Shaheen suggests in noting the trend in post-9/11 media to vilify Arab and Muslim Americans. The dangers of such propaganda are simply ignored by those responsible for its production. Finally, Salim Muwakkil points out in "Real Minority, Media Majority" that even though television and movie entertainment often suggest blacks are the majority of drug pushers and users in America, in fact, whites outnumber blacks on both counts. Both numerically and proportionally, fewer blacks than whites have used cocaine, but Bureau of Justice Statistics surveys are merely informative. They don't entertain us, and consequently people are far less aware of them.

Americans are often asked to dismiss concerns with media misrepresentations as "political correctness." It is easy to isolate a case like the "tomahawk chop" of baseball fans and to ridicule concern over its influence in our culture. Yet at some point, there is a cumulative effect to stereotypes, and the public's view of some people shifts accordingly. As Shaheen remarks in the essay included here, "Show only vilifying images of any group, incessantly, and after a while—100 years in the case of the Arab stereotype—it becomes 'natural' not to like certain people. It is a sin of omission— we omit the humanity—and of commission—we show only hateful images that make a stereotype that injures the innocent."

Admitting that popular misrepresentations harm people isn't "politically correct." It's simply correct. Countering stereotypes moves us toward fair and humane relations. What the Los Angeles-based writer Robin Deane says about the unfounded fear of black Americans rings true for all of us. "Fear of blacks should be un-American. Black Americans know that there is nothing dangerous about being black, but those who fear us must discover it too." We all have things to discover about each other.

Put On a Happy Face: Masking the Differences Between Blacks and Whites

BENJAMIN DEMOTT

Benjamin DeMott, born in 1924 in New York, was educated at Johns Hopkins University, George Washington University, and Harvard University. He has written numerous books, both fiction and non-fiction—among them works about Americans and their attitudes on race, gender, and class. In the essay that follows, DeMott examines the gulf between media images of racial harmony and the day-to-day facts of life that contradict those images. Lulled by the media into thinking all is well in multicultural America, we should, as DeMott puts it, "Never forget what we see and hear for ourselves."

◆

At the movies these days, questions about racial injustice have been amicably resolved. Watch *Pulp Fiction* or *Congo* or *A Little Princess* or any other recent film in which both blacks and whites are primary characters and you can, if you want, forget about race. Whites and blacks greet one another on the screen with loving candor, revealing their common humanity. In *Pulp Fiction*, an armed black mobster (played by Samuel L. Jackson) looks deep into the eyes of an armed white thief in the middle of a holdup (played by Tim Roth) and shares his version of God's word in Ezekiel, whereupon the two men lay aside their weapons, both more or less redeemed. The moment inverts an earlier scene in which a white boxer (played by Bruce Willis) risks his life to save another black mobster (played by Ving Rhames), who is being sexually tortured as a prelude to his execution.

Pulp Fiction (gross through July [1995]: $107 million) is one of a series of films suggesting that the beast of American racism is tamed and harmless. Close to the start of *Die Hard with a Vengeance* (gross through July [1995]: $95 million) the camera finds a white man wearing sandwich boards on the corner of Amsterdam Avenue and 138th Street in Harlem. The boards carry a horrific legend: I HATE NIGGERS. A group of young blacks approach the man with murderous intent, bearing guns and knives. They are figures straight out of a national nightmare—ugly, enraged, terrifying. No problem. A black man, again played by Jackson, appears and rescues the white man, played by Willis. The black man and white man come to know each other well. In time the white man declares flatly to the black, "I need you more than you need me." A moment later he charges the black with being a racist—with not liking whites as much as the white man likes blacks—and the two talk frankly about their racial prejudices. Near the end of the film, the men have grown so close that each volunteers to die for the other.

Pulp Fiction and *Die Hard with a Vengeance* follow the pattern of *Lethal Weapon 1, 2,* and *3,* the Danny Glover/Mel Gibson buddy vehicles that collectively grossed $357 million, and *White Men Can't Jump*, which, in the year of the L.A. riots, grossed $76 million. In *White Men Can't Jump*, a white dropout, played by Woody Harrelson, ekes out a living on black-dominated basketball courts in Los Angeles. He's arrogant and aggressive but never in danger because he has a black protector and friend, played by Wesley Snipes. At the movie's end, the white, flying above the hoop like a stereotypical black player, scores the winning basket in a two-on-two pickup game on an alley-oop pass from his black chum, whereupon the two men fall into each other's arms in joy. Later, the black friend agrees to find work for the white at the store he manages.

WHITE (*helpless*): I gotta get a job. Can you get me a job?
BLACK (*affectionately teasing*): Got any references?
WHITE (*shy grin*): You.

Such dialogue is the stuff of romance. What's dreamed of and gained is a place where whites are unafraid of blacks, where blacks ask for and need nothing from whites, and where the sameness of the races creates a common fund of sweet content.[1] The details of the dream matter less than the force that makes it come true for both races, eliminating the constraints of objective reality and redistributing resources, status, and capabilities. That cleansing social force supersedes political and economic fact or policy; that force, improbably enough, is friendship.

5   Watching the beaming white men who know how to jump, we do well to remind ourselves of what the camera shot leaves out. Black infants die in America at twice the rate of white infants. (Despite the increased numbers of middle-class blacks, the rates are diverging, with black rates actually rising.) One out of every two black children lives below the poverty line (as compared with one out of seven white children). Nearly four times as many black families exist below the poverty line as white families. More than 50 percent of African American families have incomes below $25,000. Among black youths under age twenty, death by murder occurs nearly ten times as often as among whites. Over 60 percent of births to black mothers occur out of wedlock, more than four times the rate for white mothers. The net worth of the typical white household is ten times that of the typical black household. In many states, five to ten times as many blacks as whites age eighteen to thirty are in prison.

The good news at the movies obscures the bad news in the streets and confirms the Supreme Court's recent decisions on busing, affirmative action, and redistricting. Like the plot of *White Men Can't Jump*, the Court postulates the existence of a society no longer troubled by racism. Because black-white friendship is now understood to be the rule, there is no need for integrated schools or a congressional Black Caucus or affirmative action. The Congress and state governors can guiltlessly cut welfare, food assistance, fuel assistance, Head Start, housing money, fellowship money, vaccine money. Justice Anthony Kennedy can declare, speaking for the Supreme Court majority last June, that creating a world of genuine equality and sameness requires only that "our political system and our society cleanse themselves . . . of discrimination."

The deep logic runs as follow: *Yesterday white people didn't like black people, and accordingly suffered guilt, knowing that the dislike was racist and knowing also that as moral persons they would have to atone for the guilt. They would have to ante up for welfare and Head Start and halfway houses and free vaccine and midnight basketball and summer jobs for schoolkids and graduate fellowships for promising scholars and craft-union apprenticeships and so on, endlessly. A considerable and wasteful expense. But at length came the realization that by ending dislike or hatred it would be possible to end guilt, which in turn would mean an end to redress: no more wasteful ransom money. There would be but one requirement: the regular production and continuous showing forth of evidence indisputably proving that hatred has totally vanished from the land.*

I cannot tell the reader how much I would like to believe in this sunshine world. After the theater lights brighten and I've found coins for a black beggar on the way to my car and am driving home through downtown Springfield, Massachusetts, the world invented by *Die Hard with a Vengeance* and America's highest court gives way only slowly to the familiar urban vision in my windshield—homeless blacks on trash-strewn streets, black prostitutes staked out on a corner, and signs of a not very furtive drug trade. I know perfectly well that most African Americans don't commit crimes or live in alleys. I also know that for somebody like myself, downtown Springfield in the late evening is not a good place to be.

The movies reflect the larger dynamic of wish and dream. Day after day the nation's corporate ministries of culture churn out images of racial harmony. Millions awaken each morning to the friendly sight of Katie Couric nudging a perky elbow into good buddy Bryant Gumbel's side. My mailbox and millions of demographically similar others are choked with flyers from companies (Wal-Mart, Victoria's Secret) bent on publicizing both their wares and their social bona fides by displaying black and white models at cordial ease with one another. A torrent of goodwill messages about race arrives daily—revelations of corporate largesse, commercials, news features, TV specials, all proclaiming that whites like me feel strongly positive impulses of friendship for blacks and that those same admirable impulses are effectively eradicating racial differences, rendering blacks and whites the same. BellSouth TV commercials present children singing "I am the keeper of the world"—first a white child, then a black child, then a white child, then a black child. Because Dow Chemical likes black America, it recruits young black college grads for its research division and dramatizes, in TV commercials, their tearful-joyful partings from home. ("Son, show 'em what you got," says a black lad's father.) American Express shows an elegant black couple and an elegant white couple sitting together in a theater, happy in one another's company. (The couples share the box with an oversized Gold Card.) During the evening news I watch a black mom offer Robitussin to a miserably coughing white mom. Here's *People* magazine promoting itself under a photo of John Lee Hooker, the black bluesman. "We're these kinds of people, too," *People* claims in the caption. In [a recent] production of *Hamlet* on Broadway, Horatio [was] played by a black actor. On *The 700 Club*, Pat Robertson joshes Ben Kinchlow, his black sidekick, about Ben's far-out ties.

10   What counts here is not the saccharine clumsiness of the interchanges but the bulk of them—the ceaseless, self-validating gestures of friendship, the humming, buzzing background theme: *All decent Americans extend the hand of friendship to African Americans: nothing but nothing is more auspicious for the African American future than this extended hand.* Faith in the miracle cure of racism by change-of-heart turns out to be so familiar as to have become unnoticeable. And yes, the faith has its benign aspect. Even as they nudge me and others toward belief in magic (instant pals and no-money-down equality), the images and messages of devoted relationships between blacks and whites do exert a humanizing influence.

Nonetheless, through these same images and messages the comfortable majority tells itself a fatuous untruth. Promoting the fantasy of painless answers, inspiring groundless self-approval among whites, joining the Supreme Court in treating "cleansing" as *inevitable*, the new orthodoxy of friendship incites culture-wide evasion, justifies one political step backward after another, and greases the skids along which, tomorrow, welfare block grants will slide into state highway-resurfacing budgets. Whites are part of the solution, says this orthodoxy, if we break out of the prison of our skin color, say hello, as equals, one-on-one, to a black stranger, and make a black friend. We're part of the problem if we have an aversion to black people or are frightened of them, or if we feel that the more distance we put between them and us the better, or if we're in the habit of asserting our superiority rather than acknowledging our common humanity. Thus we shift the problem away from politics—from black experience and the history of slavery—and perceive it as a matter of the suspicion and fear found within the white heart; solving the problem asks no more of us than that we work on ourselves, scrubbing off the dirt of ill will.

The approach miniaturizes, personalizes, and moralizes; it removes the large and complex dilemmas of race from the public sphere. It tempts audiences to see history as irrelevant and to regard feelings as decisive—to believe that the fate of black Americans is shaped mainly by events occurring in the hearts and minds of the privileged. And let's be frank: the orthodoxy of friendship feels *nice*. It practically *consecrates* self-flattery. The "good" Bill Clinton who attends black churches and talks with likable ease to fellow worshipers was campaigning when Los Angeles rioted in '92. "White Americans," he said, "are gripped by the isolation of their own experience. Too many still simply have no friends of other races and do not know any differently." Few black youths of working age in South-Central L.A. had been near enough to the idea of a job even to think of looking for work before the Rodney King verdict, but the problem, according to Clinton, was that whites need black friends.

Most of the country's leading voices of journalistic conscience (editorial writers, television anchorpersons, syndicated columnists) roundly endorse the doctrine of black-white friendship as a means of redressing the inequalities between the races. Roger Rosenblatt, editor of the *Columbia Journalism Review* and an especially deft supplier of warm and fuzzy sentiment, published an essay in *Family Circle* arguing that white friendship and sympathy for blacks simultaneously make power differentials vanish and create interracial identity between us, one by one. The author finds his *exemplum* in an episode revealing the personal sensitivity, to injured blacks, of one of his children.

"When our oldest child, Carl was in high school," he writes, "he and two black friends were standing on a street corner in

New York City one spring evening, trying to hail a taxi. The three boys were dressed decently and were doing nothing wild or threatening. Still, no taxi would pick them up. If a driver spotted Carl first, he might slow down, but he would take off again when he saw the others. Carl's two companions were familiar with this sort of abuse. Carl, who had never observed it firsthand before, burned with anger and embarrassment that he was the color of a world that would so mistreat his friends."

15 Rosenblatt notes that when his son "was applying to colleges, he wrote his essay on that taxi incident with his two black friends. . . . He was able to articulate what he could not say at the time—how ashamed and impotent he felt. He also wrote of the power of their friendship, which has lasted to this day and has carried all three young men into the country that belongs to them. To all of us."

In this homily white sympathy begets interracial sameness in several ways. The three classmates are said to react identically to the cabdriver's snub; i.e., they feel humiliated. "[Carl] could not find the words to express his humiliation and his friends *would* not express theirs."

The anger that inspires the younger Rosenblatt's college-admission essay on racism is seen as identical with black anger. Friendship brings the classmates together as joint, equal owners of the land of their birth ("the country that belongs to [all of] them"). And Rosenblatt supplies a still larger vision of essential black-white sameness near the end of his essay: "Our proper hearts tell the truth," he declares, "which is that we are all in the same boat, rich and poor, black and white. We are helpless, wicked, heroic, terrified, and we need one another. We need to give rides to one another."

Thus do acts of private piety substitute for public policy while the possibility of urgent political action disappears into a sentimental haze. "If we're looking for a formula to ease the tensions between the races," Rosenblatt observes, then we should "attack the disintegration of the black community" and "the desperation of the poor." Without overtly mocking civil rights activists who look toward the political arena "to erase the tensions," Rosenblatt alludes to them in a throwaway manner, implying the properly adjusted whites look elsewhere, that there was a time for politicking for "equal rights" but we've passed through it. Now is a time in which we should listen to our hearts at moments of epiphany and allow sympathy to work its wizardry, cleansing and floating us, blacks and whites "all in the same boat," on a mystical undercurrent of the New Age.

Blacks themselves aren't necessarily proof against this theme, as witness a recent essay by James Alan McPherson in the Harvard journal *Reconstruction*. McPherson, who received the 1977 Pulitzer Prize for fiction for his collection of stories *Elbow Room*, says that "the only possible steps, the safest steps . . . small ones" in the movement "toward a universal culture" will be those built not on "ideologies and formulas and programs" but on experiences of personal connectedness.

"Just this past spring," he writes, "when I was leaving a restau-   20
rant after taking a [white] former student to dinner, a black [woman on the sidewalk] said to my friend, in a rasping voice, 'Hello, girlfriend. Have you got anything to spare?'" The person speaking was a female crack addict with a child who was also addicted. "But," writes McPherson, when the addict made her pitch to his dinner companion, "I saw in my friend's face an understanding and sympathy and a shining which transcended race and class. Her face reflected one human soul's connection with another. The magnetic field between the two women was charged with spiritual energy."

The writer points the path to progress through interpersonal gestures by people who "insist on remaining human, and having human responses. . . . Perhaps the best that can be done, now, is the offering of understanding and support to the few out of many who are capable of such gestures, rather than devising another plan to engineer the many into one."

The elevated vocabulary ("soul," "spiritual") beatifies the impulse to turn away from the real-life agenda of actions capable of reducing racial injustice. Wherever that impulse dominates, the rhetoric of racial sameness thrives, diminishing historical catastrophes affecting millions over centuries and inflating the significance of tremors of tenderness briefly troubling the heart or conscience of a single individual—the boy waiting for a cab, the woman leaving the restaurant. People forget the theoretically unforgettable—the caste history of American blacks, the connection between no schools for longer than a century and bad school performance now, between hateful social attitudes and zero employment opportunities, between minority anguish and majority fear.

How could this way of seeing have become conventional so swiftly? How did the dogmas of instant equality insinuate themselves so effortlessly into courts and mass audiences alike? How can a white man like myself, who taught Southern blacks in the 1960s, find

himself seduced—as I have been more than once—by the orthodoxy
of friendship? In the civil rights era, the experience for many millions of Americans was one of discovery. A hitherto unimagined
continent of human reality and history came into view, inducing
genuine concern and at least a temporary setting aside of self-
importance. I remember with utter clarity what I felt at Mary
Holmes College in West Point, Mississippi, when a black student of
mine was killed by tailgating rednecks; my fellow tutors and I were
overwhelmed with how shamefully wrong a wrong could be. For a
time, we were released from the prisons of moral weakness and am-
biguity. In the year or two that followed—the mid-Sixties—the notion that some humans are more human than others, whites more
human than blacks, appeared to have been overturned. The next
step seemed obvious: society would have to admit that when one
race deprives another of its humanity for centuries, those who have
done the depriving are obligated to do what they can to restore
the humanity of the deprived. The obligation clearly entailed the
mounting of comprehensive *long-term* programs of developmental
assistance—not guilt-money handouts—for nearly the entire black
population. The path forward was unavoidable.

It was avoided. Shortly after the award of civil rights and the
institution, in 1966, of limited preferential treatment to remedy
employment and educational discrimination against African
Americans, a measure of economic progress for blacks did appear
in census reports. Not much, but enough to stimulate glowing
tales of universal black advance and to launch the good-news bar-
rage that continues to this day (headline in the *New York Times*,
June 18, 1995: "Moving On Up: The Greening of America's Black
Middle Class").

25   After Ronald Reagan was elected to his first term, the new
dogma of black-white sameness found ideological support in the
form of criticism of so-called coddling. Liberal activists of both
races were berated by critics of both races for fostering an allegedly enfeebling psychology of dependency that discouraged
African Americans from committing themselves to individual self-
development. In 1988, the charge was passionately voiced in an
essay in these pages. "I'm Black, You're White, Who's Innocent?"
by Shelby Steele, who attributed the difference between black
rates of advance and those of other minority groups to white folks'
pampering. Most blacks, Steele claimed, could make it on their
own—as voluntary immigrants have done—were they not held

back by devitalizing programs that presented them, to themselves and others, as somehow dissimilar to and weaker than other Americans. This argument was all-in-the-same-boatism in a different key; the claim remained that progress depends upon recognition of black-white sameness. Let us see through superficial differences to the underlying, equally distributed gift for success. Let us teach ourselves—in the words of the Garth Brooks tune— to ignore "the color of skin" and "look for . . . the beauty within."

Still further support for the policy once known as "donothingism" came from points-of-light barkers, who held that a little something might perhaps be done *if* accompanied by enough publicity. Nearly every broadcaster and publisher in America moves a bale of reportage on pro bono efforts by white Americans to speed the advance of black Americans. Example: McDonald's and the National Basketball Association distribute balloons when they announce they are addressing the dropout problem with an annual "Stay in School" scheme that gives schoolkids who don't miss a January school day a ticket to an all-star exhibition. The publicity strengthens the idea that these initiatives will nullify the social context—the city I see through my windshield. Reports of white philanthropy suggest that the troubles of this block and the next should be understood as phenomena in transition. The condition of American blacks need not be read as the fixed, unchanging consequence of generations of bottom-caste existence. Edging discreetly past a beggar posted near the entrance to Zabar's or H&H Bagels, or while walking the dog, stepping politely around black men asleep on the side walk, we need not see ourselves and our fellows as uncaring accomplices in the acts of social injustice.

Yet more powerful has been the ceaseless assault, over the past generation, on our knowledge of the historical situation of black Americans. On the face of things it seems improbable that the cumulative weight of documented historical injury of African Americans could ever be lightly assessed. Gifted black writers continue to show, in scene after scene—in their studies of middle-class blacks interacting with whites—how historical realities shape the lives of their black characters. In *Killer of Sheep*, the brilliant black filmmaker Charles Burnett dramatizes the daily encounters that suck poor blacks into will-lessness and contempt for white fairy tales of interracial harmony; he quickens his historical themes with images of faceless black meat processors gutting undifferentiated, unchoosing animal life. Here, say these images, as though talking back to Clarence Thomas, here is a basic level of black life unchanged over generations. Where there's work, it's miserably paid and ugly. Space allotments at home and at work cramp body and mind. Positive expectation withers in infancy. People fall into the habit of jeering at aspiration as though at the bidding of physical law. Obstacles at every hand prevent people from loving and being loved in decent ways, prevent children from believing their parents, prevent parents from believing they themselves know anything worth knowing. The only true self, now as in the long past, is the one mocked by one's own race. "Shit on you, nigger," says a voice in *Killer of Sheep*. "Nothing you say matters a good goddamn."

For whites, these words produce guilt, and for blacks, I can only assume, pain and despair. The audience for tragedy remains small, while at the multiplex the popular enthusiasm for historical romance remains constant and vast. During the last two decades, the entertainment industry has conducted a siege on the pertinent past, systematically excising knowledge of the consequences of the historical exploitation of African Americans. Factitious renderings of the American past blur the outlines of black-white conflict, redefine the ground of black grievances for the purposes of diminishing the grievances, restage black life in accordance with the illusory conventions of American success mythology, and present the operative influences on race history as the same as those implied to be pivotal in *White Men Can't Jump* or a BellSouth advertisement.

Although there was scant popular awareness of it at the time (1997), the television miniseries *Roots* introduced the figure of the Unscathed Slave. To an enthralled audience of more than 80 million the series intimated that the damage resulting from generations of birth-ascribed, semianimal status was largely temporary, that slavery was a product of motiveless malignity on the social margins rather than of respectable rationality, and that the ultimate significance of the institution lay in the demonstration, by freed slaves, that no force on earth can best the energies of American Individualism. ("Much like the Waltons confronting the depression," writes historian Eric Foner, a widely respected authority of American slavery, "the family in *Roots* neither seeks nor requires outside help; individual or family effort is always sufficient.") Ken Burns's much applauded PBS documentary *The Civil War* (1990) went even further than *Roots* in downscaling black injury; the series treated slavery, birth-ascribed inferiority, and the centuries-old denial of dignity as matters of slight consequence. (By "implicitly denying the brutal reality of slavery," writes historian Jeanie Attie, Burns's programs crossed "a dangerous moral threshold." To a group of historians who asked him why slavery had been so slighted, Burns said that any discussion of slavery "would have been lengthy and boring.")

Mass media treatments of the civil rights protest years carried forward the process, contributing to the "positive" erasure of difference. Big-budget films like *Mississippi Burning*, together with an array of TV biographical specials on Dr. Martin Luther King and others, presented the long-running struggle between disenfranchised blacks and the majority white culture as a heartwarming episode of interracial unity; the speed and caringness of white response to the oppression of blacks demonstrated that broadscale race conflict or race difference was inconceivable.

A consciousness that ingests either a part or the whole of this revisionism loses touch with the two fundamental truths of race in America; namely, that because of what happened in the past, blacks and whites cannot yet be the same; and that because what happened in the past was no mere matter of ill will or insult but the outcome of an established caste structure that has only very recently begun to be dismantled, it is not reparable by one-on-one goodwill. The word "slavery" comes to induce stock responses with no vital sense of a grinding devastation of mind visited upon generation after generation. Hoodwinked by the orthodoxy of friendship, the nation either ignores the past, summons for it a detached, correct "compassion," or gazes at it as though it were a set of aesthetic conventions, like twisted trees and fragmented rocks in nineteenth-century picturesque painting—lifeless phenomena without bearing on the present. The chance of striking through the mask of corporate-underwritten, feel-good, ahistorical racism grows daily more remote. The trade-off—whites promise friendship, blacks accept the status quo—begins to seem like a good deal.

Cosseted by Hollywood's magic lantern and soothed by press releases from Washington and the American Enterprise Institute, we should never forget what we see and hear for ourselves. Broken out by race, the results of every social tabulation from unemployment to life expectancy add up to a chronicle of atrocity. The history of black America fully explains—to anyone who

30

approaches it honestly—how the disaster happened and why neither guilt money nor lectures on personal responsibility can, in
and of themselves, repair the damage. The vision of friendship
and sympathy placing blacks and whites "all in the same boat,"
rendering them equally able to do each other favors, "to give rides
to one another," is a smiling but monstrous lie.

Endnote

1. I could go on with examples of movies that deliver the good news of
   friendship: *Regarding Henry, Driving Miss Daisy, Forrest Gump, The
   Shawshank Redemption, Philadelphia, The Last Boy Scout, 48 Hours
   I-II, Rising Sun, Iron Eagle I-II, Rudy, Sister Act, Hearts of Dixie, Be-
   trayed, The Power of One, White Nights, Clara's Heart, Doc Hollywood,
   Cool Runnings, Places in the Heart, Trading Places, Fried Green Toma-
   toes, Q & A, Platoon, A Mother's Courage: The Mary Thomas Story, The
   Unforgiven, The Air Up There, The Pelican Brief, Losing Isaiah, Smoke,
   Searching for Bobby Fischer, An Officer and a Gentleman, Speed,* etc.

For Discussion and Writing

1. DeMott claims that the movie *Pulp Fiction* shows an America in which
   racism is tamed. What do you think that means? Why wouldn't the taming
   of racism be a good thing? Or is it that DeMott means the opposite, that
   racism still plagues America? If you can, watch the movie again, and analyze
   for yourself some of the scenes DeMott mentions. Would you consider such
   scenes as central to the movie or incidental? Describe at least one scene in a
   movie that portrays an interracial friendship and harmony in our country.
2. In the second paragraph of the essay, DeMott describes a scene from *Die
   Hard with a Vengeance*. How does DeMott describe the young blacks depicted in this scene? How does he describe the relationship between the
   film's two stars? Characterize his tone, that is, neutral, mocking, and so on.
3. DeMott refers to a "new dogma of black-white sameness." What does he
   mean by this? When do pundits and talk show hosts refer to black-white
   equality? Do they mean it's a reality or a goal? Which do you think it is? If
   it's a goal, list three means by which it can be achieved. If it's a reality, list
   three proofs that you find in our culture. To what degree might "feel-good"
   movies mask racial dysfunction in our culture? What bridges might such
   texts build between different people in America?
4. DeMott says that the movies he examines have a "deep logic." Paraphrase
   his description of this deep logic. Why can't DeMott believe in the "sunshine
   world" suggested by the movies in question?

5. DeMott refers to a "new orthodoxy of friendship." Who is promoting this new orthodoxy? In what sense does promoting this belief incite "culture-wide evasion" of racism? How does it justify "one political step backward after another"?

6. "Thus we shift the problem away from politics—from black experience . . . ; solving the problem asks no more of us than that we work on ourselves, scrubbing off the dirt of ill will." What does DeMott mean here? Why keep the problem in the realm of politics rather than in the realm of individual self-improvement?

The Long March from Wong to Woo
Tiana Thi Thanh Nga

Tiana Thi Thanh Nga was born in Saigon, Vietnam, where her father was Minister of Information for South Vietnam. In 1966 he moved his family to the United States. Nga later returned to Vietnam and that experience is presented in her film From Hollywood to Hanoi. *As a Vietnamese American, Nga has lived in two worlds and grappled with the problems that attend having a complex identity. As an insider in the movie industry, she can speak knowledgeably about Hollywood and its presentation of Asians. In an interview for* Cineaste *magazine, she emphasized the cultural impact of movies, noting that "we live in a visual world. If you have something to say, film is a great medium, especially nonfiction film that can illuminate people as it entertains them."*

---------------- ✦ ----------------

On International Women's Day in 1994, I was honored at the Directors Guild of America by becoming the youngest recipient of the Women in Film Achievement Award. Stevie Wonder, my hero, congratulated me, and CNN Entertainment asked how I felt. Cool. Hey, I was on global television! But after struggling for two decades in Hollywood, my film work had just begun. When I was a teenager struggling for work as an actress, Asian American Screen Actors Guild members took up only two pages in the Academy Players listing of what was then called the "Orientals" category. Ouch! Conjures up images of conniving little Fu Manchus who do your shirts with extra starch. Nowadays our glossy photos fill up dozens of pages in the Academy book. We are now "Asian Pacific." Ugh. Sounds like one of those railroads our Chinese forebears died building in pursuit of the American Dream. Why can't we simply be who we are? Why do we have to be categorized at all?

Flashback to 1928: Anna May Wong explains her reason for leaving Hollywood—"I was tired of the parts I had to play. Why is it that on the screen the Chinese are nearly aways the villain of the piece, and so cruel a villain—murderous, treacherous, a snake in the grass. We are not like that. How could we be, with a civilization so many times older than that of the West? We have our rigid code of behavior, of honor. Why do they never show those on the screen?"

Jumpcut to 1995: John Woo, Hong Kong's leading director, comments on his first Hollywood film—"I feel honored, grateful and excited to work in Hollywood. . . . It's a great joy to receive such wonderful support, so that I can bring my creativity a step higher when supported by good crews and productions. It has been a great learning experience for me. It also fulfilled my dream of combining East and West and making a good film."

Seventy-five years lurk between the debut of Anna May Wong as an extra in the silent *The Red Lantern* (1919) and John Woo. During those seventy-five years, Hollywood's perception of the Asian seemed to have been derived directly from the nineteenth-century frontier view of Chinese as a subhuman species suitable for building levees, laying railroad track, doing laundry, or being dangled from trees by those ridiculous pigtails. Moviegoers were fed erotic images of the China Doll as concubine, supple in cheongsam attire, secret danger cocked in the eyes, graceful as a snow leopard. But look out! There's a dagger up her silk sleeve. Asian males fared no better, being either Ming the Merciless, the Mad Malaysian run amok, Fu Manchu, or Charlie Chan spouting those fortune-cookie one-liners.

5   Throughout the 1930s, Hollywood dabbled from time to time with Asian locales, but as Asian never got a leading role. Stars of European descent were entrusted with the plum parts; their eyelids hiked up so tightly it is a wonder they could find their marks on the sound stage floors. Typically, when MGM cast for *The Good Earth*, one of the most successful films of the decade, the

leading Chinese roles went to Paul Muni and Luise Rainer. With typical grace, the studio asked Anna May Wong to drive over to Culver City to test for the role of Lotus, an especially loathsome concubine. A furious Anna May told them, with her Oxonian accent, what they could do with that lotus of theirs.

The 1940s presented Hollywood with major casting problems. The villains of that era were the terrible Nips. But the American authorities had herded all the West Coast Japanese into detention camps. Who would play the Bad Guys? No problem. All Asians look alike. We'll use Chinese and Koreans. Thus, Philip Ahn, Richard Loo, and other non-Japanese were up to their samurai swords in work. It was Yellow Peril Time—babies on bayonets, John Wayne storming beachheads—and few Asian actors needed to collect unemployment benefits in those heady days.

An outright assault on stereotyping had to wait until 1960, when Ray Stark cast an honest to goodness, mostly Asian girl in the title role in *The World of Suzie Wong*, an East-West love story caressingly photographed in Hong Kong. Nancy Kwan, who played a Chinese prostitute, was actually permitted on screen to let a clean-cut American lad (William Holden, no less) love and cherish her, overlook the fact that she made her daily biscuits by flat-backing, and see in her only that gauzy, abiding goodness of the loving Asian mistress, willing prey to the tall, shining white knight. Sentimental? Of course. Racist? You bet. Outdated? Like the horse and buggy. But sentimental, racist, and outdated as it was, Suzie Wong was a breakthrough film in the long march from Wong to Woo. In 1928, British censors had removed a scene in one of Anna May's films in which she kissed an Englishman. The authorities argued that such a thing could not have occurred in real life.

Bruce Lee would be similarly affronted when, in spite of his awesome martial arts expertise and the indisputable genetic fact that he was Chinese, DNA from a German grandfather notwithstanding, Warner Bros. rejected him for the leading role in *Kung Fu*, a TV series based on Bruce's idea. Instead, the role went to an American actor, David Carradine. Rubbing salt into the wound, Warner Bros. initially broadcast the show only once a month, explaining, "The American public won't sit for a Chinaman appearing in their living rooms every week."

This racial rejection by Hollywood, Bruce told me, made him furious. It impelled him to leave the United States and return to

Hong Kong, where, in two dizzying years, he became an international legend. The week before he died we spoke. He was filming *Game of Death* and had just left the hospital after stunt injuries sustained on the set. He was as feisty as ever. His new film, *Enter the Dragon*, produced by Warner Bros., was due to open in the U.S. "Just watch, I'll outgross Steve McQueen and James Coburn," he declared. They were both Bruce's students and each had told him that he could never reach their star status because he was Chinese. Part of his plan to prove them wrong involved another pupil, the Oscar-winning screenwriter Stirling Silliphant, who proved to be a staunch Lee ally. Silliphant wrote a special part for Bruce in the ABC-TV show, *Longstreet*. After the show's two-hour pilot episode, "The Way of the Intercepting Fist," Bruce got more fan mail than James Franciscus, the leading man. That episode was shown to Raymond Chow in Hong Kong. The rest, as they say, is history.

10   Before Bruce left for his final destiny in Hong Kong, he and Silliphant collaborated on a script with James Coburn entitled *The Silent Flute*. In it, Bruce was to play several roles similar to but more authentic than Carradine's TV zen-chop-socky character. Warner Bros. sent the trio to India on a reconnaissance mission to see what could be done with the company's blocked rupees. Coburn was treated like a star in India while Bruce, whom everyone assumed was a lowly assistant, got what he referred to as "the broom closet." He was so bitter about the stereotyping that he made me promise him that I would never agree to play the Hollywood game—being cast as the Chinese whore or the helpless Oriental who gets raped and killed. He was clairvoyant about that. Years later, I turned down exactly such a part in Brian De Palma's Viet Nam film, *Casualties of War*. No problem, they cast a Thai girl for the part. They were shooting Thailand for Viet Nam anyway. Bruce swore to me he'd never wear a braid and play the coolie. We made a pact to take on Hollywood! We didn't know what we were up against. His road would take him back home to Hong Kong and mine, two decades later, would lead me to Viet Nam.

As the 1980s unspooled, Hollywood began to replace their nasty Asian types with more benign stereotypes—Asians seen through flickering foregrounds of candlelit, burnished temples—the old sound of one-hand-clapping routine, with Zen the buzzword. These images were balanced, yin and yang style, by the Asian martial artists who demonstrated that any monk trained in wushu could easily mop up an alley full of street toughs in, say, Hoboken, or even East St. Louis.

The long decades of demonizing Asians also spawned new stereotypes. Asian actors in minor roles were often a tad brighter than their sluggish coworkers. Got a part for the forensic expert in a police film? How about a systems analyst? That all fits in with the honor-roll images from Berkeley and Harvard. Study another set of statistics and we get another variation on the Other: Asian gang members. The Japanese were still catching hell in films like *Black Rain* and *Rising Sun*. And in *Robocop III* the long-enduring Mako got to play the ever-mysterious CEO of an octopuslike Tokyo conglomerate. Even after fifty-two years, the people who brought Americans Pearl Harbor were not to be trusted, especially when they're holding the mortgage on the Hollywood studio bungalow.

But other forces were in play as well. The flow of Asian immigrants to the United States had given birth to a rising chorus of Asian American voices. These new writers included Maxine Hong Kingston, Amy Tan, Lois-Ann Yamanaka, Carlos Bulosan, and Bharati Mukherjee. Adding another dimension to this movement were the new translated works of Vietnamese writers from Hanoi. In 1987 I discovered and interviewed Duong Thu Huong, the lady cadre, political prisoner, and beloved writer of socialist Viet Nam. *Paradise of the Blind*, her novel about postwar Viet Nam, was published by William Morrow. Bao Ninh, another Hanoi writer, had his masterpiece, *The Sorrow of War*, become a bestseller in England. Ninh writes, in a much-needed corrective, of how Vietnamese war veterans also have nightmarish, compelling images.

All of these writers provide Hollywood with a vision of the 15 Asian and Asian American experience that rips apart the old images. Their truth, held up like a crucifix before the Dracula of Hollywood, compels the studios to face the fact that Asian hearts are not so different, that Asian eyes shed tears despite the slant of their eyelids. Responding to these simple truths, American audiences have flocked to *The Joy Luck Club*, a film with real-life Asians daringly playing real-life characters with not a Shirley MacLaine, Myrna Loy, or Katharine Hepburn in the cast. The film's existence is due mainly to Executive Producer Oliver Stone's willingness to take a risk. The film is directed by Wayne Wang, an Asian American who began his career in 1982 with an honest little film, *Chan Is Missing*, shot on the streets of San Francisco for a handful of change with a dedicated Asian American cast and crew.

Have the times caught up? I can't say. The big blockbuster of last year was *Forrest Gump*. What does Gump say about his experience in Nam? "We were lookin' for some guy named Charlie." The audiences thought that was hilarious. I cringed. Was this to be our legacy? Three million Indochinese dead. The nation of Viet Nam ravished, fit now only to be the butt of a Hollywood joke? I think Steve McQueen, shot and dying in a Chinese courtyard in Robert Wise's *The Sand Pebbles*, gave a more honest answer— "What am I doing here?"

John Woo, with all the heat he generated in Hollywood after several successful Hong Kong action films, might ask the same question. Recently he stated, "The system here is very complicated and involved. There are a lot of power struggles and politics. I feel that sometimes I waste so much time and energy on meaningless rules of the game. Politics, meetings, and the ego problems of a lot of people make me confused. This affects my creative mood and depresses me. . . . I believe many American directors go through the same thing."

Yes, indeed we do. My own film, *From Hollywood to Hanoi*, made with blood, sweat, and tears over six years, was screened for the U.S. Congress in 1994 in celebration of President Clinton's decision to lift the twenty-year trade embargo against Viet Nam. This was the first American film shot in Viet Nam for Viet Nam to play in theaters. It has won major festival awards and pleased audiences enough that they have funded the prints and 35mm blow-up. I have taken the film on the college circuit from East Coast Harvard to West Coast Stanford. I've shown it in art centers as far north as Minneapolis and as far south as New Orleans. But no Hollywood studio has been willing to take it on for distribution. Distributing has been like waging war. You take a hill at a time. You go bunker by bunker. I had no choice, but I don't recommend it.

Part of the problem, of course, is that I chose to make a documentary. Unless your topic is baseball or basketball, the studios aren't usually interested. Do I have regrets about my choices? A few. Not enough hours in each day. A wrecked personal life. But I enjoy the freedom of retaining all rights to my work. We are free to play it for audiences throughout the world. I have seen my film reunite families, help change government policies, and stir the passionate but still rigid Vietnamese community. The film even succeeded in making my parents proud of their daughter, the Woman Warrior armed with a camera. Sometimes I've felt like giving up, but I believe Bruce would have been proud of me for keeping my vow with him.

Now it's time to make another one. It's called *Rice Dreams.*   20 I'm writing it, living it, and workshopping it. Before that, I'm heading out to China Beach in Central Viet Nam to shoot my summer musical comedy film, *Bingo Beach,* as the first Vietnamese-American co-production. In the meantime, I dream of Anna May. I wish I had met her. Most of all, I wish I had her to cast. A teenage Anna May and Leonardo DiCaprio on a kitchen table. Anna May and Spike Lee rapping! Tom Cruise and Anna get married in Hawaii. Thelma and Anna May. The possibilities are endless. The long march isn't complete, but maybe we do see the hint of light at the end of the Hollywood tunnel. Thank you, Anna May Wong! Best of luck, John Woo!

For Discussion and Writing

1. Nga notes that Asian actors have been classified as "Orientals" and "Asian Pacific" in the Academy Players listing. She asks, "Why do we have to be categorized at all?" What sort of answer can you offer?

2. The actor Anna May Wong objected, years ago, to narrow depictions of Chinese characters in film. What are some of the roles that were available to her, and what did these roles leave out in depicting Chinese? Think of some of the ways Chinese have been depicted in movies you've seen. How do these portrayals conform to a stereotype? If you try to name three Asian actors, who comes to mind?

3. As the author reports, Bruce Lee was rejected for the leading role in a 1970s TV show, *Kung Fu.* The part went to a Caucasian actor untrained in martial arts. Discuss the apparent ironies in this. What resistance, if any, do you think there might be to a leading TV role played by a Chinese actor today?

4. Nga mentions two movies, *Forrest Gump* and *The Sand Pebbles.* What is the point of her contrast? In what differing ways might Asian Americans and other Americans respond to the "joke" in *Forrest Gump?* What kind of film stereotypes make you uncomfortable? Why?

5. Nga notes that the "1940s presented Hollywood with major casting problems." What does she mean? In what ways might events of the 1940s have impacted conventional stereotypes of Chinese?

6. Look at a contemporary movie featuring an Asian leading man, a Jet Li or Jackie Chan movie, for example. In what ways do such movies fall into or avoid the sort of stereotypes Nga mentions?

Crimes Against Humanity
WARD CHURCHILL

Characterized by bell hooks as a "leading insurgent intellectual,"
Ward Churchill has written widely on Native Americans. His books
include Native Son: Selected Essays on Indigenism 1985–1995,
Fantasies of the Master Race: Literature, Cinema, and the Colo-
nization of American Indians *and* Since Predator Came: Notes on
the Struggle for American Indian Liberation. *He has been a mem-*
ber of the governing council of the Colorado chapter of the American
Indian Movement, and has worked on the Leonard Peltier defense
committee. In the essay below, published by Z Magazine *in 1993,*
Churchill attacks the continuing practice of naming sports teams
"Redskins," "Braves," "Chiefs," and so on. Many sports fans are com-
pletely comfortable with such names and insist that they contain no
malice and do no harm to Native Americans. Churchill takes aim at
such fans when he asks them to imagine teams named after other
ethnic groups and according to stereotypes about them. More to the
point, he asks about connections between such mainstream images
and the far less visible world of actual Native Americans.

✦

During the past couple of seasons, there has been an increasing wave of controversy regarding the names of professional
sports teams like the Atlanta "Braves," Cleveland "Indians," Washington "Redskins," and Kansas City "Chiefs." The issue extends to
the names of college teams like Florida State University "Semi-
noles," University of Illinois "Fighting Illini," and so on, right on
down to high school outfits like the Lamar (Colorado) "Savages."
Also involved have been team adoption of "mascots," replete with
feathers, buckskins, beads, spears and "warpaint" (some fans have
opted to adorn themselves in the same fashion), and nifty little
"pep" gestures like the "Indian Chant" and "Tomahawk Chop."

A substantial number of American Indians have protested that
use of native names, images and symbols as sports team mascots
and the like is, by definition, a virulently racist practice. Given the
historical relationship between Indians and non-Indians during
what has been called the "Conquest of America," American Indian
Movement leader (and American Indian Anti-Defamation Council

founder) Russell Means has compared the practice to contemporary Germans naming their soccer teams the "Jews," "Hebrews," and "Yids," while adorning their uniforms with grotesque caricatures of Jewish faces taken from the Nazis' anti-Semitic propaganda of the 1930s. Numerous demonstrations have occurred in conjunction with games—most notably during the November 15, 1992 match-up between the Chiefs and Redskins in Kansas City—by angry Indians and their supporters.

In response, a number of players—especially African-Americans and other minority athletes—have been trotted out by professional team owners like Ted Turner, as well as university and public school officials, to announce that they mean not to insult but to honor native people. They have been joined by the television networks and most major newspapers, all of which have editorialized that Indian discomfort with the situation is "no big deal," insisting that the whole thing is just "good, clean fun." The country needs more such fun, they've argued, and "a few disgruntled Native Americans" have no right to undermine the nation's enjoyment of its leisure time by complaining. This is especially the case, some have argued, "in hard times like these." It has even been contended that Indian outrage at being systematically degraded—rather than the degradation itself—creates "a serious barrier to the sort of intergroup communication so necessary in a multicultural society such as ours."

Okay, let's communicate. We are frankly dubious that those advancing such positions really believe their own rhetoric, but, just for the sake of argument, let's accept the premise that they are sincere. If what they say is true, then isn't it time we spread such "inoffensiveness" and "good cheer" around among *all* groups so that *everybody* can participate *equally* in fostering the round of national laughs they call for? Sure it is—the country can't have too much fun or "intergroup involvement"—so the more, the merrier. Simple consistency demands that anyone who thinks the Tomahawk Chop is a swell pastime must be just as hearty in his or her endorsement of the following ideas. The same logic used to defend the defamation of American Indians should help us all start yukking it up.

First, as a counterpart to the Redskins, we need an NFL team   5
called "Niggers" to honor Afro-Americans. Half-time festivities for fans might include a simulated stewing of the opposing coach in a large pot while players and cheerleaders dance around it, garbed in leopard skins and wearing fake bones in their noses.

This concept obviously goes along with the kind of gaiety attending the Chop, but also with the actions of the Kansas City Chiefs, whose team members—prominently including black team members—lately appeared on a poster looking "fierce" and "savage" by way of wearing Indian regalia. Just a bit of harmless "morale boosting," says the Chiefs' front office. You bet.

So that the newly formed Niggers sports club won't end up too out of sync while expressing the "spirit" and "identity" of Afro-Americans in the above fashion, a baseball franchise—let's call this one the "Sambos"—should be formed. How about a basketball team called the "Spearchuckers"? A hockey team called the "Jungle Bunnies"? Maybe the "essence" of these teams could be depicted by images of tiny black faces adorned with huge pairs of lips. The players could appear on TV every week or so gnawing on chicken legs and spitting watermelon seeds at one another. Catchy, eh? Well, there's "nothing to be upset about," according to those who love wearing "war bonnets" to the Super Bowl or having "Chief Illiniwik" dance around the sports arenas of Urbana, Illinois.

And why stop there? There are plenty of other groups to include. Hispanics? They can be "represented" by the Galveston "Greasers" and San Diego "Spics," at least until the Wisconsin "Wetbacks" and Baltimore "Beaners" get off the ground. Asian Americans? How about the "Slopes," "Dinks," "Gooks," and "Zipperheads"? Owners of the latter teams might get their logo ideas from editorial page cartoons printed in the nation's newspapers during World War II: slant-eyes, buck teeth, big glasses, but nothing racially insulting or derogatory, according to the editors and artists involved at the time. Indeed, this Second World War–vintage stuff can be seen as just another barrel of laughs, at least by what current editors say are their "local standards" concerning American Indians.

Let's see. Who's been left out? Teams like the Kansas City "Kikes," Hanover "Honkies," San Leandro "Shylocks," Daytona "Dagos," and Pittsburgh "Polacks" will fill a certain social void among white folk. Have a religious belief? Let's all go for the gusto and gear up the Milwaukee "Mackerel Snappers" and Hollywood "Holy Rollers." The Fighting Irish of Notre Dame can be rechristened the "Drunken Irish" or "Papist Pigs." Issues of gender and sexual preference can be addressed through creation of teams like the St. Louis "Sluts," Boston "Bimbos," Detroit "Dykes," and the Fresno "Fags." How about the Gainesville

"Gimps" and Richmond "Retards," so the physically and mentally impaired won't be excluded from our fun and games? Now, don't go getting "overly sensitive" out there. None of this is demeaning or insulting, at least not when it's being done to Indians. Just ask the folks who are doing it, or their apologists like Andy Rooney in the national media. They'll tell you—as in fact they *have* been telling you—that there's been no harm done, regardless of what their victims think, feel, or say. The situation is exactly the same as when those with precisely the same mentality used to insist that Step 'n' Fetchit was okay, or Rochester on the *Jack Benny Show,* or Amos and Andy, Charlie Chan, the Frito Bandito, or any of the other cutesy symbols making up the lexicon of American racism. Have we communicated yet?

Let's get just a little bit real here. The notion of "fun" embodied 10 in rituals like the Tomahawk Chop must be understood for what it is. There's not a single non-Indian example used above which can be considered socially acceptable in even the most marginal sense. The reasons are obvious enough. So why is it different where American Indians are concerned? One can only conclude that, in contrast to the other groups at issue, Indians are (falsely) perceived as being too few, and therefore too weak, to defend themselves effectively against racist and otherwise offensive behavior.

Fortunately, there are some glimmers of hope. A few teams and their fans have gotten the message and have responded appropriately. Stanford University, which opted to drop the name "Indians" from Stanford, has experienced no resulting drop-off in attendance. Meanwhile, the local newspaper in Portland, Oregon recently decided its long-standing editorial policy prohibiting use of racial epithets should include derogatory team names. The Redskins, for instance, are now referred to as "the Washington team," and will continue to be described in this way until the franchise adopts an inoffensive moniker (newspaper sales in Portland have suffered no decline as a result).

Such examples are to be applauded and encouraged. They stand as figurative beacons in the night, proving beyond all doubt that it is quite possible to indulge in the pleasure of athletics without accepting blatant racism into the bargain.

On October 16, 1946, a man named Julius Streicher mounted the steps of a gallows. Moments later he was dead, the sentence of an international tribunal composed of representatives of the

United States, France, Great Britain, and the Soviet Union having been imposed. Streicher's body was then cremated, and—so horrendous were his crimes thought to have been—his ashes dumped into an unspecified German river so that "no one should ever know a particular place to go for reasons of mourning his memory."

Julius Streicher had been convicted at Nuremberg, Germany, of what were termed "Crimes Against Humanity." The lead prosecutor in his case—Justice Robert Jackson of the United States Supreme Court—had not argued that the defendant had killed anyone, nor that he had personally committed any especially violent act. Nor was it contended that Streicher had held any particularly important position in the German government during the period in which the so-called Third Reich had exterminated some 6,000,000 Jews, as well as several million Gypsies, Poles, Slavs, homosexuals, and other *untermenschen* (subhumans).

15   The sole offense for which the accused was ordered put to death was in having served as publisher/editor of a Bavarian tabloid entitled *Der Stürmer* during the early-to-mid 1930s, years before the Nazi genocide actually began. In this capacity, he had penned a long series of virulently anti-Semitic editorials and "news" stories, usually accompanied by cartoons and other images graphically depicting Jews in extraordinarily derogatory fashion. This, the prosecution asserted, had done much to "dehumanize" the targets of his distortion in the mind of the German public. In turn, such dehumanization had made it possible—or at least easier—for average Germans to later indulge in the outright liquidation of Jewish "vermin." The tribunal agreed, holding that Streicher was therefore complicit in genocide and deserving of death by hanging.

During his remarks to the Nuremberg tribunal, Justice Jackson observed that, in implementing its sentences, the participating powers were morally and legally binding themselves to adhere forever after to the same standards of conduct that were being applied to Streicher and the other Nazi leaders. In the alternative, he said, the victorious allies would have committed "pure murder" at Nuremberg—no different in substance from that carried out by those they presumed to judge—rather than establishing the "permanent bench-mark for justice" which was intended.

Yet in the United States of Robert Jackson, the indigenous American Indian population had already been reduced, in a process which is ongoing to this day, from perhaps 12.5 million in the year 1500 to fewer than 250,000 by the beginning of the twentieth century. This was accomplished, according to official sources, "largely through the cruelty of [Euro-American] settlers," and an informal but clear governmental policy which had made it an articulated goal to "exterminate these red vermin," or at least whole segments of them.

Bounties had been placed on the scalps of Indians—any Indians—in places as diverse as Georgia, Kentucky, Texas, the Dakotas, Oregon, and California, and had been maintained until resident Indian populations were decimated or disappeared altogether. Entire peoples such as the Cherokee had been reduced to half their size through a policy of forced removal from their homelands east of the Mississippi River to what were then considered less preferable areas in the West.

Others, such as the Navajo, suffered the same fate while under military guard for years on end. The United States Army had also perpetrated a long series of wholesale massacres of Indians at places like Horseshoe Bend, Bear River, Sand Creek, the Washita River, the Marias River, Camp Robinson, and Wounded Knee.

Through it all, hundreds of popular novels—each competing   20
with the next to make Indians appear more grotesque, menacing, and inhuman—were sold in the tens of millions of copies in the U.S. Plainly, the Euro-American public was being conditioned to see Indians in such a way as to allow their eradication to continue. And continue it did until the Manifest Destiny of the U.S.—a direct precursor to what Hitler would subsequently call *Lebensraumpolitik* (the politics of living space)—was consummated.

By 1900, the national project of "clearing" Native Americans from their land and replacing them with "superior" Anglo-American settlers was complete; the indigenous population had been reduced by as much as 98 percent while approximately 97.5 percent of their original territory had "passed" to the invaders. The survivors had been concentrated, out of sight and mind of the public, on scattered "reservations," all of them under the self-assigned "plenary" (full) power of the federal government. There was, of course, no Nuremberg-style tribunal passing judgment on those who had fostered such circumstances in North America. No U.S. official or private citizen was ever imprisoned—never mind hanged—for implementing or propagandizing what had been done. Nor had the process of genocide afflicting Indians been completed. Instead, it merely changed form.

Between the 1880s and the 1980s, nearly half of all Native American children were coercively transferred from their own families, communities, and cultures to those of the conquering society. This was done through compulsory attendance at remote boarding schools, often hundreds of miles from their homes, where native children were kept for years on end while being systematically "deculturated" (indoctrinated to think and act in the manner of Euro-Americans rather than as Indians). It was also accomplished through a pervasive foster home and adoption program—including "blind" adoptions, where children would be permanently denied information as to who they were/are and where they'd come from—placing native youths in non-Indian homes.

The express purpose of all this was to facilitate a U.S. governmental policy to bring about the "assimilation" (dissolution) of indigenous societies. In other words, Indian cultures as such were to be caused to disappear. Such policy objectives are directly contrary to the United Nations 1948 Convention on Punishment and Prevention of the Crime of Genocide, an element of international law arising from the Nuremberg proceedings. The forced "transfer of the children" of a targeted "racial, ethnical, or religious group" is explicitly prohibited as a genocidal activity under the Convention's second article.

Article II of the Genocide Convention also expressly prohibits involuntary sterilization as a means of "preventing births among" a targeted population. Yet, in 1975, it was conceded by the U.S. government that its Indian Health Service (IHS), then a subpart of the Bureau of Indian Affairs (BIA), was even then conducting a secret program of involuntary sterilization that had affected approximately 40 percent of all Indian women. The program was allegedly discontinued, and the IHS was transferred to the Public Health Service, but no one was punished. In 1990, it came out that the IHS was inoculating Inuit children in Alaska with Hepatitis-B vaccine. The vaccine had already been banned by the World Health Organization as having a demonstrated correlation with the HIV-syndrome which is itself correlated to AIDS. As this is written, a "field test" of Hepatitis-A vaccine, also HIV-correlated, is being conducted on Indian reservations in the northern plains region.

25   The Genocide Convention makes it a "crime against humanity" to create conditions leading to the destruction of an identifiable human group, as such. Yet the BIA has utilized the government's plenary prerogatives to negotiate mineral leases "on

behalf of" Indian peoples paying a fraction of standard royalty rates. The result has been "super profits" for a number of preferred U.S. corporations. Meanwhile, Indians, whose reservations ironically turned out to be in some of the most mineral-rich areas of North America, which makes us, the nominally wealthiest segment of the continent's population, live in dire poverty.

By the government's own data in the mid-1980s, Indians received the lowest annual and lifetime per capita incomes of any aggregate population group in the United States. Concomitantly, we suffer the highest rate of infant mortality, death by exposure and malnutrition, disease, and the like. Under such circumstances, alcoholism and other escapist forms of substance abuse are endemic in the Indian community, a situation which leads both to a general physical debilitation of the population and a catastrophic accident rate. Teen suicide among Indians is several times the national average.

The average life expectancy of a reservation-based Native American man is barely forty-five years; women can expect to live less than three years longer.

Such itemizations could be continued at great length, including matters like the radioactive contamination of large portions of contemporary Indian Country, the forced relocation of traditional Navajos, and so on. But the point should be made: Genocide, as defined in international law, is a continuing fact of day-do-day life (and death) for North America's native peoples. Yet there has been—and is—only the barest flicker of public concern about, or even consciousness of, this reality. Absent any serious expression of public outrage, no one is punished and the process continues.

A salient reason for public acquiescence before the ongoing holocaust in Native North America has been a continuation of the popular legacy, often through more effective media. Since 1925, Hollywood has released more than 2,000 films, many of them rerun frequently on television, portraying Indians as strange, perverted, ridiculous, and often dangerous things of the past. Moreover, we are habitually presented to mass audiences one-dimensionally, devoid of recognizable human motivations and emotions; Indians thus serve as props, little more. We have thus been thoroughly and systematically dehumanized.

Nor is this the extent of it. Everywhere, we are used as logos, as 30 mascots, as jokes: "Big Chief" writing tablets, "Red Man" chewing tobacco, "Winnebago" campers, "Navajo" and "Cherokee" and

"Pontiac" and "Cadillac" pickups and automobiles. There are the Cleveland "Indians," the Kansas City "Chiefs," the Atlanta "Braves" and the Washington "Redskins" professional sports teams—not to mention those in thousands of colleges, high schools, and elementary schools across the country—each with their own degrading caricatures and parodies of Indians and/or things Indian. Pop fiction continues in the same vein, including an unending stream of New Age manuals purporting to expose the inner works of indigenous spirituality in everything from pseudo-philosophical to do-it-yourself styles. Blond yuppies from Beverly Hills amble about the country claiming to be reincarnated seventeenth century Cheyenne Ushamans ready to perform previously secret ceremonies.

In effect, a concerted, sustained, and in some ways accelerating effort has gone into making Indians unreal. It is thus of obvious importance that the American public begin to think about the implications of such things the next time they witness a gaggle of face-painted and war-bonneted buffoons doing the "Tomahawk Chop" at a baseball or football game. It is necessary that they think about the implications of the grade-school teacher adorning their child in turkey feathers to commemorate Thanksgiving. Think about the significance of John Wayne or Charleton Heston killing a dozen "savages" with a single bullet the next time a western comes on TV. Think about why Land-o-Lakes finds it appropriate to market its butter with the stereotyped image of an "Indian princess" on the wrapper. Think about what it means when non-Indian academics profess—as they often do—to "know more about Indians than Indians do themselves." Think about the significance of charlatans like Carlos Castaneda and Jamake Highwater and Mary Summer Rain and Lynn Andrews churning out "Indian" bestsellers, one after the other, while Indians typically can't get into print.

Think about the real situation of American Indians. Think about Julius Streicher. Remember Justice Jackson's admonition. Understand that the treatment of Indians in American popular culture is not "cute" or "amusing" or just "good, clean fun."

Know that it causes real pain and real suffering of real people. Know that it threatens our very survival. And know that this is just as much a crime against humanity as anything the Nazis ever did. It is likely that the indigenous people of the United States will never demand that those guilty of such criminal activity be punished for their deeds. But the least we have the right to expect—indeed, to demand—is that such practices finally be brought to a halt.

For Discussion and Writing

1. How many sports teams can you think of whose names refer in any way to Native Americans? How many refer to other ethnic groups? What's the difference between the names of the Atlanta Braves and the MSU Spartans?
2. Analyze Churchill's shock tactics. Who is the intended audience for his imaginary African American, Hispanic, Italian, and other teams? What would the reaction be to such teams? In what ways are the author's fictional teams fair counterparts to the actual teams named for Native Americans?
3. Why does Churchill mention the case of Julius Streicher? Evaluate Churchill's use of this material in making his own case. How effectively does the essay link historical facts of the slaughter of and criminal actions against Native Americans with cultural stereotypes?
4. How does Churchill link the practice of naming ball teams to deeper and more pernicious stereotypes? How can changing a team's name change anything else in our culture? Imagine that you are a fan who is insulted by the tomahawk chop. You call a radio talk show whose host dismisses criticism of such things as misplaced, unimportant. The host gives you time to make a one-minute response. What would it be?
5. The Internet includes many sites maintained by Native American nations. Contact several and ask for responses to a well-formed question about stereotypes in the naming of sports teams. Ask about the tomahawk chop, too. If at all possible, exchange several e-mails with the same people so that you have something like a conversation. The writing you do should come out of these exchanges and whatever other research these lead to.

The Don Juan Syndrome
JULIE CHAPA

In the following article, the freelance writer and former editor of Hispanic Magazine *Julie Chapa examines the stereotype of the Latin lover, from Rudolph Valentino back in the very early 20th century to Antonio Banderas's current work. She notes that the Latin lover is one among several recognizable roles typical for today's Latino actors: drug runner, gangster, crime lord. She is not alone in remarking on the narrowness of roles available.*

———————— ✦ ————————

Since the days of early cinema, Latin men have portrayed some of the most virile, passionate, and forbidden characters on the screen. With their swarthy good looks and smoldering eyes, these "Latin lovers" have caused female moviegoers to swoon for decades. But unlike his blond counterpart, the Latin lover was generally not cast in the leading role. He played the rogue to the Anglo gentleman. He was, however, suave and more than able to captivate even the strongest screen siren. Early screen actors such as Rudolph Valentino, Ramón Novarro, and Gilbert Roland invariably set the stage for today's Latino film roles.

While the Latin lover stereotype seems like a whimsical characterization that only existed on the big screen decades ago, its effects have seeped into the American psyche, forcing Latinos, especially those in the film industry, into a smothering, tight mold. Although no stereotype should be deemed acceptable, some argue that the Latin lover image is just a step above the other stereotypes today's Latino actors have to play—drug runners, gang members, and crime lords.

THE ROOTS OF THE LATIN LOVER

The Latin lover character evolved from other stereotypes, which were seemingly much worse. Throughout cinematic and television history, Latinos have been relegated to portraying several stereotypes, according to Charles Ramírez Berg, professor of radio-television-film at the University of Texas at Austin, in the *Howard Journal of Communications*. Some have been comic characters, such as the "male buffoon" incarnated as Sergeant Garcia in Walt Disney's *Zorro* series and Leo Carrillo's Pancho in *The Cisco Kid* television series of the early fifties. Carrillo made a career of playing the buffoon, especially in his various film portrayals of the thirties. The buffoon character usually utilized his broken English or feisty temper for comic relief.

Another unlikely precursor of the Latin lover is the "bandido." A series of early films, including *Tony the Greaser* (1911) and *The Greaser's Revenge* (1914) conceived the bandido stereotype—the greasy and/or slovenly rapist, thief, drunk, or murderer. Ramírez Berg writes that the bandido stereotype not only over-simplifes Latinos—the very definition of stereotype—but also "reinforces the cleanliness, sobriety, sanity, overall decency, and moral rectitude of the WASP in the white hat." Consciously or not, movie studios used the bandido to reaffirm white America's values and morality.

Changing the image of Latinos from murderous greasers to 5 the passionate, suave lover resulted from the loss of what the film industry sought from the beginning—money. The "greaser" movies were not embraced by all. They were virulently anti-Mexican. After ignoring a written protest from the Mexican government in 1919, Hollywood suffered a blow in 1922 when films promoting such stereotypes were banned south of the border. Hollywood's response? The "greaser" became the citizen of fictitious Latin American countries. This aura of mystery added a touch of romanticism to the character and became one of the reasons for the birth of the Latin lover image.

According to Victoria Thomas, author of *Hollywood's Latin Lovers* (Santa Monica: Angel City Press, 1998), another reason was American audiences' fascination with primitivism. "The Latin lover was created for a non-Latino audience," she says. "Latin men were a passport to the forbidden." Swashbuckling heroes were venturing into previously unchartered territory in theaters, a reflection of the real-life spirit of adventure that was sweeping across the United States. "Although the portrayal has a tang of racism, it reveals the colonial attitude of the European meeting the indigenous," continues Thomas.

EARLY SCREEN HEARTTHROBS

While most consider Italian Rudolph Valentino as the founder of the Latin lover persona, the true architect of the role was Antonio Moreno. Born Antonio Garrido Monteagudo y Moreno in Madrid, Moreno began his career in 1912 in the one-reeler *Voice of the Million*. Because of his dark features and expressive face, which "read" well on camera, he was considered a natural for early films being produced under difficult conditions and with primitive equipment. By 1923 he was Paramount's leading man. That same year, his much-publicized marriage to oil heiress Daisy Canfield Danziger gave his already successful career a boost. Later that year, his three most successful films—*The Trail of the Lonesome Pine, The Spanish Dancer,* and *My American Wife*—were released, elevating demand for motion pictures with dark, dangerous men.

Following close behind Moreno was the steamy Ramón Novarro. The actor, nicknamed Ravishing Ramón, caused a furor throughout his career, offering audiences scene-stealing performances. It usually wasn't his acting that caused the distraction. In *Ben-Hur* (1926), moviegoers were treated to visions of the bare-chested Novarro as the legendary charioteer. More scandalous than that was his appearance as the sarong-clad lead in *The Pagan* (1929). Born José Ramón Gil Samaniegos in 1899 in Durango, Mexico, Novarro's ambition led him and his brother to California with only $10 between them. To help support his mother and twelve younger siblings, Novarro took a variety of odd jobs as a grocery clerk, busboy, and theater usher, among others. A talented dancer and singer, he had no trouble finding work as a studio dance extra. He appeared in myriad films, but his first big break came in 1921 when he was discovered by director Rex Ingram, who cast him in *The Four Horsemen of the Apocalypse*, also starring Valentino. Ingram then approached Novarro about a role that would showcase Novarro's Adonis-like qualities. As Rupert von Hentzau in 1922's *The Prisoner of Zenda* and with Valentino's untimely death that same year, the title of Hollywood's premier Latin lover was bestowed upon Novarro. Responsible for more than one case of "front row fainting," Novarro's sizzling scenes and exotic roles made him one of the most popular Mexican actors in American cinema history.

Along with Valentino, Moreno and Novarro unknowingly set the precedent for the future of Latino screen roles. Although the role opened the door for many Hispanic actors, including Gilbert Roland, Ricardo Montalbán, Cesar Romero, and Fernando Lamas, the Latin playboy image has been rather difficult to shake. Many modern-day Latino actors, most notably Andy Garcia and Jimmy Smits, have played "exotic" romantic leads but have also successfully avoided being typecast, thanks to their box-office appeal.

REJECTING THE LOVER

10 For lesser-known actors trying to make their big break, the Latin lover image has made the road to stardom all the more frustrating. Manny Alfaro, an actor and executive director of the Hispanic Organization of Latin Actors (HOLA), says he has learned not to have a knee-jerk reaction to typecasting. "I'm more [incensed] when Latinos are left out," he says.

HOLA, based in New York, lists as its objective "to gain an accurate, educated, and nonstereotypical portrayal of Hispanic culture and its people through the arts and media." To achieve this objective, HOLA helps its members by providing talent referrals, professional workshops, and by publishing the *HOLA Pages*, a directory of Hispanic talent.

Nonetheless, typecasting Latinos in Hollywood still exists, partly because of the needs of audiences. According to actor James Borrego, who has worked on various film projects, including *Lone Star* (1996), American audiences have more control over the situation than actors do. "As an audience member, if you don't like the casting choices, you don't go see it," he says. "For actors, it's different. What are you going to do if that's the only game in town?"

Another factor lies in *who* is making the film. The "greaser" continued to appear in motion pictures well into the seventies in films such as *Duck, You Sucker* (1972), *Bring Me the Head of Alfredo Garcia* (1974), and *Boulevard Nights* (1979). When Latino filmmakers gained visibility in the early eighties with films like Luis Valdez's *Zoot Suit* (1981), more realistic, acceptable portrayals of Latinos in films made it to the silver screen. But even these early films were blasted, as Clint C. Wilson II and Félix Gutierrez write in *Race, Multiculturalism, and the Media* (Thousand Oaks: Sage Publications, 1995), for their "perceived glorification of the drug culture, sexist orientation, and nontraditional lifestyle of the featured characters."

It wasn't until the late eighties that Latinos were recognized as members of mainstream culture with the release of highly acclaimed motion pictures like Valdez's *La Bamba* (1987), an account of the life of Richie Valens, a Latino rock and roller of the fifties; and Ramon Menendez's *Stand and Deliver* (1988), recounting the true story of inspirational Mexican American math teacher Jaime Escalante. However, according to Wilson and Gutierrez, who also penned *Minorities and the Media* (Beverly Hills: Sage Publications, 1985), films in general still portray Latinos as hoodlums and drug runners.

Many Latino actors rode in on the wave of Latino films of the late seventies and early eighties, including Edward James Olmos, Cheech Marin, and Andy Garcia. For the most part, their characters bore no resemblance to the stereotypical Latin lover. Many of today's Latino stars got their breaks by reincarnating the "greaser," who, in today's films, has evolved into the drug lord and gang

15

member. One of today's hottest Hispanic actors, Garcia, has played a few modern-day "greaser" roles, including his sadistic gangster role in *Eight Million Ways to Die* (1986). (Not all of Garcia's gangster portrayals have been Latinos; some have been Italians.) Like most of today's Latino actors, however, he has successfully steered clear of Latin lover roles. "Today Latin actors won't play it," says author Thomas, because of the fear of being limited in acting choices.

Garcia, born Andrés Arturo Garcia-Menéndez in Havana, Cuba, immigrated to the United States in 1961 at the age of five. The extremely private actor refuses to play by Hollywood's rules, keeping reporters at bay about his family life and refusing to do nude scenes. So determined is Garcia to avoid the Latin lover label, that he has reportedly refused to continue auditions when asked to remove his shirt.

EMBRACING THE LOVER

The antithesis of Garcia, Spanish heartthrob Antonio Banderas has made a career of resurrecting the Latin lover role. Making his debut in Spanish writer-director Pedro Almodóvar's films, including *Labyrinth of Passion* (1983), *Law of Desire* (1986), and *Women on the Verge of a Nervous Breakdown* (1988), this sultan of sweat, who had previously appeared in various screen roles, exploded on the scene in his first starring role in an American film, Robert Rodriguez's *Desperado* (1995). Later that year, he costarred in *Assassins* with Sylvester Stallone. Since then, Banderas has appeared in many testosterone-driven roles, most recently in *The Mask of Zorro* (1998). In a recent *Los Angeles Times* interview, Banderas said of his sex-symbol status, "I don't care. It doesn't bother me and doesn't make me feel like a superhero."

While the character of the Latin lover is not as prevalent in films today as it was seventy years ago, Hispanic men in general are still feeling the effects. "Obviously when you have Latin features—a dark complexion and different hair type—you are placed in a special category," explains actor Fred Estrada. "Usually the only category [other than that of the Latin lover] you get called in for is the homeboy with the accent." Estrada has stopped playing to the stereotype and describes his acting style as playing basically himself. "I'm educated. I don't have an inner-city accent. But when I'm auditioning I frequently hear, 'Can you have more of an accent?' or '. . . more of a lisp?'"

Estrada, who has appeared on ABC soaps *General Hospital* and *Port Charles*, also finds himself being type-cast in his day-to-day life as well as in his acting roles. As a licensed New York attorney, Estrada says that the stigma of being a "Latin playboy" haunted him throughout his legal career. "In law school, people were always calling me to find out where the parties were. No one ever asked me to be in their study groups." Estrada also says he also experienced discrimination and sexual harassment because of his looks. "As an attorney, I had five assignments cut short because of jealousy." The frustration of not being taken seriously has followed the 30-year-old actor into his new career. "The 'ladies man' stereotype definitely hurts Latin nonactors," he says, emphatically.

It is quite possible that the Latin lover is a character that will   20 never fully go away. After all, he's not all bad. Among his redeeming qualities is his attractiveness. As Borrego reminds us, "In film and media, the emphasis is on sex appeal. It's about gorgeous people. If you're going to make it [as an actor], you have to have sex appeal." While that in itself is not a bad thing, "it unfortunately gives us an unrealistic representation [of people]," he continues. "While no stereotypes are better than others, today they are not as overt as they used to be. Today's characters are more stylized. It's now possible to *like* villains. They're no longer just ugly bandits—they can be slick dudes." Alfaro also offers hope for the future of Latino roles. "Things are changing," he says. "It's coming—it's just slow."

For Discussion and Writing

1. How does Chapa connect the image of the "greaser" to that of the lover? What do the two images have in common?

2. Consider several of Banderas's films. In what ways is he typecast? A white male actor like Harrison Ford is also typecast. Compare Banderas to other typecast actors. What, if any, patterns do you find? Why isn't there a Caucasian lover stereotype? Or is there? Can you think of some stereotypes that only work if played by white actors?

3. Suppose that the studies Chapa cites are correct, and that films generally do still portray Latinos as hoodlums and drug runners. Discuss the degree to which recent and current films create or mirror actual behavior. It might help to pick a film like *American Me* or *Scarface* for review before such a discussion.

4. Fred Estrada claims that he has felt the effects of stereotypes in both his careers. In what ways have media stereotypes influenced your view of

particular people? The influences might be slight or significant. What sort of forces or images might counteract the effects of negative representations?

5. Look into older movies and their representations of Latin characters. Discuss the ways that such movies presented Latinos to the largely white audiences who attended them. Consider the ways that such stereotypes influence our perceptions of actual people.

Hollywood Targets Arab and Muslim Americans Since Sept. 11

JACK SHAHEEN

Jack Shaheen, author, scholar, and media critic, is professor emeritus of mass communications at Southern Illinois University. A former CBS news consultant, Shaheen has published widely since his days at the Wall Street Journal. *Among his books are* The TV Arab *(1984),* Arab and Muslim Stereotyping in American Popular Culture *(1997), and* Reel Bad Arabs *(2001). In the following article, Shaheen considers the media's post-9/11 portrayal of Arab and Muslim Americans in contrast to attempts by political leaders to distinguish between Islam and terrorism.*

◆

Our country's leadership has gone out of its way to distinguish between Islam and terrorism in the aftermath of Sept. 11. Yet, Hollywood has ignored that distinction completely. Major television networks—including NBC, Fox, ABC and CBS—have not only gone to great lengths to vilify Arab Muslims since then, but have introduced a very dangerous new equation: Arab Americans and Muslim Americans equals terrorist.

A few weeks ago CBS televised the movie *The President's Man: A Line in the Sand,* with Chuck Norris. In it, swarthy-looking Arab Muslims try to set off a nuclear bomb in Texas. Islam is vilified. Assisting the Arab Muslims from overseas are Americans of Arab heritage. Such an outrageous depiction has never before appeared on television.

The movie does have a good-guy Arab-American attorney general who interviews the Arab-Muslim terrorist. His scene lasts three minutes, then he disappears. CBS was effectively saying, "Our movie has one good Arab-American character, so it's fair." That is tokenism, a lie, a network's way of trying to protect its backside.

Also on CBS: In *JAG*, Arab Muslims in the Middle East plot to blow up 30 children in an American school, and beat a female Marine who heroically blows herself up with the villains; in *The District*, Arab fathers are labeled brutish to their children, and a mosque president destroys his mosque (such an incident has never happened, but vandals have destroyed more than a dozen U.S. mosques); in *The Agency*, Arab Muslim terrorists blow up a London department store, killing thousands including children (since Oct. 4, CBS has run this episode three times); on *Family Law*, an attorney defending an Arab American is betrayed when his client skips town on bail (you just can't trust "those people").

NBC's *The West Wing* and ABC's *Alias* have also made carica-   5
tures out of Arabs and Muslims, making them hateful.

Do Arab women even exist on television? You never see them. In the history of television, there has never been an Arab American woman in a starring or supporting role. Arab women in the Middle East are portrayed mainly as bundles of black cloth, submissive harem maidens or carrying jugs on their heads. They have no identities whatsoever. And they're always mute.

Anybody who has ever been to the Middle East knows who runs everything there—don't think the men do. There, you know who's in charge of the home, who flies the airplane, works on the computers, serves as the nurse. But on U.S. TV, the image of Arab women is as bad as—if not worse than—the image of the Arab male.

Hollywood has chosen to focus on a few stock caricatures and repeat these images over and over again. These images project American Arabs, American Muslims, Arabs and Muslims as members of a lunatic fringe. We come to think all "those people" are this way. We are never allowed to see, for example, Arabs and Muslims who do what normal people do—go out on picnics, go to work, love their children.

This has a profound impact even within our own community. It breeds anxiety and a sense of helplessness, particularly in children. You hear some say, "I'm not Arab, I'm Spanish," or "I'm Italian." The pervasive negative images breed a denial of heritage, a fear, a sort of shying away. It makes some not even want to speak the language.

10   It is not only the Arab and Muslim communities in the United States that are affected. In more than 150 nations, American TV and movies are hugely popular. Recently, I met with a group of Middle Eastern students at Vanderbilt University, and I asked if they watched American movies. Everyone had. "When you see Islam being vilified as a faith of violence, when you see yourselves portrayed as terrorists, what do you think?" I asked.

"We ask ourselves why Hollywood hates us," they said.

Show only vilifying images of any group, incessantly, and after a while—100 years in the case of the Arab stereotype—it becomes "natural" not to like certain people. It is a sin of omission—we omit the humanity—and of commission—we show only hateful images that make a stereotype that injures the innocent.

One reason these images and stereotypes continue is politics. The Arab-Israeli conflict has played a paramount role in shaping these images. Many of the movies I write about in my book *Reel Bad Arabs* were shot in Israel, with the cooperation of the Israeli government. It is naïve to overlook this. Another reason is that there is no American Arab or American Muslim presence in Hollywood moviemaking.

However, the primary responsibility rests with men and women who know exactly what they're doing and continue to do it because they know they can get away with it. They do it because they are prejudiced and greedy—these movies make money.

15   We've been programmed to hate "these people" they distort, and as a result, no one really cares.

Things are bad, and getting worse. Innocent Americans are being brought into the Hollywood stereotype. "Worse" isn't a strong enough word—it's dangerous.

For Discussion and Writing

1. What does the author mean by "tokenism" in his account of *The President's Man: A Line in the Sand?*

2. "Anybody who has been to the Middle East knows who runs everything there—don't think the men do," writes Shaheen. But if you haven't been to the Middle East, where do you get information about that area of the world? Make a casual list of your own recent "sources" of such information (e.g., newspaper stories, TV news, gossip, movies, TV shows). Compare your list with those of classmates.

3. What does Shaheen mean when he says, "It is a sin of omission—we omit the humanity . . ."? What do you think he would want to see included in Hollywood portrayals of Middle Easterners and Muslims? In your view, what kinds of portrayals humanize the people of another culture?

Real Minority, Media Majority
SALIM MUWAKKIL

Salim Muwakkil (né Alonzo Canady Jr.) was born in New York City in 1947. Educated in New Jersey, he graduated from Rutgers with a B.A. in political science in 1973. He was working as a news writer in the Associated Press Newark bureau at that time. A contributor to numerous books, Muwakkil has been an observer of the political scene for many years. His column "The Third Coast" currently runs in the progressive magazine In These Times.

──────────── ✦ ────────────

Chicago cops have just finished a big drug bust on the city's South Side. Local television crews are on hand, taping young black men, their heads bowed and hands cuffed, as they file into the police wagon. Later in the evening, those images will be shown on all the major television stations, filling up TV screens across the Chicago metropolitan area with the sight of young, black offenders.

Such scenes are par for the course on television news programs in major urban areas. But do these images accurately reflect the problems of race and crime in American cities? A number of recent studies show that the media—especially television—often present commonly held stereotypes about blacks, whites and criminal behavior, rather than the more complicated realities. They do so to the great detriment of the black community—and to race relations in general.

African-American men comprise about 6 percent of the U.S. population, yet they represent 51 percent of the prison population, according to the Sentencing Project. Nearly one-third of all black men in their 20s are under the control of the criminal justice system. Black Americans are eight times as likely to be incarcerated as are whites. And in 12 states and the District of

Columbia, that ratio is more than 10-to-1. Most are in prison for drug possession or other drug-related crimes.

This difference in incarceration rates is no secret. Most Americans are aware of the disparity, and attribute it to black people being more involved in the drug trade than white people. Thus, most Americans would probably be stumped by this question. What percentage of America's drug users are black? According to a 1996 study by the Justice Department's Bureau of Justice Statistics, 12 percent are black and 70 percent are white—roughly the same as in the population at large.

5   One reason for this disparate treatment, a number of academics argue, is negative stereotypes projected through the media. William Drummond, a professor of journalism at the University of California-Berkeley, studies how blacks are depicted on television. "News media have taken the lead in equating young African-American males with aggressiveness, lawlessness and violence," he says. "And entertainment media have eagerly taken their cue from journalists." The most common stereotype, says Drummond, "is that African-American men engage in drug abuse in disproportionate numbers."

In a recent article, Drummond cites data from the 1996 Bureau of Justice Statistics survey showing that only 6 percent of African-Americans have used cocaine even once in their lives, and that the great majority of those—65.5 percent—have tried it 10 times or less. Among white respondents, 10.6 percent had used cocaine. "This is not the impression one gets from watching the evening news or even an episode of a television program like *Cops*," says Drummond.

Why does the media seem to reflect a different notion of reality? For years, television stations have insisted that they are rooting out bias. But old stereotypes die hard, especially those that are useful to reporters as culture shorthand. When a newscaster described a community as "gang-ravaged," he or she imparts crucial information without having to bother with details or context. "I'll never forget the time a news director sent a camera crew out to tape some welfare mothers in public housing, and one of our more rebellious black cameramen chose to tape white mothers at one of the city's few integrated public housing projects," recalls Monroe Anderson, community affairs director at WBBM-TV, Chicago's CBS affiliate. "He came back with some shots of white welfare mothers and the news director exploded in anger. He didn't want images of white welfare mothers. He wanted footage that was authenticated by traditional stereotypes."

Of course, racial stereotyping of African-Americans has a long history in the United States, going all the way back to the slave codes. But the association of blackness with crime became most prevalent during and immediately after Reconstruction, when whites re-enslaved blacks under the ruthless system of Jim Crow. The legal system was a crucial component of this process. For example, vagrancy laws in many states allowed blacks to be arrested for the "crime" of being unemployed. "After the Civil War, the crime problem in the South became equated with the 'Negro Problem' as black prisoners began to outnumber white prisoners in all southern prisons," writes sociologist Shirley Vinning-Brown. "The terms 'slave,' 'Negro' and 'convict' were interchangeable."

By the late 1880s, when the influence of newspapers began to explode, most of the country's prestigious publications routinely projected vile stereotypes of blacks. When historian Rayford Logan surveyed the popular media from 1901 to 1912, he found that many described African-Americans with words like "brutes," "savages," "imbeciles" and "moral degenerates." Even after Jim Crow laws were firmly in place, the media set out on a mission to protect white Americans from what a February 1905 *Boston Evening Transcript* editorial called the "scourge of black crime." Popular entertainment was no less racist. Thomas Dixon's popular 1905 novel, *Clansman*, glorified the Ku Klux Klan and demonized former slaves. A few years later, D. W. Griffith transformed it into a groundbreaking and immensely popular movie, *Birth of a Nation*.

Although such crude expressions of bias are no longer routine fare, seemingly neutral code words have come to embody many of the same racist assumptions. Terms like "gang-related," "drug turf," "crack plague," "crack babies," "welfare queens" and "inner-city pathologies" impart the same biased message as did the indelicate phrases of the openly racist past. The power of institutional racism lies in its familiarity, normality and indirectness. By popularizing familiar, negative stereotypes, the media become one of the institutions that reinforces racism.

Take, for example, the findings of Children Now, an Oakland, Calif., children's rights organization. Children most often associate positive qualities—financial and academic success, leadership, intelligence—with whites, and associate negative qualities—lawbreaking, financial hardship, laziness, goofy behavior—with minorities, particularly blacks. Children of all races say the news media tend to portray blacks and Latinos more negatively than whites and Asians, particularly when reporting about young people. "You always see black people doing drugs and carrying around drugs, shooting people and stealing things," one white girl told the Children Now researchers.

Amy Jordan, who directs children's television research at the University of Pennsylvania's Annenberg Public Policy Center, says that those results are consistent with other research on minorities and television. Minorities, she argues, are also underrepresented in entertainment television, where they are also more likely to be cast as criminals or buffoons, or as having low-class jobs. Television recycles successful formulas, which often are "rooted in stereotypes," Jordan says.

Fortunately, several organizations are working to change U.S. media coverage. San Francisco State University's Center for Integration and Improvement of Journalism has compiled a list of recommendations. The center argues that news shows should cover a variety of stories about minorities, not just those related to race, and that they should find out how issues affect different segments of society. Reporters and editors should become more familiar with the communities they cover, expand their Rolodexes to include minorities who can provide authoritative opinions on a variety of subjects, and keep an informal checklist of every story's cultural implications. Meanwhile, newsroom management ought to redefine and expand its concept of what constitutes "news," so that they don't only assign negative stories about minorities.

Most experts on the issue agree that the most important factor is to include more African-Americans and other minorities as editors and other decision-makers. Unfortunately, to that end, the American Society of Newspaper Editors (ASNE) recently rescinded its goal of achieving parity between the newsrooms and the African-American population by 2000. Although there has been some progress since ASNE made its commitment, a spokesman for the group conceded that the problem is more difficult than it originally anticipated.

15   The public representation of "blackness" is a distorted one. African-Americans are routinely portrayed as marginal, deviant members of society. The exceptions to these portrayals—and there have been some—have been insufficient to alter the public's perceptions. Our public language on the problems of race and crime

makes it difficult to redress these habits of media stereotyping. But if we don't attend to the issue, those problems will just get worse.

For Discussion and Writing

1. Most Americans are aware that African Americans represent a disproportionate number of prison inmates. They think black people are simply more involved in the drug trade. How does the 1996 Bureau of Justice study refute this assumption? Why, in your view, haven't this study and similar statistical evidence shaped popular ideas about blacks and crime?

2. According to the same study mentioned above, more whites than blacks have used cocaine. What reasons does the author give for the media's indifference to such facts? What reasons can you offer?

3. What is the "ruthless system of Jim Crow" that Muwakkil mentions? Who was D. W. Griffith?

4. How does Muwakkil link media stereotypes and children's perceptions of race? What do you make of his suggestions for redressing distorted public representations of "blackness" in our culture? To what degree do news and entertainment shows on TV shape your perceptions of race? Before you answer, you might keep a log for a week or two of all the negative portrayals of African Americans or other groups on TV and in the news. You might use the log to help you write a brief critique of media stereotyping.

Reading, Research, and Writing

1. Movies and TV sometimes suggest that racial harmony is a fact of life. Keep a log of TV shows for a week or so. Note how many programs depict friendships across racial lines. Which groups get along? What are they shown to have in common? How ordinary or unusual do they seem to you? Compare such images of harmony with an example to the contrary taken from life, such as this excerpt from a 1999 keynote address at the First National Meeting of the Regional People of Color Legal Scholarship Conferences:

   In the hot New Orleans summer of 1996, neighborhood tension erupted in a street brawl between Tho Nguyen's son and Ulysses Narcisse. African American residents and the Committee for Justice boycotted Nguyen's PNT grocery store. They accused the owners of assault and discrimination as well as "refusing to accept pennies, taxing food stamps and allowing neighborhood drunkards to loiter." The Nguyens brought charges of their own about African Americans' untrustworthiness and years of tolerating obscene language and repeated taunts to "go back to your own country."

   Erik K. Yamamoto, "Healing Our Own"

2. Visit a Web site that generally avoids crude racism while at the same time working to support "race talk" and stereotypes. You might try the Web site for the Council of Conservative Citizens, for example. Write a paper that reviews several such sites. Analyze their tactics. Who is the intended audience? Are their messages aimed at audience fears? In what ways do the sites evoke negative stereotypes? What sort of authority is used to bolster their credibility (crime statistics, science, religious references, etc.)? What do you think the site designers want from their audience?

3. Read a Fu Manchu novel. Many libraries carry Sax Rohmer's fiction, so finding a copy should be easy enough. Analyze the book's representation of Chinese people. What sort of moral failings are attributed to Asians in the book? In what ways are these failings contrasted with the virtues of the European characters? You might also compare Fu Manchu with more recent Asian villains featured in Tom Clancy's *Debt of Honor*, or his *Bear and the Dragon*. Or, if you can get hold of them, read *Her Father's Daughter* by Gene Stratton-Porter or Wallace Irwin's *Seed of the Sun*. Compare villains and stereotypes in several such texts.

4. Is there a mosque in your community? Visit it and try to interview people there about their daily lives. Plan your interview, so that you have prepared several well-formed questions that could lead to ample responses. Do they feel any particular animosity from non-Muslims in the area? In what ways does Islam impact their lives at work, or at home? Consider beforehand what sorts of things you would like to learn from them. After all this, write an essay that compares your living subjects with media images of Arabs and Muslims.

5. To prepare for the writing of this assignment, closely view several movies that present Arab culture, even if only as background for the main drama (*Indiana Jones* comes to mind, as does *The Mummy*). Ask a video library or rental store employee for movie suggestions. Or search the Web. *Into the Night*, *Rollover*, and *The Sheik* were among the movies mentioned on a recently available Web site critical of Hollywood presentations of Arabs (http://www.peak.sfu.ca/the-peak/2002-1/issue6/fe-mots.html). A Google search will no doubt turn up many more. Look for patterns, for simplistic stereotypes, and also look for well-rounded characters. Are there any? Is all of the Middle East simply an exotic background for dramas involving Westerners? Are Arabs generally portrayed in your selected movies as wealthy, sinister, or exotic? Raise lots of questions and find in them an approach to a critical review of Hollywood's Arabs.

Confinement Within Stereotypes

Today at the beach my chubby-legged, brown-skinned daughter ran laughing into the water as fast as she could. My wife and I laughed watching her, until we heard behind us a low guttural curse and then an unpleasant voice raised in an imitation war whoop.

I turned to see a fat man in a bathing suit, white and soft as a grub, as he covered his mouth and prepared to make the Indian war cry again.

Lewis (Johnson) Sawaquat

The white kids were going to have a chance to become Galileos and Madame Curies and Edisons and Gauguins, and our boys (the girls weren't even in on it) would try to be Jesse Owenses and Joe Louises.

Maya Angelou

Combating negative ethnic and racial stereotypes—the violent black man, the tomahawk-wielding Indian, the "ideal" Asian, the lazy Mexican—continues to be a challenge to the American dream of a multicultural society. It's important to explore where these stereotypes begin and how they are reinforced through media and popular cultural images, but it's also important to understand how confining and debilitating these stereotypes are for those who are labeled. Understanding the impact of stereotypes on actual human beings may be the first step in actively combating such stereotypes. For example, how do individuals—through the "innocent" retelling of ethnic jokes and the reliance on media images rather than direct experience—reinforce the confinement of "the other" through reiteration of stereotypes?

97

Some stereotypes no doubt begin with some semblance to actual events and actual experience. At one time in our history, there were no doubt Indians who used tomahawks. Poverty and addiction in some poor communities of African Americans may produce some black men who react violently. And the success of some Asians in math and science certainly occurs. But when these images are abstracted to fit the whole of a race or an ethnic group, people need to raise questions and challenge the results that lead to overgeneralization.

One of the problems is, of course, the whole idea of categories. As human beings, we need categories in order to manage our observations and our experiences. If we couldn't make generalizations, every day humans would have to decide anew what something means, how it relates to things that are the same and different. In very basic ways, we need categories: We categorize food groups, subject matter, personality traits, landscapes, weather, family, and friends—the list is endless. Categories help us organize our world. But categories can lead to stereotypes, to overgeneralizations that lead to misunderstanding rather than understanding, to overgeneralizations that, in fact, may be misleading, or even wrong.

Each of the writers in this chapter seeks to combat the overgeneralizations that create harmful effects on the identities of people within racial or ethnic groups. Maya Angelou's "Graduation" story recounts how stereotypes generated by someone who did not know her or her community took joy from what should have been one of her happiest days. On Angelou's eighth-grade graduation day, it was a young man's refusal to be belittled by ignorant stereotypes that allowed others to be restored in their community's sense of self and remembrance of its history and tradition. Kesaya E. Noda in "Growing Up Asian in America" looks at some historical stereotypes and compares them with her knowledge of her family in Japan, California, and New York to challenge their validity in establishing her identity.

Lewis (Johnson) Sawaquat describes the complexity and subtlety of stereotypes of American Indians in "For My Indian Daughter." While some Americans demonstrate a sort of admiration for Indian history and Indian culture, such as white "hobbyists" masquerading as Indians on weekends and Boy Scouts doing imitation Indian dances, Sawaquat argues that these activities demonstrate a mindless perpetuation of long-time stereotypes.

C. N. Le argues that Asian Americans are stuck with the designation of "model minority" that never quite covers all the many Asian groups in the United States. Le considers the statistical generalizations that come with that very general term to challenge the stereotypes of Asian Americans. In examining the well-being of subgroups of that category, he discovers that many Asian Americans struggle financially and educationally, as well as being discriminated against because of race.

Luis Valdez's play *Los Vendidos* provides a bitingly satirical picture of stereotypes that plague the Hispanic community—in this case, Mexican Americans. The 1970s stereotypes that Valdez's "models" of Mexican men represent are still images that remain prevalent in the 21st century. "The Myth of the Latin Woman: I Just Met a Girl Named Maria" by Judith Ortiz Cofer demonstrates in very personal ways not only how Latinas become "Evitas" or "Marias," but also how freely people act on stereotypes without examining their assumptions.

Generalizations, often growing out of direct encounters, lead to stereotypes. Everyone makes use of them, but thinking people learn to question them.

Graduation
Maya Angelou

Maya Angelou has authored 12 best-selling books including I Know Why the Caged Bird Sings *and her recent* A Song Flung Up to Heaven. *In addition, she has worked as a poet, educator, historian, actress, playwright, civil rights activist, producer, and director. In January 1993 she had the honor of writing original work for, and reciting it at, the presidential inauguration of Bill Clinton. Angelou has a lifetime position as the Reynolds Professor of American Studies at Wake Forest University. Born in 1928 in St. Louis, Missouri, Angelou describes growing up in Stamps, Arkansas, in her autobiography,* I Know Why the Caged Bird Sings, *from which the following is excerpted.*

✦

The children in Stamps trembled visibly with anticipation. Some adults were excited too, but to be certain the whole young population had come down with graduation epidemic. Large classes were graduating from both the grammar school and the high school. Even those who were years removed from their own day of glorious release were anxious to help with preparations as a kind of dry run. The junior students who were moving into the vacating classes' chairs were tradition-bound to show their talents for leadership and management. They strutted through the school and around the campus exerting pressure on the lower grades. Their authority was so new that occasionally if they pressed a little too hard it had to be overlooked. After all, next term was coming, and it never hurt a sixth grader to have a play sister in the eighth grade, or a tenth-year student to be able to call a twelfth grader Bubba. So all was endured in a spirit of shared understanding. But the graduating classes themselves were the nobility. Like travelers with exotic destinations on their minds, the graduates were remarkably forgetful. They came to school without their books, or tablets or even pencils. Volunteers fell over themselves to secure replacements for the missing equipment. When accepted, the willing workers might or might not be thanked, and it was of no importance to the pregraduation rites. Even teachers were respectful of the now quiet and aging seniors, and tended to speak to them, if not as equals, as beings only slightly lower than themselves. After tests were returned and grades given, the student body, which acted like an extended family, knew who did well, who excelled, and what piteous ones had failed.

Unlike the white high school, Lafayette County Training School distinguished itself by having neither lawn, nor hedges, nor tennis court, nor climbing ivy. Its two buildings (main classrooms, the grade school and home economics) were set on a dirt hill with no fence to limit either its boundaries or those of bordering farms. There was a large expanse to the left of the school which was used alternately as a baseball diamond or a basketball court. Rusty hoops on the swaying poles represented the permanent recreational equipment, although bats and balls could be borrowed from the P.E. teacher if the borrower was qualified and if the diamond wasn't occupied.

Over this rocky area relieved by a few shady tall persimmon trees the graduating class walked. The girls often held hands and no longer bothered to speak to the lower students. There was a sadness about them, as if this old world was not their home and they were bound for higher ground. The boys, on the other hand, had become more friendly, more outgoing. A decided change from the closed attitude they projected while studying for finals. Now they seemed not ready to give up the old school, the familiar paths and classrooms. Only a small percentage would be continuing on to college—one of the South's A & M (agricultural and mechanical) schools, which trained Negro youths to be carpenters, farmers, handymen, masons, maids, cooks and baby nurses. Their future rode heavily on their shoulders, and blinded them to the collective joy that had pervaded the lives of the boys and girls in the grammar school graduating class.

Parents who could afford it had ordered new shoes and ready-made clothes for themselves from Sears and Roebuck or Montgomery Ward. They also engaged the best seamstresses to make the floating graduating dresses and to cut down second-hand pants which would be pressed to a military slickness for the important event.

Oh, it was important, all right. Whitefolks would attend the 5 ceremony, and two or three would speak of God and home and the Southern way of life, and Mrs. Parsons, the principal's wife, would play the graduation march while the lower-grade graduates paraded down the aisles and took their seats below the platform. The high school seniors would wait in empty classrooms to make their dramatic entrance.

In the Store I was the person of the moment. The birthday girl. The center. Bailey had graduated the year before, although to do so he had had to forfeit all pleasures to make up for his time lost in Baton Rouge.

My class was wearing butter-yellow pique dresses, and Momma launched out on mine. She smocked the yoke into tiny crisscrossing puckers, then shirred the rest of the bodice. Her dark fingers ducked in and out of the lemony cloth as she embroidered raised daisies around the hem. Before she considered herself finished she had added a crocheted cuff on the puff sleeves, and a pointy crocheted collar.

I was going to be lovely. A walking model of all the various styles of fine hand sewing and it didn't worry me that I was only twelve years old and merely graduating from the eighth grade. Besides, many teachers in Arkansas Negro schools had only that diploma and were licensed to impart wisdom.

The days had become longer and more noticeable. The faded beige of former times had been replaced with strong and sure colors. I began to see my classmates' clothes, their skin tones, and the dust that waved off pussy willows. Clouds that lazed across the sky were objects of great concern to me. Their shiftier shapes might have held a message that in my new happiness and with a little bit of time I'd soon decipher. During that period I looked at the arch of heaven so religiously my neck kept a steady ache. I had taken to smiling more often, and my jaws hurt from the unaccustomed activity. Between the two physical sore spots, I suppose I could have been uncomfortable, but that was not the case. As a member of the winning team (the graduating class of 1940) I had outdistanced unpleasant sensations by miles. I was headed for the freedom of open fields.

10   Youth and social approval allied themselves with me and we trammeled memories of slights and insults. The wind of our swift passage remodeled my features. Lost tears were pounded to mud and then to dust. Years of withdrawal were brushed aside and left behind, as hanging ropes of parasitic moss.

My work alone had awarded me a top place and I was going to be one of the first called in the graduating ceremonies. On the classroom blackboard, as well as on the bulletin board in the auditorium, there were blue stars and white stars and red stars. No absences, no tardinesses, and my academic work was among the best of the year. I could say the preamble to the Constitution even faster than Bailey. We timed ourselves often: "Wethepeopleofthe-UnitedStatesinordertoformamoreperfectunion. . . ." I had memorized the Presidents of the United States from Washington to Roosevelt in chronological as well as alphabetical order.

My hair pleased me too. Gradually the black mass had lengthened and thickened, so that it kept at last to its braided pattern, and I didn't have to yank my scalp off when I tried to comb it.

Louise and I had rehearsed the exercises until we tired out ourselves. Henry Reed was class valedictorian. He was a small, very black boy with hooded eyes, a long, broad nose and an oddly shaped head. I had admired him for years because each term he and I vied for the best grades in our class. Most often he bested me, but instead of being disappointed I was pleased that we shared top places between us. Like many Southern Black children, he lived with his grandmother, who was as strict as Momma and as kind as she knew how to be. He was courteous, respectful and soft-spoken to elders, but on the playground he chose to play the roughest games. I admired him. Anyone, I reckoned, sufficiently afraid or sufficiently dull could be polite. But to be able to operate at a top level with both adults and children was admirable.

His valedictory speech was entitled "To Be or Not to Be." The rigid tenth-grade teacher had helped him to write it. He'd been working on the dramatic stresses for months.

The weeks until graduation were filled with heady activities.   15 A group of small children were to be presented in a play about buttercups and daisies and bunny rabbits. They could be heard throughout the building practicing their hops and their little songs that sounded like silver bells. The older girls (nongraduates, of course) were assigned the task of making refreshments for the night's festivities. A tangy scent of ginger, cinnamon, nutmeg and chocolate wafted around the home economics building as the budding cooks made samples for themselves and their teachers.

In every corner of the workshop, axes and saws split fresh timber as the woodshop boys made sets and stage scenery. Only the graduates were left out of the general bustle. We were free to sit in the library at the back of the building or look in quite detachedly, naturally, on the measures being taken for our event.

Even the minister preached on graduation the Sunday before. His subject was "Let your light so shine that men will see your good works and praise your Father, Who is in Heaven." Although the sermon was purported to be addressed to us, he used the occasion to speak to backsliders, gamblers and general ne'er-do-wells. But since he had called our names at the beginning of the service we were mollified.

Among Negroes the tradition was to give presents to children going only from one grade to another. How much more important this was when the person was graduating at the top of the class. Uncle Willie and Momma had sent away for a Mickey Mouse watch like Bailey's. Louise gave me four embroidered handkerchiefs. (I gave her three crocheted doilies.) Mrs. Sneed, the minister's wife, made me an underskirt to wear for graduation, and nearly every customer gave me a nickel or maybe even a dime with the instruction "Keep on moving to higher ground," or some such encouragement.

Amazingly the great day finally dawned and I was out of bed before I knew it. I threw open the back door to see it more clearly, but Momma said, "Sister, come away from that door and put your robe on."

20   I hoped the memory of that morning would never leave me. Sunlight was itself still young, and the day had none of the insistence maturity would bring it in a few hours. In my robe and barefoot in the backyard, under cover of going to see about my new beans, I gave myself up to the gentle warmth and thanked God that no matter what evil I had done in my life He had allowed me to live to see this day. Somewhere in my fatalism I had expected to die, accidentally, and never have the chance to walk up the stairs in the auditorium and gracefully receive my hardearned diploma. Out of God's merciful bosom I had won reprieve.

Bailey came out in his robe and gave me a box wrapped in Christmas paper. He said he had saved his money for months to pay for it. It felt like a box of chocolates, but I knew Bailey wouldn't save money to buy candy when we had all we could want under our noses.

He was as proud of the gift as I. It was soft-leather-bound copy of a collection of poems by Edgar Allan Poe, or, as Bailey and I called him, "Eap." I turned to "Annabel Lee" and we walked up and down the garden rows, the cool dirt between our toes, reciting the beautifully sad lines.

Momma made a Sunday breakfast although it was only Friday. After we finished the blessing, I opened my eyes to find the watch on my plate. It was a dream of a day. Everything went smoothly and to my credit I didn't have to be reminded or scolded for anything. Near evening I was too jittery to attend to chores, so Bailey volunteered to do all before his bath.

Days before, we had made a sign for the Store and as we turned out the lights Momma hung the cardboard over the doorknob. It read clearly: CLOSED. GRADUATION.

25   My dress fitted perfectly and everyone said that I looked like a sunbeam in it. On the hill, going toward the school, Bailey walked behind with Uncle Willie, who muttered, "Go on, Ju." He wanted him to walk ahead with us because it embarrassed him to have to walk so slowly. Bailey said he'd let the ladies walk together, and the men would bring up the rear. We all laughed, nicely.

Little children dashed by out of the dark like fireflies. Their crepe-paper dresses and butterfly wings were not made for running and we heard more than one rip, dryly, and the regretful "uh uh" that followed.

The school blazed without gaiety. The windows seemed cold and unfriendly from the lower hill. A sense of ill-fated timing crept over me, and if Momma hadn't reached for my hand I would have drifted back to Bailey and Uncle Willie, and possibly beyond. She made a few slow jokes about my feet getting cold, and tugged me along to the now-strange building.

Around the front steps, assurance came back. There were my fellow "greats," the graduating class. Hair brushed back, legs oiled, new dresses and pressed pleats, fresh pocket handkerchiefs and little handbags, all homesewn. Oh, we were up to snuff, all right. I joined my comrades and didn't even see my family go in to find seats in the crowded auditorium.

The school band struck up a march and all classes filed in as had been rehearsed. We stood in front of our seats, as assigned, and on a signal from the choir director, we sat. No sooner had this been accomplished than the band started to play the national anthem. We rose again and sang the song, after which we recited the pledge of allegiance. We remained standing for a brief minute before the choir director and the principal signaled to us, rather desperately I thought, to take our seats. The command was so un- usual that our carefully rehearsed and smooth-running machine was thrown off. For a full minute we fumbled for our chairs and bumped into each other awkwardly. Habits change or solidify un- der pressure, so in our state of nervous tension we had been ready to follow our usual assembly pattern: the American National Anthem, then the pledge of allegiance, then the song every Black person I knew called the Negro National Anthem. All done in the same key, with the same passion and most often standing on the same foot.

Finding my seat at last, I was overcome with a presentiment   30
of worse things to come. Something unrehearsed, unplanned, was going to happen, and we were going to be made to look bad. I distinctly remember being explicit in the choice of pronoun. It was "we," the graduating class, the unit, that concerned me then.

The principal welcomed "parents and friends" and asked the Baptist minister to lead us in prayer. His invocation was brief and punchy, and for a second I thought we were getting back on the high road to right action. When the principal came back to the dais, however, his voice had changed. Sounds always affected me profoundly and the principal's voice was one of my favorites. Dur- ing assembly it melted and lowed weakly into the audience. It had not been in my plan to listen to him, but my curiosity was piqued and I straightened up to give him my attention.

He was talking about Booker T. Washington, our "late great leader," who said we can be as close as the fingers on the hand, etc. . . . Then he said a few vague things about friendship and the friendship of kindly people to those less fortunate than themselves. With that his voice nearly faded, thin, away. Like a river diminishing to a stream and then to a trickle. But he cleared his throat and said, "Our speaker tonight, who is also our friend, came from Texarkana to deliver the commencement address, but due to the irregularity of the train schedule, he's going to, as they say, 'speak and run.'" He said that we understood and wanted the man to know that we were most grateful for the time he was able to give us and then something about how we were willing always to adjust to another's program, and without more ado—"I give you Mr. Edward Donleavy."

Not one but two white men came through the door offstage. The shorter one walked to the speaker's platform, and the tall one moved over to the center seat and sat down. But that was our principal's seat, and already occupied. The dislodged gentleman bounced around for a long breath or two before the Baptist minister gave him his chair, then with more dignity than the situation deserved, the minister walked off the stage.

Donleavy looked at the audience once (on reflection, I'm sure that he wanted only to reassure himself that we were really there), adjusted his glasses and began to read from a sheaf of papers.

35   He was glad "to be here and to see the work going on just as it was in the other schools."

At the first "Amen" from the audience I willed the offender to immediate death by choking on the word. But Amen's and Yes, sir's began to fall around the room like rain through a ragged umbrella.

He told us of the wonderful changes we children in Stamps had in store. The Central School (naturally, the white school was Central) had already been granted improvements that would be in use in the fall. A well-known artist was coming from Little Rock to teach art to them. They were going to have the newest microscopes and chemistry equipment for their laboratory. Mr. Donleavy didn't leave us long in the dark over who made these improvements available to Central High. Nor were we to be ignored in the general betterment scheme he had in mind.

He said that he had pointed out to people at a very high level that one of the first-line football tacklers at Arkansas Agricultural and Mechanical College had graduated from good old Lafayette County Training School. Here fewer Amen's were heard. Those few that did break through lay dully in the air with the heaviness of habit.

He went on to praise us. He went on to say how he had bragged that "one of the best basketball players at Fisk sank his first ball right here at Lafayette County Training School."

The white kids were going to have a chance to become   40 Galileos and Madame Curies and Edisons and Gauguins, and our boys (the girls weren't even in on it) would try to be Jesse Owenses and Joe Louises.

Owens and the Brown Bomber were great heroes in our world, but what school official in the white-goddom of Little Rock had the right to decide that those two men must be our only heroes? Who decided that for Henry Reed to become a scientist he had to work like George Washington Carver, as a bootblack, to buy a lousy microscope? Bailey was obviously always going to be too small to be an athlete, so which concrete angel glued to what country seat had decided that if my brother wanted to become a lawyer he had to first pay penance for his skin by picking cotton and hoeing corn and studying correspondence books at night for twenty years?

The man's dead words fell like bricks around the auditorium and too many settled in my belly. Constrained by hard-learned manners I couldn't look behind me, but to my left and right the proud graduating class of 1940 had dropped their heads. Every girl in my row had found something new to do with her handkerchief. Some folded the tiny squares into love knots, some into triangles, but most were wadding them, then pressing them flat on their yellow laps.

On the dais, the ancient tragedy was being replayed. Professor Parsons sat, a sculptor's reject, rigid. His large, heavy body seemed devoid of will or willingness, and his eyes said he was no longer with us. The other teachers examined the flag (which was draped stage right) or their notes, or the window which opened on our now-famous playing diamond.

Graduation, the hush-hush magic time of frills and gifts and congratulations and diplomas, was finished for me before my name was called. The accomplishment was nothing. The meticulous maps, drawn in three colors of ink, learning and spelling decasyllabic words, memorizing the whole of *The Rape of Lucrece*—it was nothing. Donleavy had exposed us.

45   We were maids and farmers, handymen and washerwomen, and anything higher that we aspired to was farcical and presumptuous. Then I wished that Gabriel Prosser and Nat Turner had killed all whitefolks in their beds and that Abraham Lincoln had been assassinated before the signing of the Emancipation Proclamation, and that Harriet Tubman had been killed by that blow on her head and Christopher Columbus had drowned in the *Santa Maria*.

It was awful to be Negro and have no control over my life. It was brutal to be young and already trained to sit quietly and listen to charges brought against my color with no chance of defense. We should all be dead. I thought I should like to see us all dead, one on top of the other. A pyramid of flesh with the whitefolks on the bottom, as the broad base, then the Indians with their silly tomahawks and teepees and wigwams and treaties, the Negroes with their mops and recipes and cotton sacks and spirituals sticking out of their mouths. The Dutch children should all stumble in their wooden shoes and break their necks. The French should choke to death on the Louisiana Purchase (1803) while silkworms ate all the Chinese with their stupid pigtails. As a species, we were an abomination. All of us.

Donleavy was running for election, and assured our parents that if he won we could count on having the only colored paved playing field in that part of Arkansas. Also—he never looked up to acknowledge the grunts of acceptance—also, we were bound to get some new equipment for the home economics building and the workshop.

He finished, and since there was no need to give any more than the most perfunctory thank-you's, he nodded to the men on the stage, and the tall white man who was never introduced joined him at the door. They left with the attitude that now they were off to something really important. (The graduation ceremonies at Lafayette County Training School had been a mere preliminary.)

The ugliness they left was palpable. An uninvited guest who wouldn't leave. The choir was summoned and sang a modern arrangement of "Onward, Christian Soldiers," with new words pertaining to graduates seeking their place in the world. But it didn't work. Elouise, the daughter of the Baptist minister, recited "Invictus," and I could have cried at the impertinence of "I am the master of my fate: I am the captain of my soul."

My name had lost its ring of familiarity and I had to be   50
nudged to go and receive my diploma. All my preparations had
fled. I neither marched up to the stage like a conquering Amazon,
nor did I look in the audience for Bailey's nod of approval. Mar-
guerite Johnson, I heard the name again, my honors were read,
there were noises in the audience of appreciation, and I took my
place on the stage as rehearsed.

I thought about colors I hated: ecru, puce, lavender, beige and
black.

There was shuffling and rustling around me, then Henry
Reed was giving his valedictory address, "To Be or Not to Be."
Hadn't he heard the whitefolks? We couldn't *be*, so the question
was a waste of time. Henry's voice came out clear and strong. I
feared to look at him. Hadn't he got the message? There was no
"nobler in the mind" for Negroes because the world didn't think
we had minds, and they let us know it. "Outrageous fortune"?
Now, that was a joke. When the ceremony was over I had to tell
Henry Reed some things. That is, if I still cared. Not "rub," Henry,
"erase." "Ah, there's the erase." Us.

Henry had been a good student in elocution. His voice rose
on tides of promise and fell on waves of warnings. The English
teacher had helped him to create a sermon winging through
Hamlet's soliloquy. To be a man, a doer, a builder, a leader, or to
be a tool, an unfunny joke, a crusher of funky toadstools. I mar-
veled that Henry could go through with the speech as if we had a
choice.

I had been listening and silently rebutting each sentence with
my eyes closed; then there was a hush, which in an audience
warns that something unplanned is happening. I looked up and
saw Henry Reed, the conservative, the proper, the A student, turn
his back to the audience and turn to us (the proud graduating
class of 1940) and sing, nearly speaking,

Lift ev'ry voice and sing
Till earth and heaven ring
Ring with the harmonies of Liberty . . .[1]

It was the poem written by James Weldon Johnson. It was the   55
music composed by J. Rosamond Johnson. It was the Negro National Anthem. Out of habit we were singing it.

Our mothers and fathers stood in the dark hall and joined the hymn of encouragement. A kindergarten teacher led the small children onto the stage and the buttercups and daisies and bunny rabbits marked time and tried to follow:

Stony the road we trod
Bitter the chastening rod
Felt in the days when hope, unborn, had died.
Yet with a steady beat
Have not our weary feet
Come to the place for which our fathers sighed?

Every child I knew had learned that song with his ABC's and along with "Jesus Loves Me This I Know." But I personally had never heard it before. Never heard the words, despite the thousands of times I had sung them. Never thought they had anything to do with me.

On the other hand, the words of Patrick Henry had made such an impression on me that I had been able to stretch myself tall and trembling and say, "I know not what course others may take, but as for me, give me liberty or give me death."

And now I heard, really for the first time:

We have come over a way that with tears has been watered,
We have come, treading our path through the blood of the slaughtered.

While echoes of the song shivered in the air, Henry Reed bowed his head, said "Thank you," and returned to his place in the line. The tears that slipped down many faces were not wiped away in shame.

We were on top again. As always, again. We survived. The depths had been icy and dark, but now a bright sun spoke to our souls. I was no longer simply a member of the proud graduating class of 1940; I was a proud member of the wonderful, beautiful Negro race.

Oh, Black known and unknown poets, how often have your auctioned pains sustained us? Who will compute the lonely nights made less lonely by your songs, or the empty pots made less tragic by your tales?

If we were a people much given to revealing secrets, we might raise monuments and sacrifice to the memories of our poets, but slavery cured us of that weakness. It may be enough, however, to have it said that we survive in exact relationship to the dedication of our poets (include preachers, musicians and blues singers).

Endnote

1. "Lift Ev'ry Voice and Sing"—words by James Weldon Johnson and music by J. Rosamond Johnson. © Copyrighted: Edward B. Marks Music Corporation. Used by permission.

For Discussion and Writing

1. Compare the description of the mood and atmosphere at the beginning of this excerpt with that at the end. What descriptions and images does Angelou use that best capture the change in the feeling about the day?
2. What can you say about Donleavy's understanding of his audience on the basis of his speech? How does the way he sees the young people differ from how they see themselves? What affect does his stereotyping have on Angelou and others in the audience?
3. When Henry and then the audience and children begin to sing the "Negro National Anthem," Angelou says, "Never heard the words, despite the thousands of times I had sung them. Never thought they had anything to do with me." What changed for Angelou in those moments? Why?
4. Find the "Negro National Anthem" (it is readily available online). Read (and perhaps listen to) it. How does the image of the African American represented in the anthem differ from many stereotypes of African Americans that have been a part of American history and tradition?
5. Have you ever been in a situation where someone has stereotyped you with no recognition of who you are or your own sense of self? Describe and characterize that experience.

Growing Up Asian in America
KESAYA E. NODA

In the following essay Kesaya E. Noda describes "encountering the stereotypes of my race perpetrated by non-Japanese people (primarily white) who may or may not have had contact with other Japanese in America" As a Japanese American born in the United States, Noda struggles with the identities that others impose on her. This essay was published in Making Waves *in 1989. Noda teaches at Lesley College in Massachusetts.*

———————— ✦ ————————

Sometimes when I was growing up, my identity seemed to hurtle toward me and paste itself right to my face. I felt that way, encountering the stereotypes of my race perpetuated by non-Japanese people (primarily white) who may or may not have had contact with other Japanese in America. "You don't like cheese, do you?" someone would ask. "I know your people don't like cheese." Sometimes questions came making allusions to history. That was another aspect of the identity. Events that had happened quite apart from the me who stood silent in that moment connected my face with an incomprehensible past. "Your parents were in California? Were they in those camps during the war?" And sometimes there were phrases or nicknames: "Lotus Blossom." I was sometimes addressed or referred to as racially Japanese, sometimes as Japanese-American, and sometimes as an Asian woman. Confusions and distortions abounded.

How is one to know and define oneself? From the inside—within a context that is self-defined from a grounding in community and a connection with culture and history that are comfortably accepted? Or from the outside—in terms of messages received from the media and people who are often ignorant? Even as an adult I can still see two sides of my face and past. I can see from the inside out, in freedom. And I can see from the outside in, driven by the old voices of childhood and lost in anger and fear.

I AM RACIALLY JAPANESE

A voice from my childhood says: "You are other. You are less than. You are unalterably alien." This voice has its own history. We have indeed been seen as other and alien since the early years of our arrival in the United States. The very first immigrants were welcomed and sought as laborers to replace the dwindling numbers of Chinese, whose influx had been cut off by the Chinese Exclusion Act of 1882. The Japanese fell natural heir to the same anti-Asian prejudice that had arisen against the Chinese. As soon as they began striking for better wages, they were no longer welcomed.

I can see myself today as a person historically defined by law and custom as being forever alien. Being neither "free white," nor "African," our people in California were deemed "aliens, ineligible for citizenship," no matter how long they intended to stay here. Aliens ineligible for citizenship were prohibited from owning, buying, or leasing land. They did not and could not belong here. The voice in me remembers that I am always a *Japanese*-American in the eyes of many. A third-generation German-American is an American. A third-generation Japanese-American is a Japanese-American. Being Japanese means being a danger to the country during the war and knowing how to use chopsticks. I wear this history on my face.

I move to the other side. I see a different light and claim a dif- 5 ferent context. My race is a line that stretches across ocean and time to link me to the shrine where my grandmother was raised. Two high, white banners lift in the wind at the top of the stone steps leading to the shrine. It is time for the summer festival. Black characters are written against the sky as boldly as the clouds, as lightly as kites, as sharply as the big black crows I used to see above the fields in New Hampshire. At festival time there is liquor and food, ritual, discipline, and abandonment. There is music and drunkenness and invocation. There is hope. Another season has come. Another season has gone.

I am racially Japanese. I have a certain claim to this crazy place where the prayers intoned by a neighboring Shinto priest (standing in for my grandmother's nephew who is sick) are drowned out by the rehearsals for the pop singing contest in which most of the villagers will compete later that night. The village elders, the priest, and I stand respectfully upon the immaculate, shinning wooden floor of the outer shrine, bowing our heads before the hidden powers. During the patchy intervals when I can hear him, I notice the priest has a stutter. His voice flutters up to my ears only occasionally because two men and a woman are singing gustily into a microphone in the compound, testing the sound system. A prerecorded tape of guitars, samisens, and drums accompanies them. Rock music and Shinto prayers. That night, to loud applause and cheers, a young man is given the award for the most *netsuretsu*—passionate, burning—rendition of a song. We roar our approval of the reward. Never mind that his voice had wandered and slid, now slightly above, now slightly below the given line of the melody. Netsuretsu. Netsuretsu.

In the morning, my grandmother's sister kneels at the foot of the stone stairs to offer her morning prayers. She is too crippled to climb the stairs, so each morning she kneels here upon the path. She shuts her eyes for a few seconds, her motions as matter of fact as when she washes rice. I linger longer than she does, so reluctant to leave, savoring the connection I feel with my grandmother in America, the past, and the power that lives and shines in the morning sun.

Our family has served this shrine for generations. The family's need to protect this claim to identity and place outweighs any individual claim to any individual hope. I am Japanese.

I Am a Japanese-American

"Weak." I hear the voice from my childhood years. "Passive," I hear. Our parents and grandparents were the ones who were put into those camps. They went without resistance; they offered cooperation as proof of loyalty to America. "Victim," I hear. And, "Silent."

10   Our parents are painted as hard workers who were socially uncomfortable and had difficulty expressing even the smallest opinion. Clean, quiet, motivated, and determined to match the American way; that is us, and that is the story of our time here.

"Why did you go into those camps?" I raged at my parents, frightened by my own inner silence and timidity. "Why didn't you do anything to resist? Why didn't you name it the injustice it was?" Couldn't our parents even think? Couldn't they? Why were we so passive?

I shift my vision and my stance. I am in California. My uncle is in the midst of the sweet potato harvest. He is pressed, trying to get the harvesting crews onto the field as quickly as possible, worried about the flow of equipment and people. His big pickup is pulled off to the side, motor running, door ajar. I see two tractors in the yard in front of an old shed. The flatbed harvesting platform on which the workers will stand has already been brought over from the other field. It's early morning. The workers stand loosely grouped and at ease, but my uncle looks as harried and tense as a police officer trying to unsnarl a New York City traffic jam. Driving toward the shed, I pull my car off the road to make way for an approaching tractor. The front wheels of the car sink luxuriously into the soft, white sand by the roadside and the car slides to a dreamy halt, tail still on the road. I try to move forward. I try to move back. The front bites contentedly into the sand, the back lifts itself at a jaunty angle. My uncle sees me and storms down the road, running. He is shouting before he is even near me. "What's the matter with you?" he screams. "What the hell are you doing?" In his frenzy, he grabs his hat off his head and slashes it through the air across his knee. He is beside himself. "Don't you know how to drive in sand? What's the matter with you? You've blocked the whole roadway. How am I supposed to get my tractors out of here? Can't you use your head? You've cut off the whole roadway, and we've got to get out of here."

I stand on the road before him helplessly thinking, "No, I don't know how to drive in sand. I've never driven in sand."

"I'm sorry, uncle," I say, burying a smile beneath a look of sin-   15 cere apology. I notice my deep amusement and my affection for him with great curiosity. I am usually devastated by anger. Not this time.

During the several years that follow I learn about the people and the place, and much more about what has happened in this California village where my parents grew up. The issei, our grandparents, made this settlement in the desert. Their first crops were eaten by rabbits and ravaged by insects. The land was so barren that men walking from house to house sometimes got lost. Women came here too. They bore children in 114-degree heat, then carried the babies with them into the fields to nurse when they reached the end of each row of grapes or other truck-farm crops.

I had had no idea what it meant to buy this kind of land and make it grow green. Or how, when the war came, there was no space at all for the subtlety of being who we were—Japanese-Americans. Either/or was the way. I hadn't understood that people were literally afraid for their lives then, that their money had been frozen in banks; that there was a five-mile travel limit; that when the early evening curfew came and they were inside their houses, some of them watched helplessly as people they knew went into their barns to steal their belongings. The police were patrolling the road, interested only in violators of curfew. There was no help for them in the face of thievery. I had not been able to imagine before what it must have felt like to be an American—to know absolutely that one is an American—and yet to have almost everyone else deny it. Not only deny it, but challenge that identity with machine guns and troops of white American soldiers. In those circumstances it was difficult to say, "I'm a Japanese-American." "American" had to do.

But now I can say that I am a Japanese-American. It means I have a place here in this country, too. I have a place here on the East Coast, where our neighbor is so much a part of our family that my mother never passes her house at night without glancing at the lights to see if she is home and safe; where my parents have hauled hundreds of pounds of rocks from fields and arduously planted Christmas trees and blueberries, lilacs, asparagus, and crab apples, where my father still dreams of angling a stream to a new bed so that he can dig a pond in the field and fill it with water and fish. "The neighbors already came for their Christmas tree?" he asks in December. "Did they like it? Did they like it?"

I have a place on the West Coast where my relatives still farm, where I heard the stories of feuds and backbiting, and where I saw that people survived and flourished because fundamentally they trusted and relied upon one another. A death in the family is not just a death in a family; it is a death in the community. I saw people help each other with money, materials, labor, attention, and time. I saw men gather once a year, without fail, to clean the grounds of a ninety-year-old woman who had helped the community before, during, and after the war. I saw her remembering them with birthday cards sent to each of their children.

20   I come from a people with a long memory and a distinctive grace. We live our thanks. And we are Americans. Japanese-Americans.

I Am a Japanese-American Woman

Woman. The last piece of my identity. It has been easier by far for me to know myself in Japan and to see my place in America than it has been to accept my line of connection with my own mother. She was my dark self, a figure in whom I thought I saw all that I feared most in myself. Growing into womanhood and looking for some model of strength, I turned away from her. Of course, I could not find what I sought. I was looking for a black feminist or a white feminist. My mother is neither white nor black.

My mother is a woman who speaks with her life as much as with her tongue. I think of her with her own mother. Grandmother had Parkinson's disease and it had frozen her gait and set her fingers, tongue, and feet jerking and trembling in a terrible dance. My aunts and uncles wanted her to be able to live in her own home. They fed her, bathed her, dressed her, awoke at midnight to take her for one last trip to the bathroom. My aunts (her daughters-in-law) did most of the care, but my mother went from New Hampshire to California each summer to spend a month living with Grandmother because she wanted to and because she wanted to give my aunts at least a small rest. During those hot summer days, mother lay on the couch watching the television or reading, cooking foods that Grandmother liked, and speaking little. Grandmother thrived under her care.

The time finally came when it was too dangerous for Grandmother to live alone. My relatives kept finding her on the floor beside her bed when they went to wake her in the mornings. My mother flew to California to help clean the house and make arrangements for Grandmother to enter a local nursing home. On her last day at home, while Grandmother was sitting in her big, overstuffed armchair, hair combed and wearing a green summer dress, my mother went to her and knelt at her feet. "Here, Mamma," she said. "I've polished your shoes." She lifted Grandmother's legs and helped her into the shiny black shoes. My Grandmother looked down and smiled slightly. She left her house walking, supported by her children, carrying her pocket book, and wearing her polished black shoes. "Look, Mamma," my mom had said, kneeling. "I've polished your shoes."

Just the other day, my mother came to Boston to visit. She had recently lost a lot of weight and was pleased with her new shape and her feeling of good health. "Look at me, Kes," she exclaimed, turning toward me, front and back, as naked as the day she was born. I saw her small breasts and the wide, brown scar, belly button to pubic hair, that marked her because my brother and I were both born by Caesarean section. Her hips were small. I was not a large baby, but there was so little room for me in her that when she was carrying me she could not even being to bend over toward the floor. She hated it, she said.

"Don't I look good? Don't you think I look good?"   25

I looked at my mother smiling and as happy as she, thinking of all the times I have seen her naked. I have seen both my parents naked throughout my life, as they have seen me. From childhood through adulthood we've had our naked moments, sharing baths, idle conversations picked up as we moved between showers and closets, hurried moments at the beginning of days, quiet moments at the end of days.

I know this to be Japanese, this ease with the physical, and it makes me think of an old Japanese folk song. A young nursemaid, a fifteen-year-old girl, is singing a lullaby to a baby who is strapped to her back. The nursemaid has been sent as a servant to a place far from her own home. "We're the beggars," she says, "and they are the nice people. Nice people wear fine sashes. Nice clothes."

If I should drop dead,
bury me by the roadside!
I'll give a flower
to everyone who passes.
What kind of flower?
The cam-cam-camellia *[tsun-tsun-tsunaki]*
watered by Heaven:
alms water.

The nursemaid is the intersection of heaven and earth, the intersection of the human, the natural world, the body, and the soul. In this song, with clear eyes, she looks steadily at life, which is sometimes so very terrible and sad. I think of her while looking at my mother, who is standing on the red and purple carpet before me, laughing, without any clothes.

I am my mother's daughter. And I am myself.
I am a Japanese-American woman.

30

Epilogue

I recently heard a man from West Africa share some memories of his childhood. He was raised Muslim but when he was a young man, he found himself deeply drawn to Christianity. He struggled against his inner impulse for years, trying to avoid the church yet feeling pushed to return to it again and again. "I would have done *anything* to avoid the change," he said. At last, he became Christian. Afterwards he was afraid to go home, fearing that he would not be accepted. The fear was groundless, he discovered, when at last he returned—he had separated himself, but his family and friends (all Muslim) had not separated themselves from him.

The man, who is now a professor of religion, said that in the Africa he knew as a child and a young man, pluralism was embraced rather than feared. There was "a kind of tolerance that did not deny your particularity," he said. He alluded to zestful, spontaneous debates that would sometimes loudly erupt between Muslims and Christians in the village's public spaces. His memories of an atheist who harangued the villagers when he came to visit them once a week moved me deeply. Perhaps the man was an agricultural advisor or inspector. He harassed the women. He would say: "Don't go to the fields! Don't even bother to go to the fields. Let God take care of you. He'll send you the food. If you believe in God, why do you need to work? You don't need to work! Let God put the seeds in the ground. Stay home."

The professor said, "The women laughed, you know? They just laughed. Their attitude was, 'Here is a child of God. When will he come home?'"

The storyteller, the professor of religion, smiled a most fantastic tender smile as he told this story. "In my country, there is a deep affirmation of the oneness of God," he said. "The atheist and the women were having quite different experiences in their encounter, though the atheist did not know this. He saw himself as quite separate from the women. But the women did not see themselves as being separate from him. 'Here is a child of God,' they said. 'When will he come home?'"

For Discussion and Writing

1. What use does Noda make of the history of the Japanese to explain her conflicted identity? What sources does she identify as debilitating stereotypes? What sources does she find enriching?
2. What stories does Noda tell about her family in Japan and in California? How do you think these stories affect Noda's sense of self? How do her experiences with her Japanese relatives contrast with her experiences in New York? How does she seem to use them to make sense of herself and her identity?
3. Noda asks questions everyone must ask: "How is one to know and define oneself? From the inside . . .? Or from the outside?" What are the influences that make establishing an identity difficult? How do you encounter similar conflicting inside and/or outside influences on your identity?
4. Noda focuses on three aspects of her identity—her Japanese race, her Japanese American nationality, and her gender. What does each contribute to her self-understanding? How does she turn stereotypes into positive elements? Are there positive and negative aspects of your identity? How do you integrate them?
5. Why does Noda include the epilogue about a man from West Africa? How does the story relate to her themes of identity and stereotyping?

For My Indian Daughter
LEWIS (JOHNSON) SAWAQUAT

The following essay by Lewis Sawaquat appeared in Newsweek's *"My Turn" column in 1983. The great-grandson of the last official chief of the Potawatomi Ottawas in Harbor Springs, Michigan, Sawaquat grew up hearing stories about his family's history and traditions. Nonetheless, he lived a "white" life for a number of years before rediscovering his heritage through the Indian political activity of the 1960s and 1970s. Sawaquat is active in the Grand Traverse Band of Ottawa and Chippewa Indians in Michigan.*

———————— ✦ ————————

My little girl is singing herself to sleep upstairs, her voice mingling with the sounds of the birds outside in the old maple trees. She is two and I am nearly 50, and I am very taken with her. She came along late in my life, unexpected and unbidden, a startling gift.

Today at the beach my chubby-legged, brown-skinned daughter ran laughing into the water as fast as she could. My wife and I laughed watching her, until we heard behind us a low guttural curse and then an unpleasant voice raised in an imitation war whoop.

I turned to see a fat man in a bathing suit, white and soft as a grub, as he covered his mouth and prepared to make the Indian war cry again. He was middle-aged, younger than I, and had three little children lined up next to him, grinning foolishly. My wife suggested we leave the beach, and I agreed.

I knew the man was not unusual in his feelings against Indians. His beach behavior might have been socially unacceptable to more civilized whites, but his basic view of Indians is expressed daily in our small town, frequently on the editorial pages of the county newspaper, as white people speak out against Indian fishing rights and land rights, saying in essence, "Those Indians are taking our fish, our land." It doesn't matter to them that we were here first, that the U.S. Supreme Court has ruled in our favor. It matters to them that we have something they want, and they hate us for it. Backlash is the common explanation of the attacks on Indians, the bumper stickers that say, "Spear an Indian, Save a Fish," but I know better. The hatred of Indians goes back to the beginning when white people came to this country. For me it goes back to my childhood in Harbor Springs, Michigan.

Harbor Springs is now a summer resort for the very affluent, but a hundred years ago it was the Indian village of my Ottawa ancestors. My grandmother, Anna Showanessy, and other Indians like her, had their land there taken by treaty, by fraud, by violence, by theft. They remembered how whites had burned down the village at Burt Lake in 1900 and pushed the Indians out. These were the stories in my family.

When I was a boy my mother told me to walk down the alleys in Harbor Springs and not to wear my orange football sweater out of the house. This way I would not stand out, not be noticed, and not be a target.

I wore my orange sweater anyway and deliberately avoided the alleys. I was the biggest person I knew and wasn't really afraid. But I met my comeuppance when I enlisted in the U.S. Army. One night all the men in my barracks gathered together and, gang-fashion, pulled me into the shower and scrubbed me down with rough brushes used for floors, saying, "We won't have any dirty Indians in our outfit." It is a point of irony that I was cleaner than any of them. Later in Korea I learned how to kill, how to bully, how to hate Koreans. I came out of the war tougher than ever and, strangely, white.

I went to college, got married, lived in La Porte, Indiana, worked as a surveyor and raised three boys. I headed Boy Scout groups, never thinking it odd when the Scouts did imitation Indian dances, imitation Indian lore.

One day when I was 35 or thereabouts I heard about an Indian powwow. My father used to attend them and so with great curiosity and a strange joy at discovering a part of my heritage, I decided the thing to do to get ready for this big event was to have my friend make me a spear in his forge. The steel was fine and blue and iridescent. The feathers on the shaft were bright and proud.

In a dusty state fairground in southern Indiana, I found white people dressed as Indians. I learned they were "hobbyists," that is, it was their hobby and leisure pastime to masquerade as Indians on weekends. I felt ridiculous with my spear, and I left.

It was years before I could tell anyone of the embarrassment of this weekend and see any humor in it. But in a way it was that weekend, for all its silliness, that was my awakening. I realized I didn't know who I was. I didn't have an Indian name. I didn't speak the Indian language. I didn't know the Indian customs. Dimly I remembered the Ottawa word for dog, but it was a baby word, *kahgee*, not the full word, *muhkahgee*, which I was later to learn. Even more hazily I remembered a naming ceremony (my own). I remembered legs dancing around me, dust. Where had that been? Who had I been? "Suwaukquat," my mother told me when I asked, "where the tree begins to grow."

That was 1968, and I was not the only Indian in the country who was feeling the need to remember who he or she was. There were others. They had powwows, real ones, and eventually I found them. Together we researched our past, a search that for me culminated in the Longest Walk, a march on Washington in 1978. Maybe because I now know what it means to be Indian, it surprises me that others don't. Of course there aren't very many of us left. The chances of an average person knowing an average Indian in an average lifetime are pretty slim.

Still, I was amused one day when my small, four-year-old neighbor looked at me as I was hoeing in my garden and said, "You aren't a real Indian, are you?" Scotty is little, talkative, likable. Finally I said, "I'm a real Indian." He looked at me for a moment and then said, squinting into the sun, "Then where's your horse and feathers?" The child was simply a smaller, whiter version of my own ignorant self years before. We'd both seen too much TV, that's all. He was not to be blamed. And so, in a way, the moronic man on the beach today is blameless. We come full circle to realize other people are like ourselves, as discomfiting as that may be sometimes.

As I sit in my old chair on my porch, in a light that is fading so the leaves are barely distinguishable against the sky, I can picture my girl asleep upstairs. I would like to prepare her for what's to come, take her each step of the way saying, there's a place to avoid, here's what I know about this, but much of what's before her she must go through alone. She must pass through pain and joy and solitude and community to discover her own inner self that is unlike any other and come through that passage to the place where she sees all people are one, and in so seeing may live her life in a brighter future.

For Discussion and Writing

1. Early in the essay, Sawaquat describes a man at the beach as "a fat man in a bathing suit, white and soft as a grub" who utters a "low guttural curse" and has "an unpleasant voice raised in an imitation war whoop." What other

details are included about this man and his family? How is the description of the man and his behavior juxtaposed with that of the daughter? How do these contrasting descriptions affect your judgments?

2. Sawaquat describes the Scouts' use of "imitation Indian dances, imitation Indian lore" and white "hobbyists" whose pastime is to "masquerade as Indians on the weekends." Sawaquat also says that "the hatred of Indians goes back to the beginning when white people came to this country." Account for this apparent contradiction. Why do you suppose "Indians" are regarded with such ambivalence in this country?

3. Serving in the Army in Korea Sawaquat says he "learned how to kill, how to bully, how to hate Koreans. I came out of the war tougher than ever and, strangely, white." What ironies and contradictions are underscored in Sawaquat's Army experience?

4. Sawaquat apparently grew up hearing stories and having experiences related to his Indian heritage, became "white" in his adulthood, only to have an "awakening" in which he reclaimed his culture in 1968. Analyze the ways in which he accounts for these shifts in perceptions and loyalties. What motivates him to rediscover that past?

5. Sawaquat doesn't blame his little neighbor or the fat man on the beach for their stereotypes of Indians. On what basis does he dismiss them? Do you agree with his position on the "blamelessness" of people who hold stereotypes? Why or why not?

6. Sawaquat wrote this essay in 1983. How have things changed since then? What instances of "backlash" that he describes are evident today? What are some current common stereotypes of Indians?

The Model Minority Image
C. N. Le

In the following article, C. N. Le looks closely at statistics to see what underlies them. Arguing that numbers may, in fact, lie, Le draws on the 2000 Census to show the comparative measures for whites, blacks, Hispanic or Latino Americans, Native Americans, and Asian Americans in terms of such categories as schooling, income, poverty levels, public assistance, and home ownership. Le breaks down the category of Asian American to demonstrate that Vietnamese, Laotians, Cambodians, and Khmer are still struggling to gain access to the "American dream." A Vietnamese American,

*Le earned his bachelor's degree at the University of California,
Irvine, and his Ph.D. at the University of Albany, SUNY, in sociol-
ogy. He has presented papers and written extensively about Asian
Americans and Vietnamese Americans and their place in American
society and has worked as a research assistant at the Center for
Technology in Government.*

———————— ✦ ————————

In a lot of ways, Asian Americans have done remarkably well in
achieving "the American dream" of getting a good education,
working at a good job, and earning a good living. So much so that
the image many have of Asian Americans is that we are the "model
minority"—a bright, shining example of hard work and patience
whose example other minority groups should follow. However, the
practical reality is slightly more complicated than that.

STATISTICS DON'T LIE . . . DO THEY?

Once in a great while, statistics don't lie. It is true that in many
ways, Asian Americans have done very well socially and economi-
cally. The data in the following tables was calculated using the
2000 Census Public Use Microdata Samples, and they compare
the major racial/ethnic groups among different measures of what
sociologists call "socioeconomic achievement." The numbers in
bold represent the group with the highest (most successful) attainment, while the group with the italic number has the lowest
(least successful) attainment levels.

These numbers tell you that among the five major racial/
ethnic groups in the U.S., Asian Americans have the highest college degree attainment rate, rates of having an advanced degree
(professional or Ph.D.), median family income, being in the labor
force, rate of working in a "high skill" occupation (executive, professional, technical, or upper management), and median Socioeconomic Index (SEI) score that measures occupational prestige.
Yes, in these categories, Asians even outperform Whites. Asian
Americans seem to have done so well that magazines such as
Newsweek and respected television shows such as *60 Minutes* proclaim us to be the "model minority."

Selected Socioeconomic Characteristics of the Five Major Racial/Ethnic Groups in the U.S.

	Whites	Blacks	Hispanics/ Latinos	Native Americans	Asian Americans
Less than High School	**15.3**	29.1	*48.5*	27.4	19.5
College Degree	25.3	13.6	*9.9*	10.8	**42.9**
Advanced Degree	3.0	1.2	1.6	*0.9*	**6.5**
Median Personal Income	**$23,640**	$16,300	*$14,400*	$14,500	$20,200
Median Family Income	$48,500	$33,300	$36,000	*$32,240*	**$59,000**
Living in Poverty	*9.4*	24.9	21.4	**25.1**	11.5
Public Assistance	*1.3*	4.5	3.5	**6.1**	2.2
Homeowner	**78.2**	54.4	*52.4*	64.2	62.0
In Labor Force	63.6	*59.8*	61.5	61.2	**65.3**
High Skill Occupation	21.4	12.3	*9.6*	11.9	**34.6**
Median SEI Score	47.0	44.0	*26.0*	44.0	**49.0**

Data Source: 2000 Census 1% Public Use Microdata Samples (PUMS)

They point to statistics like this and say how well Asian Americans are doing in society and that we've overcome past instances of prejudice and discrimination without resorting to political or violent confrontations with Whites. Further, our success should serve as an example for other racial/ethnic minority groups to follow in their own quest to overcome barriers in their way to achieving the American dream.

5   Many people go even further and argue that since Asian Americans are doing so well, we **no longer experience any discrimination** and that Asian Americans no longer need public services such as bilingual education, government documents in multiple languages, and welfare. Further, using the first stereotype of Asian Americans, many just assume that all Asian Americans are successful and that none of us are struggling.

On the surface, it may sound rather benign and even flattering to be described in those terms. However, we need to take a much closer look at these numbers. As we will see, many other statistics show that Asian Americans are still the targets of racial inequality and institutional discrimination and that the **model minority image is a myth.**

WHEN GOOD NUMBERS GO BAD

Again, we need to remember that not all Asian Americans are the same. For every Chinese American or South Asian who has a college degree, the same number of Southeast Asians are still struggling to adapt to their lives in the U.S. For example, as shown in the tables in the *Socioeconomic Statistics & Demographics* article, Vietnamese Americans only have a college degree attainment rate of 20%, less than half the rate for other Asian American ethnic groups. The rates for Laotians, Cambodians, and Khmer are even lower at less than 10%.

The results show that as a whole Asian American families have higher median incomes than White families. However, this is because in most cases, the typical Asian American family tends to have more members who are working than the typical White family. It's not unusual for an Asian American family to have four, five, or more members working. A more telling statistic is **median personal income** (also known as per capita income). The results above show that Asian Americans still trail Whites on this very important measure.

Case in point, another reason why Asian American families tend to make more than White families is because, as described in the *Population Statistics* page, Asian Americans are much more likely to concentrate in metropolitan areas where the **cost of**

living is much higher. Anyone who has lived in New York City (yours truly included) can attest to just how expensive it is to live in these cities. Therefore, Asian Americans may earn more but they also have to spend more to survive. In fact, research shows that within these metropolitan areas, Asian American incomes still trail that of Whites.

"SUCCESS" MAY ONLY BE SKIN-DEEP

Another telling statistic is how much more money a person earns   10 with each additional year of schooling completed, or what sociologists call "returns on education." One of the first in-depth studies that looked at per capita income between Asian Americans and other racial/ethnic groups came from Robert Jiobu and is cited in *Asian Americans: An Interpretive History* by Sucheng Chan. Using this measure, research consistently shows that for each additional year of education attained, Whites earn another $522.

That is, beyond a high school degree, a White with 4 more years of education (equivalent to a college degree) can expect to earn $2088 per year in salary. In contrast, returns on each additional year of education for a Japanese American is only $438. For a Chinese American, it's $320. For Blacks, it's even worse at only $284. What this means is that basically, a typical Asian American has to get more years of education **just to make the same amount of money** that a typical White makes with less education.

Recent research from scholars such as Timothy Fong, Roderick Harrison, and Paul Ong, to name just a few, continues to confirm these findings that controlling for other variables, Asian Americans still earn less money than Whites with virtually equal qualifications. Once again, for each statistic that suggests everything is picture-perfect for Asian Americans, there is another that proves otherwise.

As another example, in California, almost 40% of all Vietnamese refugees are on public assistance and in Minnesota and Wisconsin, an equal number of Cambodians, Hmong, and Laotians also receive public assistance. Another example is that of many Korean immigrants who come to the U.S. with very high levels of education. But for various reasons (i.e., not being fluent in English), many are not able to get decent jobs that pay well.

Therefore, they are forced to to work as janitors, waiters, bus-boys, or go into business for themselves to survive. The only rea-son why many Korean small business owners are able to make a small profit is that they have no paid employees and work 20 hours a day.

ALWAYS CHECK BELOW THE SURFACE

Another point is that even despite the real successes we've achieved, Asian Americans are still significantly underrepre-sented in positions of **political leadership** at the local, regional, state, and federal levels (despite the successes of a few individu-als such as Norman Mineta and Elaine Chao)—just like Blacks, Latinos, and American Indians. In the corporate world, Asian Americans are underrepresented as CEOs, board members, and high-level supervisors—just like Blacks, Latinos, and American Indians.

15   This is not to say that there aren't Asians Americans out there who are quite successful and have essentially achieved the American dream. As their socioeconomic attainment levels clearly illustrate for example, Asian Indians consistently outperform not only other Asian ethnic groups but Whites in several achievement measures, sometimes by a large margin. And of course, you'll find plenty of examples of Asian Americans who are quite affluent and successful, and as Asian Americans, we should rightly feel proud of these examples of success.

The point is that just because many Asian Americans have "made it," it does not mean that **all** Asian Americans have made it. In many ways, Asian Americans are still the targets of much prejudice, stereotypes, and discrimination. For instance, the per-sistent belief that "all Asians are smart" puts a tremendous amount of pressure on many Asian Americans. Many, particularly Southeast Asians, are not able to conform to this unrealistic ex-pectation and in fact, have the **highest high school dropout rates** in the country.

Asian Americans are also increasingly becoming the targets of hate crimes. In fact, research shows that Asian Americans are the fastest growing victims of hate crimes in the U.S. Asian Indians and other successful Asian Americans may have extraor-dinary levels of socioeconomic achievement but it's very unlikely that many of them will say that they no longer experience discrimination because of their Asian ethnicity. Ultimately, the process of achieving socioeconomic success among Asian Americans is very complex. There are many examples of affluence and prosperity within the Asian American population but in many ways, we still face the same types of racism, social inequality, and institutional discrimination that other groups of color face. Therefore, the image that the entire Asian American community is the "model minority" is a myth.

For Discussion and Writing

1. What sorts of limitations does Le demonstrate about the use of statistical information? How can statistics lie? What complexities might the other categories be overlooking?
2. What might be learned about stereotyping from Le's essay? What are some other practices—besides the use of statistics—that might create the basis for stereotyping?
3. How does Le suggest that even positive stereotypes—such as being smart—can create problems for Asian Americans? Can you think of other examples where positive stereotypes are disadvantageous?
4. What can you learn about Le through this essay? How does knowing he's Vietnamese influence your reading of this essay?

Los Vendidos
Luis Valdez

Los Vendidos is a satirical one-act play that addresses head-on the issue of the stereotyping of Mexican American men. Often called the father of Chicano theater, Luis Valdez is perhaps best known for his play Zoot Suit *(1978) that was adapted into a film in 1981. Valdez has written, co-written, and directed many plays depicting the Hispanic experience, including* La Carpa de los Rasquachis *(1973),* El Fin del Mundo *(1976), and* Tibercio Vasquez *(1980). He also directed the box-office smash movie* La Bamba *in 1987. Valdez began writing plays as a student at San José State University. Working with migrant farmers as a union organizer after he graduated from college, he combined his interests in equity and theater by founding El Teatro Campesino, which produced one-act plays, often without stage, script, or props, that reflected the circumstances of the migrant worker.*

———————— ✦ ————————

CHARACTERS

HONEST SANCHO
SECRETARY
FARM WORKER
JOHNNY
REVOLUCIONARIO
MEXICAN-AMERICAN

Scene: HONEST SANCHO'S *Used Mexican Lot and Mexican Curio Shop. Three models are on display in* HONEST SANCHO'S *shop: to the right, there is a* REVOLUCIONARIO, *complete with sombrero, carrilleras, and carabina 30–30. At center, on the floor, there is the* FARM WORKER, *under a broad straw sombrero. At stage left is the* PACHUCO, *filero in hand.*

(HONEST SANCHO *is moving among his models, dusting them off and preparing for another day of business.*)

SANCHO: Bueno, bueno, mis monos, vamos a ver a quien vendemos ahora, ¿no? (*To audience.*) ¡Quihubo! I'm Honest Sancho and this is my shop. Antes fui contratista pero ahora longré tener mi negocito. All I need now is a customer (*A bell rings offstage.*) Ay, a customer!

SECRETARY: (*Entering*) Good morning, I'm Miss Jiménez from—

SANCHO: ¡Ah, una chicana! Welcome, welcome Señorita Jiménez.

SECRETARY: (*Anglo pronunciation*) JIM-enez.

SANCHO: ¿Qué?

SECRETARY: My name is Miss JIM-enez. Don't you speak English? What's wrong with you?

SANCHO: Oh, nothing, Señorita JIM-enez. I'm here to help you.

SECRETARY: That's better. As I was starting to say, I'm a secretary from Governor Reagan's office, and we're looking for a Mexican type for the administration.

SANCHO: Well, you come to the right place, lady. This is Honest Sancho's Used Mexican lot, and we got all types here. Any particular type you want?

SECRETARY: Yes, we were looking for somebody suave—

SANCHO: Suave.

SECRETARY: Debonair.

SANCHO: De buen aire.

SECRETARY: Dark.

SANCHO: Prieto.

SECRETARY: But of course not too dark.

SANCHO: No muy prieto.

SECRETARY: Perhaps, beige.

SANCHO: Beige, just the tone. Así como cafecito con leche, ¿no?

SECRETARY: One more thing. He must be hard-working.

SANCHO: That could only be one model. Step right over here to the center of the shop, lady. (*They cross to the* FARM WORKER.) This is our standard farm worker model. As you can see, in the words of our beloved Senator George Murphy, he is "built close to the ground." Also take special notice of his four-ply Goodyear huaraches, made from the rain tire. This wide-brimmed sombrero is an extra added feature—keeps off the sun, rain, and dust.

SECRETARY: Yes, it does look durable.

SANCHO: And our farm worker model is friendly. Muy amable. Watch. (*Snaps his fingers.*)

FARM WORKER: (*Lifts up head*) Buenos días, señorita. (*His head drops.*)

SECRETARY: My, he's friendly.

SANCHO: Didn't I tell you? Loves his patrones! But his most attractive feature is that he's hard-working. Let me show you. (*Snaps fingers.* FARM WORKER *stands.*)

FARM WORKER: ¡El jale! (*He begins to work.*)

SANCHO: As you can see, he is cutting grapes.

SECRETARY: Oh, I wouldn't know.

SANCHO: He also picks cotton. (*Snap.* FARM WORKER *begins to pick cotton.*)

SECRETARY: Versatile isn't he?

SANCHO: He also picks melons. (*Snap.* FARM WORKER *picks melons.*) That's his slow speed for late in the season. Here's his fast speed. (*Snap.* FARM WORKER *picks faster.*)

SECRETARY: ¡Chihuahua! . . . I mean, goodness, he sure is a hard worker.

SANCHO: (*Pulls the* FARM WORKER *to his feet*) And that isn't the half of it. Do you see these little holes on his arms that appear to be pores? During those hot sluggish days in the field, when the vines or the branches get so entangled, it's almost impossible to move; these holes emit a certain grease that allow our model to slip and slide right through the crop with no trouble at all.

SECRETARY: Wonderful. But is he economical?

SANCHO: Economical? Señorita, you are looking at the Volkswagen of Mexicans. Pennies a day is all it takes. One plate of beans and tortillas will keep him going all day. That, and chile. Plenty of chile. Chile jalapenos, chile verde, chile colorado. But, of course, if you do give him chile (*Snap.* FARM WORKER *turns left face.* Snap. FARM WORKER *bends over.*) then you have to change his oil filter once a week.

SECRETARY: What about storage?

SANCHO: No problem. You know these new farm labor camps our Honorable Governor Reagan has built out by Parlier or Raisin City? They were designed with our model in mind. Five, six, seven, even ten in one of those shacks will give you no trouble at all. You can also put him in old barns, old cars, river banks. You can even leave him out in the field overnight with no worry!

SECRETARY: Remarkable.

SANCHO: And here's an added feature: Every year at the end of the season, this model goes back to Mexico and doesn't return, automatically, until next Spring.

SECRETARY: How about that. But tell me: does he speak English?

SANCHO: Another outstanding feature is that last year this model was programmed to go out on STRIKE! (*Snap.*)

FARM WORKER: ¡HUELGA! ¡HUELGA! Hermanos, sálganse de esos files. (*Snap. He stops.*)

SECRETARY: No! Oh no, we can't strike in the State Capitol.

SANCHO: Well, he also scabs. (*Snap.*)

FARM WORKER: Me vendo barato, ¿y qué? (*Snap.*)

SECRETARY: That's much better, but you didn't answer my question. Does he speak English?

SANCHO: Bueno . . . no pero he has other—

SECRETARY: No.

SANCHO: Other features.

SECRETARY: NO! He just won't do!

SANCHO: Okay, okay pues. We have other models.

SECRETARY: I hope so. What we need is something a little more sophisticated.

Sancho: Sophisti—¿qué?

Secretary: An urban model.

Sancho: Ah, from the city! Step right back. Over here in this corner of the shop is exactly what you're looking for. Introducing our new 1969 JOHNNY PACHUCO model! This is our fastback model. Streamlined. Built for speed, low-riding, city life. Take a look at some of these features. Mag shoes, dual exhausts, green chartreuse paint-job, dark-tint windshield, a little poof on top. Let me just turn him on. (*Snap.* JOHNNY *walks to stage center with a pachuco bounce.*)

Secretary: What was that?

Sancho: That, señorita, was the Chicano shuffle.

Secretary: Okay, what does he do?

Sancho: Anything and everything necessary for city life. For instance, survival: He knife fights. (*Snap.* JOHNNY *pulls out switch blade and swings at* SECRETARY.)

(SECRETARY *screams.*)

Sancho: He dances. (*Snap.*)

Johnny: (*Singing.*) "Angel Baby, my Angel Baby . . ." (*Snap.*)

Sancho: And here's a feature no city model can be without. He gets arrested, but not without resisting, of course. (*Snap.*)

Johnny: ¡En la madre, la placa! I didn't do it! I didn't do it! (JOHNNY *turns and stands up against an imaginary wall, legs spread out, arms behind his back.*)

Secretary: Oh no, we can't have arrests! We must maintain law and order.

Sancho: But he's bilingual!

Secretary: Bilingual?

Sancho: Simón que yes. He speaks English! Johnny, give us some English. (*Snap.*)

Johnny: (*Comes downstage.*) Fuck-you!

Secretary: (*Gasps*) Oh! I've never been so insulted in my whole life!

Sancho: Well, he learned it in your school.

Secretary: I don't care where he learned it.

Sancho: But he's economical!

Secretary: Economical?

Sancho: Nickels and dimes. You can keep Johnny running on hamburgers, Taco Bell tacos, Lucky Lager beer, Thunderbird wine, yesca—

SECRETARY: Yesca?

SANCHO: Mota.

SECRETARY: Mota?

SANCHO: Leños . . . Marijuana. (*Snap;* JOHNNY *inhales on an imaginary joint.*)

SECRETARY: That's against the law!

JOHNNY: (*Big smile, holding his breath*) Yeah.

SANCHO: He also sniffs glue. (*Snap.* JOHNNY *inhales glue, big smile.*)

JOHNNY: Tha's too much, ése.

SECRETARY: No, Mr. Sancho, I don't think this—

SANCHO: Wait a minute, he has other qualities I know you'll love. For example, an inferiority complex. (*Snap.*)

JOHNNY: (*To* SANCHO) You think you're better than me, huh ése? (*Swings switch blade.*)

SANCHO: He can also be beaten and he bruises, cut him and he bleeds; kick him and he—(*He beats, bruises and kicks* PACHUCO.) would you like to try it?

SECRETARY: Oh, I couldn't.

SANCHO: Be my guest. He's a great scapegoat.

SECRETARY: No, really.

SANCHO: Please.

SECRETARY: Well, all right. Just once. (*She kicks* PACHUCO.) Oh, he's so soft.

SANCHO: Wasn't that good? Try again.

SECRETARY: (*Kicks* PACHUCO) Oh, he's so wonderful! (*She kicks him again.*)

SANCHO: Okay, that's enough, lady. You ruin the merchandise. Yes, our Johnny Pachuco model can give you many hours of pleasure. Why, the L.A.P.D. just bought twenty of these to train their rookie cops on. And talk about maintenance. Señorita, you are looking at an entirely self-supporting machine. You're never going to find our Johnny Pachuco model on the relief rolls. No, sir, this model knows how to liberate.

SECRETARY: Liberate?

SANCHO: He steals. (*Snap.* JOHNNY *rushes the* SECRETARY *and steals her purse.*)

JOHNNY: ¡Dame esa bolsa, vieja! (*He grabs the purse and runs. Snap by* SANCHO. *He stops.*)

(SECRETARY *runs after* JOHNNY *and grabs purse away from him, kicking him as she goes.*)

SECRETARY: No, no, no! We can't have any *more* thieves in the State Administration. Put him back.

SANCHO: Okay, we still got other models. Come on, Johnny, we'll sell you to some old lady. (SANCHO *takes* JOHNNY *back to his place.*)

SECRETARY: Mr. Sancho, I don't think you quite understand what we need. What we need is something that will attract the women voters. Something more traditional, more romantic.

SANCHO: Ah, a lover. (*He smiles meaningfully.*) Step right over here, señorita. Introducing our standard Revolucionario and/or Early California Bandit type. As you can see he is well-built, sturdy, durable. This is the International Harvester of Mexicans.

SECRETARY: What does he do?

SANCHO: You name it, he does it. He rides horses, stays in the mountains, crosses deserts, plains, rivers, leads revolutions, follows revolutions, kills, can be killed, serves as a martyr, hero, movie star—did I say movie star? Did you ever see *Viva Zapata? Viva Villa? Villa Rides? Pancho Villa Returns? Pancho Villa Goes Back? Pancho Villa Meets Abbot and Costello*—

SECRETARY: I've never seen any of those.

SANCHO: Well, he was in all of them. Listen to this. (*Snap.*)

REVOLUCIONARIO: (*Scream.*) ¡VIVA VILLAAAAA!

SECRETARY: That's awfully loud.

SANCHO: He has a volume control. (*He adjusts volume. Snap.*)

REVOLUCIONARIO: (*Mousey voice*) ¡Viva Villa!

SECRETARY: That's better.

SANCHO: And even if you didn't see him in the movies, perhaps you saw him on TV. He makes commercials. (*Snap.*)

REVOLUCIONARIO: Is there a Frito Bandito in your house?

SECRETARY: Oh yes, I've seen that one!

SANCHO: Another feature about this one is that he is economical. He runs on raw horsemeat and tequila!

SECRETARY: Isn't that rather savage?

SANCHO: Al contrario, it makes him a lover. (*Snap.*)

REVOLUCIONARIO: (*To* SECRETARY) ¡Ay, mamasota, cochota, ven pa'ca! (*He grabs* SECRETARY *and folds her back—Latin-lover style.*)

SANCHO: (*Snap.* REVOLUCIONARIO *goes back upright.*) Now wasn't that nice?

SECRETARY: Well, it was rather nice.

SANCHO: And finally, there is one outstanding feature about this model I KNOW the ladies are going to love: He's a GENUINE antique! He was made in Mexico in 1910!

SECRETARY: Made in Mexico?

SANCHO: That's right. Once in Tijuana, twice in Guadalajara, three times in Cuernavaca.

SECRETARY: Mr. Sancho, I thought he was an American product.

SANCHO: No, but—

SECRETARY: No, I'm sorry. We can't buy anything but American-made products. He just won't do.

SANCHO: But he's an antique!

SECRETARY: I don't care. You still don't understand what we need. It's true we need Mexican models such as these, but it's more important that he be *American*.

SANCHO: American?

SECRETARY: That's right, and judging from what you've shown me, I don't think you have what we want. Well, my lunch hour's almost over; I better—

SANCHO: Wait a minute! Mexican but American?

SECRETARY: That's correct.

SANCHO: Mexican but . . . (*A sudden flash.*) AMERICAN! Yeah, I think we've got exactly what you want. He just came in today! Give me a minute. (*He exits. Talks from backstage.*) Here he is in the shop. Let me just get some papers off. There. Introducing our new 1970 Mexican-American! Ta-ra-ra-ra-ra-ra-RA-RAAA!

(SANCHO *brings out the* MEXICAN-AMERICAN *model, a clean-shaven middle-class type in business suit, with glasses.*)

SECRETARY: (*Impressed*) Where have you been hiding this one?

SANCHO: He just came in this morning. Ain't he a beauty? Feast your eyes on him! Sturdy US STEEL frame, streamlined, modern. As a matter of fact, he is built exactly like our Anglo models except that he comes in a variety of darker shades: naugahyde, leather, or leatherette.

SECRETARY: Naugahyde.

SANCHO: Well, we'll just write that down. Yes, señorita, this model represents the apex of American engineering! He is bilingual, college educated, ambitious! Say the world "acculturate" and he accelerates. He is intelligent, well-mannered, clean—did I say clean? (*Snap.* MEXICAN-AMERICAN *raises his arm.*) Smell.

SECRETARY: (*Smells*) Old Sobaco, my favorite.

SANCHO: (*Snap.* MEXICAN-AMERICAN *turns toward* SANCHO.) Eric! (*To* SECRETARY.) We call him Eric Garcia. (*To* ERIC.) I want you to meet Miss JIM-enez, Eric.

MEXICAN-AMERICAN: Miss JIM-enez, I am delighted to make your acquaintance. (*He kisses her hand.*)

SECRETARY: Oh, my, how charming!

SANCHO: Did you feel the suction? He has seven especially engineered suction cups right behind his lips. He's a charmer all right!

SECRETARY: How about boards? Does he function on boards?

SANCHO: You name them, he is on them. Parole boards, draft boards, school boards, taco quality control boards, surf boards, two-by-fours.

SECRETARY: Does he function in politics?

SANCHO: Señorita, you are looking at a political MACHINE. Have you ever heard of the OEO, EOC, COD, WAR ON POVERTY? That's our model! Not only that, he makes political speeches.

SECRETARY: May I hear one?

SANCHO: With pleasure. (*Snap.*) Eric, give us a speech.

MEXICAN-AMERICAN: Mr. Congressman, Mr. Chairman, members of the board, honored guests, ladies and gentlemen. (SANCHO *and* SECRETARY *applaud.*) Please, please, I come before you as a Mexican-American to tell you about the problems of the Mexican. The problems of the Mexican stem from one thing and one thing alone: He's stupid. He's uneducated. He needs to stay in school. He needs to be ambitious, forward-looking, harder-working. He needs to think American, American, American, AMERICAN, AMERICAN, AMERICAN. GOD BLESS AMERICA! GOD BLESS AMERICA!! (*He goes out of control.*)

(SANCHO *snaps frantically and the* MEXICAN-AMERICAN *finally slumps forward, bending at the waist.*)

SECRETARY: Oh my, he's patriotic too!

SANCHO: Sí, señorita, he loves his country. Let me just make a little adjustment here. (*Stands* MEXICAN-AMERICAN *up.*)

SECRETARY: What about upkeep? Is he economical?

SANCHO: Well, no, I won't lie to you. The Mexican-American costs a little bit more, but you get what you pay for. He's worth every extra cent. You can keep him running on dry martinis, Langendorf bread.

SECRETARY: Apple pie?

SANCHO: Only Mom's. Of course, he's also programmed to eat Mexican food on ceremonial functions, but I must warn you: an overdose of beans will plug up his exhaust.

SECRETARY: Fine! There's just one more question: HOW MUCH DO YOU WANT FOR HIM?

SANCHO: Well, I tell you what I'm gonna do. Today and today only, because you've been so sweet, I'm gonna let you steal this model from me! I'm gonna let you drive him off the lot for the simple price of—let's see taxes and license included— $15,000.

SECRETARY: Fifteen thousand DOLLARS? For a MEXICAN!

SANCHO: Mexican? What are you talking, lady? This is a Mexican-AMERICAN! We had to melt down two pachucos, a farm worker and three gabachos to make this model! You want quality, but you gotta pay for it! This is no cheap run-about. He's got class!

SECRETARY: Okay, I'll take him.

SANCHO: You will?

SECRETARY: Here's your money.

SANCHO: You mind if I count it?

SECRETARY: Go right ahead.

SANCHO: Well, you'll get your pink slip in the mail. Oh, do you want me to wrap him up for you? We have a box in the back.

SECRETARY: No, thank you. The Governor is having a luncheon this afternoon, and we need a brown face in the crowd. How do I drive him?

SANCHO: Just snap your fingers. He'll do anything you want.

(SECRETARY *snaps.* MEXICAN-AMERICAN *steps forward.*)

MEXICAN-AMERICAN: RAZA QUERIDA, ¡VAMOS LEVANTANDO ARMAS PARA LIBERARNOS DE ESTOS DESGRACIADOS GABACHOS QUE NOS EXPLOTAN! VAMOS.

SECRETARY: What did he say?

SANCHO: Something about lifting arms, killing white people, etc.

SECRETARY: But he's not supposed to say that!

SANCHO: Look, lady, don't blame me for bugs from the factory. He's your Mexican-American; you bought him, now drive him off the lot!

SECRETARY: But he's broken!

SANCHO: Try snapping another finger.

(SECRETARY *snaps.* MEXICAN-AMERICAN *comes to life again.*)

MEXICAN-AMERICAN: ¡ESTA GRAN HUMANIDAD HA DICHO BASTA! Y SE HA PUESTO EN MARCHA! ¡BASTA! ¡BASTA! ¡VIVA LA RAZA! ¡VIVA LA CAUSA! ¡VIVA LA HUELGA! ¡VIVAN LOS BROWN BERETS! ¡VIVAN LOS ESTUDIANTES! ¡CHICANO POWER!

(*The* MEXICAN-AMERICAN *turns toward the* SECRETARY, *who gasps and backs up. He keeps turning toward the* PACHUCO, FARM WORKER, *and* REVOLUCIONARIO, *snapping his fingers and turning each of them on, one by one.*)

PACHUCO: (*Snap. To* SECRETARY) I'm going to get you, baby! ¡Viva La Raza!

FARM WORKER: (*Snap. To* SECRETARY) ¡Viva la huelga! ¡Viva la Huelga! ¡VIVA LA HUELGA!

REVOLUCIONARIO: (*Snap. To* SECRETARY) ¡Viva la revolución! ¡VIVA LA REVOLUCIÓN!

REVOLUCIONARIO: (*Snap. To* SECRETARY) ¡Viva la revolución! ¡VIVA LA REVOLUCIÓN!

(*The three models join together and advance toward the* SECRETARY *who backs up and runs out of the shop screaming.* SANCHO *is at the other end of the shop holding his money in his hand. All freeze. After a few seconds up silence, the* PACHUCO *moves and stretches, shaking his arms and loosening up. The* FARM WORKER *and* REVOLUCIONARIO *do the same.* SANCHO *stays where he is, frozen to his spot.*)

JOHNNY: Man, that was a long one, ése. (*Others agree with him.*)

FARM WORKER: How did we do?

JOHNNY: Pretty good, look all that lana, man! (*He goes over to* SANCHO *and removes the money from his hind.* SANCHO *stays where he is.*)

REVOLUCIONARIO: En la madre, look at all the money.

JOHNNY: We keep this up, we're going to be rich.

FARM WORKER: They think we're machines.

REVOLUCIONARIO: Burros.

JOHNNY: Puppets.

MEXICAN-AMERICAN: The only thing I don't like is—how come I always got to play the goddamn Mexican-American?

JOHNNY: That's what you get for finishing high school.

FARM WORKER: How about our wages, ése?

JOHNNY: Here it comes right now. $3,000 for you, $3,000 for you, $3,000 for you, and $3,000 for me. The rest we put back into the business.

MEXICAN-AMERICAN: Too much, man. Heh, where you vatos going tonight?

FARM WORKER: I'm going over to Concha's. There's a party.

JOHNNY: Wait a minute, vatos. What about our salesman? I think he needs an oil job.

REVOLUCIONARIO: Leave him to me.

(*The* PACHUCO, FARM WORKER, *and* MEXICAN-AMERICAN *exit, talking loudly about their plans for the night. The* REVOLUCIONARIO *goes over to* SANCHO, *removes his derby hat and cigar, lifts him up and throws him over his shoulder.* SANCHO *hangs loose, lifeless.*)

REVOLUCIONARIO: (*To audience*) He's the best model we got! ¡Ajua! (*Exit.*)

For Discussion and Writing

1. There are myriad common stereotypes of Mexicans in this play. Create a list. How does Valdez treat these stereotypes? How would you characterize the tone of this piece? Why do you suppose Valdez chose this approach?

2. What stereotypes in the piece are familiar to you? What are their sources? How do these stereotypes show up in the news media and popular culture?

3. Why do you think Valdez wrote this play? Who is the audience? How might different audiences—poor whites, middle-class whites, poor Mexican Americans, middle-class Mexican Americans, people of other ethnicities—respond to this play? Explain why you think these audiences might respond in the ways you speculate.

4. This piece is presented to audiences—and here—without translating the Spanish into English. What is the impact of that? What political statement is made by the decision not to translate? If you do not know Spanish, obtain a Spanish/English dictionary and translate some of the words Valdez uses. How do your translations affect your perceptions of the play?

5. Why does Señorita Jiménez insist on a particular pronunciation of her name? What do her questions and objections to the various models tell us about her political values and opinions?

6. The play's Early California Bandit model, Sancho says, was made in Mexico in 1910. When Señorita Jiménez asks, "Made in Mexico?," Sancho answers,

"That's right. Once in Tijuana, twice in Guadalajara, three times in Cuernavaca." An Internet search will provide you with a sketch of the Mexican Revolution of 1910. What significance do these references have to the meaning of the play? What other terms ("la huelga" and "Villa," e.g.) might give you further insight into the political meaning of this play?

The Myth of the Latin Woman: I Just Met a Girl Named Maria
JUDITH ORTIZ COFER

Born in Puerto Rico in 1952, Judith Ortiz Cofer moved to Paterson, New Jersey, when she was two years old and her father, who had joined the U.S. Navy, was stationed in the United States. Her first novel, The Line of the Sun, *published in 1989 was nominated for the Pulitzer Prize. Other works include poems, stories, and essays in such collections as* Silent Dancing: A Partial Remembrance of a Puerto Rican Childhood *(1991),* The Latin Deli *(1993),* The Year of the Revolution *(1998), and* Woman in Front of the Sun: On Becoming a Writer *(2000). Among her awards are the Pushcart Prize for Non-Fiction (1990) and the Anisfield-Wolf Book Award (1993). A professor of English and creative writing at the University of Georgia, Ortiz Cofer focuses on the difficulties facing Latino immigrants, and in the following piece describes experiences in which stereotypes of Latinas limit women's possibilities.*

◆

On a bus trip to London from Oxford University where I was earning some graduate credits one summer, a young man, obviously fresh from a pub, spotted me and as if struck by inspiration went down on his knees in the aisle. With both hands over his heart he broke into an Irish tenor's rendition of "Maria" from *West Side Story.* My politely amused fellow passengers gave his lovely voice the round of gentle applause it deserved. Though I was not quite as amused, I managed my version of an English smile: no show of teeth, no extreme contortions of the facial muscles—I was at this time of my life practicing reserve and cool. Oh, that British control, how I coveted it. But Maria had followed me to London, reminding me of a prime fact of my life: you can leave the Island, master the English language, and travel as far as you can, but if you are a Latina, especially one like me who so obviously belongs to Rita Moreno's gene pool, the Island travels with you.

This is sometimes a very good thing—it may win you that extra minute of someone's attention. But with some people, the same things can make *you* an island—not so much a tropical paradise as an Alcatraz, a place nobody wants to visit. As a Puerto Rican girl growing up in the United States and wanting like most children to "belong," I resented the stereotype that my Hispanic appearance called forth from many people I met. . . .

It is surprising to some of my professional friends that some people, including those who should know better, still put others "in their place." Though rarer, these incidents are still common-place in my life. It happened to me most recently during a stay at a very classy metropolitan hotel favored by young professional couples for their weddings. Late one evening after the theater, as I walked toward my room with my new colleague (a woman with whom I was coordinating an arts program), a middle-aged man in a tuxedo, a young girl in satin and lace on his arm, stepped directly into our path. With his champagne glass extended toward me, he exclaimed "Evita!"

Our way blocked, my companion and I listened as the man half-recited, half-bellowed "Don't Cry for Me, Argentina." When he finished, the young girl said: "How about a round of applause for my daddy?" We complied, hoping this would bring the silly spectacle to a close. I was becoming aware that our little group was attracting the attention of the other guests.

5   "Daddy" must have perceived this too, and he once more barred the way as we tried to walk past him. He began to shout-sing a ditty to the tune of "La Bamba"—except that the lyrics were about a girl named Maria whose exploits all rhymed with her name and gonorrhea. The girl kept saying "Oh, Daddy" and look-ing at me with pleading eyes. She wanted me to laugh along with the others. My companion and I stood silently waiting for the man to end his offensive song. When he finished, I looked not at him but at his daughter. I advised her calmly never to ask her fa-ther what he had done in the army. Then I walked between them and to my room. My friend complimented me on my cool han-dling of the situation. I confessed to her that I really had wanted to push the jerk into the swimming pool. I knew that this same

man—probably a corporate executive, well educated, even worldly by most standards—would not have been likely to regale a white woman with a dirty song in public. He would perhaps have checked his impulse by assuming that she could be somebody's wife or mother, or at least *somebody* who might take offense. But to him, I was just an Evita or a Maria: merely a character in his cartoon-populated universe.

Because of my education and my proficiency with the English language, I have acquired many mechanisms for dealing with the anger I experience. This was not true for my parents, nor is it true for the many Latin women working at menial jobs who must put up with stereotypes about our ethnic group such as: "They make good domestics." This is another fact of the myth of the Latin woman in the United States. Its origin is simple to deduce. Work as domestics, waitressing, and factory jobs are all that's available to women with little English and few skills. The myth of the Hispanic menial has been sustained by the same media phenomenon that made "Mammy" from *Gone With the Wind* America's ideal of the black woman for generations; Maria, the housemaid or counter girl, is now indelibly etched into the national psyche. The big and the little screens have presented us with the picture of the funny Hispanic maid, mispronouncing words and cooking up a spicy storm in a shiny California kitchen.

This media-engendered image of the Latina in the United States has been documented by feminist Hispanic scholars, who claim that such portrayals are partially responsible for the denial of opportunities for upward mobility among Latinas in the professions. I have a Chicana friend working on a Ph.D. in philosophy at a major university. She says her doctor still shakes his head in puzzled amazement at all the "big words" she uses. Since I do not wear my diplomas around my neck for all to see, I too have on occasion been sent to that "kitchen," where some think I obviously belong.

One such incident that has stayed with me, though I recognize it as a minor offense, happened on the day of my first public poetry reading. It took place in Miami in a boat-restaurant where we were having lunch before the event. I was nervous and excited as I walked in with my notebook in my hand. An older woman motioned me to her table. Thinking (foolish me) that she wanted me to autograph a copy of my brand new slender volume of verse, I went over. She ordered a cup of coffee from me, assuming that

I was the waitress. Easy enough to mistake my poems for menus, I suppose. I know that it wasn't an intentional act of cruelty, yet of all the good things that happened that day, I remember that scene most clearly, because it reminded me of what I had to overcome before anyone would take me seriously. In retrospect I understand that my anger gave my reading fire, that I have almost always taken doubts in my abilities as a challenge—and that the result is, most times, a feeling of satisfaction at having won a convert when I see the cold, appraising eyes warm to my words, the body language change, the smile that indicates that I have opened some avenue for communication. That day I read to that woman and her lowered eyes told me that she was embarrassed at her little faux pas, and when I willed her to look up at me, it was my victory, and she graciously allowed me to punish her with my full attention. We shook hands at the end of the reading, and I never saw her again. She has probably forgotten the whole thing, but maybe not.

Yet I am one of the lucky ones. My parents made it possible for me to acquire a stronger footing in the mainstream culture by giving me the chance at an education. And books and art have saved me from the harsher forms of ethnic and racial prejudice that many of my Hispanic *compañeras* have had to endure. I travel a lot around the United States, reading from my books of poetry and my novel, and the reception I most often receive is one of positive interest by people who want to know more about my culture.

10   There are, however, thousands of Latinas without the privilege of an education or the entrée into society that I have. For them life is a struggle against the misconceptions perpetuated by the myth of the Latina as whore, domestic, or criminal. We cannot change this by legislating the way people look at us. The transformation, as I see it, has to occur at a much more individual level.

My personal goal in my public life is to try to replace the old pervasive stereotypes and myths about Latinas with a much more interesting set of realities. Every time I give a reading, I hope the stories I tell, the dreams and fears I examine in my work, can achieve some universal truth which will get my audience past the particulars of my skin color, my accent, or my clothes.

I once wrote a poem in which I called us Latinas "God's brown daughters." This poem is really a prayer of sorts, offered upward, but also, through the human-to-human channel of art, outward. It is a prayer for communication, and for respect. In it, Latin women pray "in Spanish to an Anglo God / with a Jewish heritage," and they are "fervently hoping / that if not omnipotent, / at least He be bilingual."

For Discussion and Writing

1. How would you characterize Ortiz Cofer's reactions to people who stereotype her? How does she distinguish her own ability to cope with negative experiences compared with that of other Latinas?
2. What impact does Ortiz Cofer believe stereotypes have on Latina women? Ortiz Cofer blames the "media-engendered image of the Latina in the United States" for stereotypes of Latinas. Describe the stereotypes you have encountered in your own experience through the media and through discussions with friends and family about Latinas. If you are Latina, have you had experiences similar to Ortiz Cofer's in which people impose a stereotype on you?
3. Ortiz Cofer says that we cannot change unfair stereotyping "by legislating the way people look at us. The transformation, as I see it, has to occur at a much more individual level." Describe some ways that negative stereotypes might be countered by you and others learning about diversity.
4. Ortiz Cofer ends with a part of one of her poems. How would you characterize the tone of these lines? Why do you suppose she ends the piece this way?

Reading, Research, and Writing

1. The essays and play in this chapter focus primarily on general stereotypes of racial groups. However, gender also affects how people are stereotyped. How are women of various racial groups stereotyped? Noda explores this as a Japanese American woman. What are some common stereotypes of black women? Asian women? Mexican women? Women from other ethnic and racial groups? Choose one racial or ethnic group and describe the stereotypes of women in that group. Where do they come from? How are they reproduced in our culture?
2. Most of the readings in this chapter focus on how whites stereotype people of other races. Why might this sort of stereotyping be considered the most powerful or the most dangerous? Of course, however, it's possible for any group to stereotype any other group—because of race,

ethnicity, age, traditions, and so forth. Explore the nature of stereotype. If you are black, what are some common stereotypes of whites that you notice African Americans have? If you are a member of another racial or ethnic group, what are some ways your group stereotypes members of other ethnicities? If you are white, learn more about how other racial groups represent white people and white culture. Write an analysis of the ways in which these stereotypes are formed and their basis in reality.

3. Sawaquat says that his grandmother and people like her in Harbor Springs, Michigan, "had their land there taken by treaty, by fraud, by violence, by theft." Explore the history of Indians in Michigan—or your own region—to discover more stories of how Indians lost their land. Or, look into the event at Burt Lake in 1900 in which Sawaquat claims whites burned down the village in Burt Lake and "pushed the Indians out." What validity can you find in Sawaquat's claims? What images of whites are created by a historical examination of the ways whites have treated American Indians? How might American Indians stereotype whites on the basis of their experiences? Write a paper in which you describe white people from an American Indian's historical perspective.

4. In this chapter, the essays focus on Asian Americans and Hispanic Americans as general groups, and more specifically on African Americans and Mexican Americans. What other groups are victims of stereotypes? Choose a group that is not examined in this section—Arab Americans, Cuban Americans, Puerto Rican Americans, Jewish Americans, Italian Americans—and examine the stereotypes common in our culture. Where did these stereotypes originate? How are they reproduced? Write a paper that demonstrates your findings.

5. To learn more about the impact of stereotypes on people's ideas and thinking, conduct a survey about people's attitudes toward various racial groups. Choose one or more groups to learn about common stereotypes among your circle of friends and acquaintances. Create a list of questions that ask people to describe the traits they think describe particular racial groups. Ask them how they have learned about these traits. Write a paper that analyzes stereotypes and their roots in people's thinking.

The Reality
of the Personal

My mother thought a nose job was a good idea.... Can it be that for all the strides made against racism and anti-Semitism, Americans still want to expunge their ethnicity from their looks as much as possible?

Lisa Miya-Jervis

Someone once told me I was lucky to be biracial because I have the best of both worlds.... But looking at the big picture, American society makes being biracial feel less like a blessing than a curse.

Brian A. Courtney

There are many ways that we learn about the world we live in—how we view the world and how the world views us: through our families, through how we are represented in the media and in popular culture, through our relationships with other people. "Experience is the best teacher" is an old cliché. But it's one that has resonance, because all of us have had profound experiences that teach us who we are and how we should relate to others.

The value in reading essays about personal experience is that they take us beyond statistics and reports. We need numbers and analyses of those numbers in order to understand the large picture of such issues as education, employment, income, legal matters, social mobility, and so forth. Numbers and reports give us an overview of how we are progressing in creating equity and eliminating discrimination. Numbers and reports allow us to develop

147

arguments for instituting change. However, numbers and reports are impersonal and disembodied. They are broad and abstract. Educator James Moffett has said abstraction sacrifices a loss in reality for a gain in control. Abstraction allows us to grasp the large features of an issue. Experience, however, provides the reality. When we learn about personal experiences, we gain insight into people's thoughts and feelings, into how they have been affected directly by issues of racial discrimination, identity, self-image, and so forth.

The essays in this chapter focus on personal experiences. Some of these experiences are positive and uplifting; others show how, because of their race, people can be limited and diminished; and still others give us insight into efforts to transcend race to understand what humans have in common.

In "Mother's English," Amy Tan describes growing up and being ashamed of her mother's English, even though she recognized the positive influence of her mother's language in shaping her own rich, literary language. Moreover, Tan laments how her mother's "limited" English "limits people's perceptions of her." Gary Soto's essay "Like Mexicans" describes his experiences as a child and a young adult with friends and family who want him to marry a Mexican. Soto grapples with the idea of race, class, and difference, when he chooses to marry a Japanese woman. Racial identity is also a consideration in bell hooks's exploration of dolls in "Baby." Although she plays with Barbie dolls, it is her "brown like light milk chocolate" doll that she most cherishes. She reflects on why the appearance of this doll is so important to her. Lisa Miya-Jervis also focuses on how she looks in her exploration of "the ideal of beauty" in "My Jewish Nose." In her case she sees her physical being as a marker of her ethnicity that she wants to preserve.

Patricia J. Williams's experience in purchasing a house in a "white" neighborhood demonstrated for her that her status as an academic professional was not as important as her status as a person of color. When her bank learned that she was African American, she faced "great resistance and much more debt." Brian A. Courtney struggles with his "biracial" identity in "Freedom from Choice." As the child of a white mother and an African American father, Courtney argues for a new category so that he won't be "pressured to choose one side of [my] heritage over the other."

Mother's English

AMY TAN

Amy Tan, a Chinese American born in Oakland, California, in 1952, gave the following speech to a conference of California English teachers in 1990. Tan graduated from the University of California-San José with a B.A. in English in 1973 and an M.A. in linguistics in 1974. Tan worked as a language development specialist with people who had mental disabilities and as a technical freelance writer until she began, in the 1980s, writing about her family's immigrant past and present. Her prize-winning novel, The Joy Luck Club *(1989), about immigrant Chinese women and their American daughters, was made into a film. She has also written* The Kitchen God's Wife *and* The Hundred Secret Senses, *as well as short stories and books for children. In the following piece, she describes the experience of moving between her various versions of English and her mother's expressive English, as well as the power that a certain kind of English has in the world.*

------------------ ✦ ------------------

As you know, I am a writer and by that definition I am someone who has always loved language. I think that is first and foremost with almost every writer I know. I'm fascinated by language in daily life. I spend a great deal of time thinking about the power of language—the way it can evoke an emotion, a visual image, a complex idea, or a simple truth. As a writer, language is the tool of my trade and I use them all, all the Englishes I grew up with.

A few months back, I was made keenly aware of the Englishes I do use. I was giving a talk to a large group of people, the same talk I had given many times before and also with notes. And the nature of the talk was about my writing, my life, and my book *The Joy Luck Club*. The talk was going along well enough until I remembered one major difference that made the whole thing seem wrong. My mother was in the room, and it was perhaps the first time she had heard me give a lengthy speech, using a kind of English I had never used with her. I was saying things like "the intersection of memory and imagination," and "there is an aspect of my fiction that relates to this and thus." A speech filled with carefully wrought grammatical sentences, burdened to me it seemed with nominalized forms, past perfect tenses, conditional phrases, all the forms of standard English that I had learned in school and through books, a form of English I did not use at home or with my mother.

Shortly after that I was walking down the street with my mother and my husband and I became self-conscious of the English I was using, the English that I do use with her. We were talking about the price of new and used furniture and I heard myself saying to her, "Not waste money that way." My husband was with me as well, and he didn't notice any switch in my English. And then I realized why: because over the twenty years that we've been together he's often used that English with me and I've used that with him. It is sort of the English that is our language of intimacy, the English that relates to family talk, the English that I grew up with.

I'd like to give you some idea what my family talk sounds like and I'll do that by quoting what my mother said during a recent conversation which I video-taped and then transcribed. During this conversation, my mother was talking about a political gangster and who had the same last name as her family, Du, and how the gangster in his early years wanted to be adopted by her family which was by comparison very rich. Later the gangster became more rich, more powerful than my mother's family and one day showed up at my mother's wedding to pay his respects. And here's what she said about that, in part, "Du Yu Sung having business like food stand, like off the street kind; he's Du like Du Zong but not Tsung-ming Island people. The local people call him Du, from the river east side. He belong that side, local people. That man want to ask Du Zong father take him in become like own family. Du Zong father look down on him but don't take seriously until that man become big like, become a Mafia. Now important person, very hard inviting him. Chinese way: come only to show respect, don't stay for dinner. Respect for making big celebration; he shows up. Means gives lots of respect, Chinese custom. Chinese social life that way—if too important, won't have to stay too long. He come to my wedding; I didn't see it I heard it. I gone to boy's side. They have YMCA dinner; Chinese age I was nineteen."

5   You should know that my mother's expressive command of English belies how much she actually understands. She reads the *Forbes Report*, listens to *Wall Street Week*, converses daily with her stock broker, reads all of Shirley MacLaine's books with ease, all kinds of things I can't begin to understand. Yet some of my

friends tell me that they understand 50% of what my mother says. Some say maybe they understand maybe 80%. Some say they understand almost nothing at all. As a case in point, a television station recently interviewed my mother and I didn't see this program when it was first aired, but my mother did. She was telling me what happened. She said that everything she said, which was in English, was subtitled in English, as if she had been speaking in pure Chinese. She was understandably puzzled and upset. Recently a friend gave me that tape and I saw that same interview and I watched. And sure enough—subtitles—and I was puzzled because listening to that tape it seemed to me that my mother's English sounded perfectly clear and perfectly natural. Of course, I realize that my mother's English is what I grew up with. It is literally my mother tongue, not Chinese, not standard English, but my mother's English which I later found out is almost a direct translation of Chinese.

Her language as I hear it is vivid and direct, full of observation and imagery. That was the language that helped shape the way that I saw things, expressed things, made sense of the world. Lately I've been giving more thought to the kind of English that my mother speaks. Like others I have described it to people as broken or fractured English, but I wince when I say that. It has always bothered me that I can think of no other way to describe it than broken, as if it were damaged or needed to be fixed, that it lacked a certain wholeness or soundness to it. I've heard other terms used, "Limited English" for example. But they seem just as bad, as if everything is limited, including people's perceptions of the Limited English speaker.

I know this for a fact, because when I was growing up my mother's limited English limited my perception of her. I was ashamed of her English. I believed that her English reflected the quality of what she had to say. That is, because she expressed it imperfectly, her thoughts were imperfect as well. And I had plenty of empirical evidence to support me: The fact that people in department stores, at banks, at supermarkets, at restaurants did not take her as seriously, did not give her good service, pretended not to understand her, or even acted as if they did not hear her.

My mother has long realized the limitations of her English as well. When I was fifteen she used to have me call people on the phone to pretend I was she. In this guise, I was forced to ask for information or oftentimes to complain and yell at people that had been rude to her. One time it was a call to her stock broker in New York. She had cashed out her small portfolio and it just so happened that we were going to New York the next week, our very first trip outside of California. I had to get on the phone and say in my adolescent voice, which was not very convincing, "This is Mrs. Tan." And my mother was in the back whispering loudly, "Why don't he send me check already? Two weeks late. So mad he lie to me, losing me money." Then I said in perfect English, "Yes I'm getting rather concerned. You had agreed to send the check two weeks ago, but it hasn't arrived." And she began to talk more loudly, "What you want—I come to New York, tell him front of his boss you cheating me?" And I was trying to calm her down, making her be quiet, while telling this stock broker, "I can't tolerate any more excuses. If I don't receive the check immediately I'm going to have to speak to your manager when I arrive in New York." And sure enough the following week, there we were in front of this astonished stock broker. And there I was, red-faced and quiet, and my mother the real Mrs. Tan was shouting at his boss in her impeccable broken English.

We used a similar routine a few months ago for a situation that was actually far less humorous. My mother had gone to the hospital for an appointment to find out about a benign brain tumor a CAT scan had revealed a month ago. And she had spoken very good English she said—her best English, no mistakes. Still she said the hospital had not apologized when they said they had lost the CAT scan and she had come for nothing. She said that they did not seem to have any sympathy when she told them she was anxious to know the exact diagnosis since her husband and son had both died of brain tumors. She said they would not give her any more information until the next time; she would have to make another appointment for that, so she said she would not leave until the doctor called her daughter. She wouldn't budge, and when the doctor finally called her daughter, me, who spoke in perfect English, lo-and-behold, we had assurances the CAT scan would be found, they promised a conference call on Monday, and apologies were given for any suffering my mother had gone through for a most regrettable mistake. By the way, apart from the distress of that episode, my mother is fine.

10   But it has continued to disturb me how much my mother's English still limits people's perceptions of her. I think my mother's English almost had an effect on limiting my possibilities as well.

Sociologists and linguists will probably tell you that a person's developing language skills are more influenced by peers. But I do think the language spoken by the family, especially immigrant families, which are more insular, plays a large role in shaping the language of the child. . . . While this may be true, I always wanted, however, to capture what language ability tests can never reveal—her intent, her passion, her imagery, the rhythms of her speech, and the nature of her thoughts. Apart from what any critic had to say about my writing, I knew I had succeeded where it counted when my mother finished reading my first book and gave me her verdict. "So easy to read."

For Discussion and Writing

1. Tan uses the word "Englishes" in her speech. What do you suppose she means by this term? What are some of the varieties of Englishes you have encountered? How many different Englishes do you use?
2. Analyze the excerpt Tan gives us of her mother's English. Why does Tan call her mother's language at the stockbroker's office "her impeccable broken English"?
3. What relationship does Tan draw between how people speak and how they are treated? Analyze the validity of the claim that limited English indicates or reflects limited thinking. Draw on what you know about Tan's mother and on your own observations and experiences.
4. On the basis of Tan's observations and your own, what do you think the relative influence of peers and families is on the language of children? Do some research into the language learning of first- and second-generation immigrant families.
5. Read *The Joy Luck Club* or watch the movie version, and further analyze the use of English by immigrant Chinese and their families, as represented in it.

Like Mexicans
Gary Soto

Gary Soto is the author of poems, novels, and stories for young people and adults. His New and Selected Poems *was a 1995 finalist for both the* Los Angeles Times *Book Award and the National Book Award. His memoir* Living Up the Streets *(1985) won an American Book Award. He is a graduate of Fresno State University in California. The following essay is from a collection of reminiscences entitled*

Small Faces *(1986). In it he describes his family's response to his desire to marry a Japanese woman and his own response to her family.*

─────────── ✦ ───────────

My grandmother gave me bad advice and good advice when I was in my early teens. For the bad advice, she said that I should become a barber because they made good money and listened to the radio all day. "Honey, they don't work como burros," she would say every time I visited her. She made the sound of donkeys braying. "Like that, honey!" For the good advice, she said that I should marry a Mexican girl. "No Okies, hijo"—she would say—"Look, my son. He marry one and they fight every day about I don't know what and I don't know what." For her, everyone who wasn't Mexican, black, or Asian were Okies. The French were Okies, the Italians in suits were Okies. When I asked about Jews, whom I had read about, she asked for a picture. I rode home on my bicycle and returned with a calendar depicting the important races of the world. "Pues si, son Okies tambien!"[1] she said, nodding her head. She waved the calendar away and we went to the living room where she lectured me on the virtues of the Mexican girl: first, she could cook and, second, she acted like a woman, not a man, in her husband's home. She said she would tell me about a third when I got a little older.

I asked my mother about it—becoming a barber and marrying Mexican. She was in the kitchen. Steam curled from a pot of boiling beans, the radio was on, looking as squat as a loaf of bread. "Well, if you want to be a barber—they say they make good money." She slapped a round steak with a knife, her glasses slipping down with each strike. She stopped and looked up. "If you find a good Mexican girl, marry her of course." She returned to slapping the meat and I went to the backyard where my brother and David King were sitting on the lawn feeling the inside of their cheeks.

"This is what girls feel like," my brother said, rubbing the inside of his cheek. David put three fingers inside his mouth and scratched. I ignored them and climbed the back fence to see my best friend, Scott, a second-generation Okie. I called him and his mother pointed to the side of the house where his bedroom was, a small aluminum trailer, the kind you gawk at when they're flipped over on the freeway, wheels spinning in the air. I went around to find Scott pitching horseshoes.

I picked up a set of rusty ones and joined him. While we played, we talked about school and friends and record albums. The horseshoes scuffed up dirt, sometimes ringing the iron that threw out a meager shadow like a sundial. After three argued-over games, we pulled two oranges apiece from his tree and started down the alley still talking school and friends and record albums. We pulled more oranges from the alley and talked about who we would marry. "No offense, Scott," I said with an orange slice in my mouth, "but I would never marry an Okie." We walked in step, almost touching, with a sled of shadows dragging behind us. "No offense, Gary," Scott said, "but I would *never* marry a Mexican." I looked at him: a fang of orange slice showed from his munching mouth. I didn't think anything of it. He had his girl and I had mine. But our seventh-grade vision was the same: to marry, get jobs, buy cars and maybe a house if we had money left over.

We talked about our future lives until, to our surprise, we   5
were on the downtown mall, two miles from home. We bought a bag of popcorn at Penneys and sat on a bench near the fountain watching Mexican and Okie girls pass. "That one's mine," I pointed with my chin when a girl with eyebrows arched into black rainbows ambled by. "She's cute," Scott said about a girl with yellow hair and a mouthful of gum. We dreamed aloud, our chins busy pointing out girls. We agreed that we couldn't wait to become men and lift them onto our laps.

But the woman I married was not Mexican but Japanese. It was a surprise to me. For years, I went about wide-eyed in my search for the brown girl in a white dress at a dance. I searched the playground at the baseball diamond. When the girls raced for grounders, their hair bounced like something that couldn't be caught. When they sat together in the lunchroom, heads pressed together, I knew they were talking about us Mexican guys. I saw them and dreamed them. I threw my face into my pillow, making up sentences that were good as in the movies.

But when I was twenty, I fell in love with this other girl who worried my mother, who had my grandmother asking once again to see the calendar of the Important Races of the World. I told her I had thrown it away years before. I took a much-glanced-at snapshot from my wallet. We looked at it together, in silence. Then grandma reclined in her chair, lit a cigarette, and said, "Es pretty." She blew and asked with all her worry pushed up to her forehead: "Chinese?"

I was in love and there was no looking back. She was the one. I told my mother who was slapping hamburger into patties. "Well, sure if you want to marry her," she said. But the more I talked, the more concerned she became. Later I began to worry. Was it all a mistake? "Marry a Mexican girl," I heard my mother say in my mind. I heard it at breakfast. I heard it over math problems, between Western Civilization and cultural geography. But then one afternoon while I was hitchhiking home from school, it struck me like a baseball in the back: my mother wanted me to marry someone of my own social class—a poor girl. I considered my fiancee, Carolyn, and she didn't look poor, though I knew she came from a family of farm workers and pull-yourself-up-by-your-bootstraps ranchers. I asked my brother, who was marrying Mexican poor that fall, if I should marry a poor girl. He screamed "Yeah" above his terrible guitar playing in his bedroom. I considered my sister who had married Mexican. Cousins were dating Mexican. Uncles were remarrying poor women. I asked Scott, who was still my best friend, and he said, "She's too good for you, so you better not."

I worried about it until Carolyn took me home to meet her parents. We drove in her Plymouth until the houses gave way to farms and ranches and finally her house fifty feet from the highway. When we pulled into the drive, I panicked and begged Carolyn to make a U-turn and go back so we could talk about it over a soda. She pinched my cheek, calling me a "silly boy." I felt better, though, when I got out of the car and saw the house: the chipped paint, a cracked window, boards for a walk to the back door. There were rusting cars near the barn. A tractor with a net of spiderwebs under a mulberry. A field. A bale of barbed wire like children's scribbling leaning against an empty chicken coop. Carolyn took my hand and pulled me to my future mother-in-law who was coming out to greet us.

10 We had lunch: sandwiches, potato chips, and iced tea. Carolyn and her mother talked mostly about neighbors and the congregation at the Japanese Methodist Church in West Fresno. Her father, who was in khaki work clothes, excused himself with a wave that was almost a salute and went outside. I heard a truck start, a dog bark, and then the truck rattle away.

Carolyn's mother offered another sandwich, but I declined with a shake of my head and a smile. I looked around when I could, when I was not saying over and over that I was a college student, hinting that I could take care of her daughter. I shifted my chair. I saw newspapers piled in corners, dusty cereal boxes and vinegar bottles in corners. The wallpaper was bubbled from rain that had come in from a bad roof. Dust. Dust lay on lamp shades and window sills. These people are just like Mexicans, I thought. Poor people.

Carolyn's mother asked me through Carolyn if I would like a *sushi*. A plate of black and white things were held in front of me. I took one, wide-eyed, and turned it over like a foreign coin. I was biting into one when I saw a kitten crawl up the window screen over the sink. I chewed and the kitten opened its mouth of terror as she crawled higher, wanting in to paw the leftovers from our plates. I looked at Carolyn who said that the cat was just showing off. I looked up in time to see it fall. It crawled up, then fell again.

We talked for an hour and had apple pie and coffee, slowly. Finally, we got up with Carolyn taking my hand. Slightly embarrassed, I tried to pull away but her grip held me. I let her have her way as she led me down the hallway with her mother right behind me. When I opened the door, I was startled by a kitten clinging to the screen door, its mouth screaming "cat food, dog biscuits, *sushi*. . . . " I opened the door and the kitten, still holding on, whined in the language of hungry animals. When I got into Carolyn's car, I looked back: the cat was still clinging. I asked Carolyn if it were possibly hungry, but she said the cat was being silly. She started the car, waved to her mother, and bounced us over the rain-poked drive, patting my thigh for being her lover baby. Carolyn waved again. I looked back, waving, then gawking at a window screen where there were now three kittens clawing and screaming to get in. Like Mexicans, I thought. I remembered the Molinas and how the cats clung to their screens—cats they shot down with squirt guns. On the highway, I felt happy, pleased by it all. I patted Carolyn's thigh. Her people were like Mexicans, only different.

Endnote

1. Well yes, they're Okies too.

For Discussion and Writing

1. Soto writes that as he talked to his family about Carolyn, he "began to worry," and that as he approached her family's house, he "panicked." What are the sources of his worry and his panic? How do they get resolved?

2. What role does Soto's friend Scott play in this piece? Characterize their relationship and their discussions of friendship and romance among people of different races. Why do you suppose Soto includes Scott's views?

3. Why does Soto focus on the kittens climbing up the screen? What do they represent to him?

4. Why does Soto's best friend Scott say, "She's too good for you, so you better not"?

5. How do issues of race and class become tied together in the various concerns expressed about Soto's marrying a Japanese woman?

6. Why is the calendar of "Important Races of the World" important to Soto's grandmother? What might be learned from such a calendar? If you were to make one today, what would it look like?

Baby

BELL HOOKS

The following is taken from one of bell hooks's essay collections, Bone Black. *hooks, born in 1952, is a distinguished professor of English at the City College of New York. bell hooks (née Gloria Watkins) was born in Hopkinsville, Kentucky, and received her B.A. from Stanford University in 1973, her M.A. in 1976 from the University of Wisconsin, and her Ph.D. in 1983 from the University of California, Santa Cruz. An important feminist thinker and writer, she's written nearly 20 books on wide-ranging topics, including gender, race, language, teaching, and the media in contemporary culture. In addition, hooks has written two memoirs. In this essay, she describes her desire as a child to have a baby doll of her own color to love and care for.*

------------------------ ✦ ------------------------

We learn early that it is important for a woman to marry. We are always marrying our dolls to someone. He of course is always invisible, that is until they made the Ken doll to go with Barbie. One of us has been given a Barbie doll for Christmas. Her skin is not white white but almost brown from the tan they have painted on her. We know she is white because of her blond hair. The newest Barbie is bald, with many wigs of all different colors. We spend hours dressing and undressing her, pretending she is going somewhere important. We want to make new clothes for her. We want to buy the outfits made just for her that we see in the store but they are too expensive. Some of them cost as much as real clothes for real people. Barbie is anything but real, that is why we like her. She never does housework, washes dishes, or has children to care for. She is free to spend all day dreaming about the Kens of the world. Mama laughs when we tell her there should be more than one Ken for Barbie, there should be Joe, Sam, Charlie, men in all shapes and sizes. We do not think that Barbie should have a girlfriend. We know that Barbie was born to be alone—that the fantasy woman, the soap opera girl, the girl of *True Confessions*, the Miss America girl was born to be alone. We know that she is not us.

My favorite doll is brown, like light milk chocolate. She is a baby doll and I give her a baby doll name, Baby. She is almost the same size as a real baby. She comes with no clothes, only a pink diaper, fastened with tiny gold pins and a plastic bottle. She has a red mouth the color of lipstick slightly open so that we can stick the bottle in it. We fill the bottle with water and wait for it to come through the tiny hole in Baby's bottom. We make her many new diapers, but we are soon bored with changing them. We lose the bottle and Baby can no longer drink. We still love her. She is the only doll we will not destroy. We have lost Barbie. We have broken the leg of another doll. We have cracked open the head of an antique doll to see what makes the crying sound. The little thing inside is not interesting. We are sorry but nothing can be done—not even mama can put the pieces together again. She tells us that if this is the way we intend to treat our babies she hopes we do not have any. She laughs at our careless parenting. Sometimes she takes a minute to show us the right thing to do. She too is terribly fond of Baby. She says that she looks so much like a real newborn. Once she came upstairs, saw Baby under the covers, and wanted to know who had brought the real baby from downstairs.

She loves to tell the story of how Baby was born. She tells us that I, her problem child, decided out of nowhere that I did not want a white doll to play with, I demanded a brown doll, one that would look like me. Only grown-ups think that the things children say come out of nowhere. We know they come from the deepest parts of ourselves. Deep within myself I had begun to worry that all this loving care we gave to the pink and white flesh-colored dolls meant that somewhere left high on the shelves were boxes of unwanted, unloved brown dolls covered in dust. I thought that they would remain there forever, orphaned and alone, unless someone began to want them, to want to give them love and care, to want them more than anything. At first they ignored my wanting. They complained. They pointed out that white dolls were easier to find, cheaper. They never said where they found Baby but I know. She was always there high on the shelf, covered in dust—waiting.

For Discussion and Writing

1. Compare the kind of play hooks describes with Barbie and the kind of play she describes with Baby. How does her mother figure differently in her play with Barbie and her play with Baby? How do these kinds of play reflect expectations for women?
2. Throughout the essay, hooks uses "we" and "they" to describe the activities of children and adults in her world. What's the effect of using those pronouns?
3. How does hooks's description of play with the two dolls reflect how she feels about them?
4. Go to a toy store and examine the dolls. What sorts of dolls are available for little girls and their parents to choose from? What does taking care of or playing with these dolls teach young girls about their roles as girls and women?

My Jewish Nose
Lisa Miya-Jervis

Lisa Miya-Jervis is editor and publisher of the zine Bitch: A Feminist Response to Pop Culture. *The following essay was published in* Utne *in its July/August 1999 issue and appeared in the anthology* Body Outlaws *in 2000. In addition, Miya-Jervis's work has appeared in* Ms., *the* San Francisco Chronicle, Mother Jones, *the* Women's Review of Books, Bust, HUES, Salon, Girlfriends, Punk Planet, Sex and Single Girls *(Seal Press, 2000), and* The Bust Guide to the New World Order *(Penguin, 1999). She is also co-editor of* Young Wives Tales: New Adventures in Love and Partnership *(2001). She lives in Oakland, California, with her husband. In the following essay, Miya-Jervis describes why she refuses to get a "nose job" and speculates on why this cosmetic surgery is so important to some Jews: Do they want to "expunge their ethnicity from their looks" or do they simply want to fit the image of "ideal beauty"?*

✦

'm a Jew. I'm not even slightly religious. Aside from attending friends' *bat mitzvahs*, I've been to temple maybe twice. I don't know Hebrew; when given the option of religious education, my junior-high self easily chose to sleep in on Sunday mornings. My family skips around the Passover Haggadah to get to the food faster. Before having dated someone from an observant family, I wouldn't have known a *mezuzah* if it bit me on the butt. I was born assimilated.

But still, I'm a Jew—even though my Jewish identity has very little to do with religion, organized or otherwise. I'm an ethnic Jew of a very specific variety: a godless, New York City–raised, neurotic middle-class girl from a solidly liberal Democrat family, who attended largely Jewish, "progressive" schools that thought they were integrated and nonracist. Growing up, almost everyone around me was Jewish; I was stunned when I found out that Jews make up only two percent of the American population. But what being Jewish meant to me was that on Christmas day my family went out for Chinese food (some years, Indian) and took in the new Woody Allen movie. It also meant that I had a big honkin' nose.

And I still do. By virtue of my class and its sociopolitical trappings, the option of having my nose surgically altered was ever-present. From adolescence on, I've had a standing offer from my mother to get a nose job.

"It's not such a big deal." "Doctors do such individual-looking noses these days, it'll look really natural." "It's not too late, you know," she would say to me for years after I flat-out refused to let someone break my nose, scrape part of it out and reposition it into a smaller, less obtrusive shape. "I'll still pay." As if money were the reason I was resisting.

My mother thought a nose job was a good idea. See, she   5 hadn't wanted one either. But when she was sixteen, her parents demanded that she get that honker "fixed," and they didn't take no for an answer. She insists that she's been glad ever since, although she usually rationalizes that it was good for her social life. (She even briefly dated a guy she met in the surgeon's waiting room: a boxer having his deviated septum corrected.)

Even my father is a believer. He says that without my mother's nose job, my sister and I wouldn't exist, because he never would have gone out with Mom. But I take this with an entire salt lick. My father's a guy who thinks that dressing up means wearing dark sneakers; that pants should be purchased every twenty years, and only if the old ones are literally falling apart at the seams; and that haircuts should cost ten dollars and take as many minutes. The only thing he notices about appearances is to say, "You have some crud . . ." as he picks a piece of lint off your sleeve. But he cared about the nose? Whatever.

Even though my mother was happy with her tidy little surgically altered nose, she wasn't going to put me through the same thing, and for that I am truly grateful. I'm also unspeakably glad that her comments stayed far from the "you'd just be so pretty if you did" angle. ("Yours isn't as big as mine was," she would say. "You don't *need* it.") I know a few people who weren't so lucky. Not that they were dragged kicking and screaming to the doctor's office; no, they were coerced and shamed into it. Seems it was their family's decision more than their own—usually older Jewish female relatives: mothers, grandmothers, aunts.

What's the motivation for that kind of pressure? Can it be that for all the strides made against racism and anti-Semitism, Americans still want to expunge their ethnicity from their looks as much as possible? Were these mothers and grandmothers trying to fit their offspring into a more white, gentile mode? Possibly. Well, definitely. But on purpose? Probably not. Their lust for the button nose is probably more a desire for a typical, "pretty" femininity than for any specific de-ethnicizing. But given the society in which we live, the proximity of white features to the ideal of beauty is no coincidence. I think that anyone who opts for a nose job today (or who pressured her daughter to do so) would say that the reason is to look "better" or "prettier." But when we scratch the surface of what "prettier" means, we find that we might as well be saying "whiter" or "more gentile" (I would add "bland," but that's my personal opinion).

Or perhaps the reason is to become unobtrusive. The stereotypical Jewish woman is loud, pushy—qualities that girls really aren't supposed to have. So is it possible that the nose job is supposed to usher in not only physical femininity but a psychological, traditional femininity as well? Ditch the physical and emotional ties to your ethnicity in one simple procedure: Bob your nose, and become feminine in both mind and body. (This certainly seems to be the way it has worked with someone like Courtney Love, although her issue is class more than ethnicity. But it's undeniable that her new nose comes on a Versace-shilling, largely silent persona, in stark contrast to her old messy, outspoken self.)

10   Thankfully, none of the women I know have become meek and submissive from their nose jobs. But *damn*, do they have

regrets. One told me it was the biggest mistake of her life; another confessed to wanting her old nose back just a few short years after the surgery. They wish they'd stood up to their families and kept their natural features.

Even though I know plenty of women with their genetically determined schnozzes still intact, women who either refused or never considered surgery, sometimes I still feel like an oddity. From what my mother tells me, nose jobs were as compulsory a rite of passage for her peers as multiple ear-piercings are for mine. Once, when I was still in high school, I went with my mother to a Planned Parenthood fundraiser. It was a cocktail party–type thing in some lovely apartment, with lovely food and drink and a lovely short speech by Wendy Wasserstein. But I was confused: We were at a lefty charity event in Manhattan, and all the women in attendance had little WASP noses. (Most of them were blond, too, but that didn't really register. I guess hair dye is a more universal ritual.)

"Why are there no Jewish women here?" I whispered to my mother. She laughed, but I think she was genuinely shocked. "What do you mean? All of these women are Jewish." And then it hit me: We were wall-to-wall rhinoplasties. And worse, there was no reason to be surprised. These were women my mother's age or older who came of age in the late '50s or before, when anti-Semitism in this country was much more overt than it is today. That kind of surface assimilation was practically the norm for Jews back then, and those honkers were way too, ahem, big a liability on the dating and social scenes. Nose jobs have declined since then. They're no longer in the top five plastic surgery procedures performed, edged out by liposuction and laser skin resurfacing. (I guess now it's more important to be young and trim than gentile, what with societal forces of youth-and-beauty worship replacing post–World War II fear and hatred. . . .)

I don't think it's a coincidence that I didn't consider my nose an ethnic feature growing up in New York. I didn't have to, because almost everyone around me had that feature (and that ethnicity) too. It wasn't until I graduated from college and moved to California that I realized how marked I was by my nose and my vaguely ethnic, certainly Jewish appearance. I also then realized how much I liked being marked that way, being instantly recognizable to anyone who knew how to look. I once met another Jewish woman at a conference in California. In the middle of our conversation, she randomly popped out with, "You're Jewish, right?" I replied, "With this nose and this hair, you gotta ask?" We both laughed. I was right: The question was just a formality, and we both knew it.

Living in California, I'm particularly in need of those little moments of recognition. I know that a Jew living in, say, Tennessee might laugh at me for saying this, but there are no Jews in California. I feel conspicuously Semitic here in a way that I never did anywhere else (not even at my small Ohio liberal arts college—after all, that place was filled with New York Jews). Few of my friends are Jewish, and those random "bagel and lox" references just don't get understood the way I'm used to.

15   Only once did I feel uneasy about being "identified." At my first job out of college, my boss asked, after I mentioned an upcoming trip to see my family in New York, "So, are your parents just like people in Woody Allen movies?" I wondered if I had a big sign on my forehead reading, "Big Yid Here." His comment brought up all those insecurities American Jews can have about our ethnicity that, not coincidentally, Woody Allen loves to play on—and overemphasize for comic effect: Am I *that* Jewish? Is it *that* obvious? I felt conspicuous, exposed. But regardless of that incident, I'm glad I have the sign on my face, even if it's located a tad lower than my forehead.

See, I don't have a whole lot of Jewish heritage to hold on to. My family's name was changed—it's not as if "Jervis" is particularly gentile, but it sure is a lot less obvious than "Jersowitz," which my grandfather jettisoned before my father can remember. Temple was never a part of my life—I'm an atheist. I don't know what Purim is about. Hell, it takes me a minute to remember how many candles go in the menorah—and last week I used mine for a candlelight dinner with my husband-to-be, a half-Christian, half-Buddhist Japanese American whose thoughts on God's existence are along the lines of "I don't know, and I don't really care."

But in a larger sense, Judaism is the only identity in which culture and religion are supposedly bound closely: If you're Irish and aren't a practicing Catholic, you can still be fully Irish; being Buddhist doesn't specify a race or an ethnic identity. African Americans can practice any religion, and it doesn't make them any less black. But "Jewish" is a funny ethnicity. Is it a race; is it a set of beliefs? Color doesn't have much to do with it. In fact, the question of whether or not Jews are white can be answered in as many different ways as there are people who have an opinion on the topic.

To me, being a Jew is cultural. But for me it's a culture tied only marginally—even hypothetically—to religion, and mostly to geography (New York Jews are different from California Jews, lemme tell ya) and sensibility/temperament (hyperintellectual, food-lovin', neurotic, worrywartish, perfectionistic). So the question for me is: What happens when Jewish identity becomes untied from religion? I don't know for sure. And that means I'll grab onto anything I need to keep that identity—including my nose.

For Discussion and Writing

1. Miya-Jervis emphasizes her desire to maintain her ethnic identity. Why is her view of her nose as a marker of identity different from her mother's view? Why does her mother argue in favor of plastic surgery? And why does Miya-Jervis resist?

2. How does Miya-Jervis think the Jewish woman stereotype affects women's desire to get a nose job? On the basis of your observations and experience, analyze the validity of this claim. How do people's physical selves affect their behavior?

3. Watch a Woody Allen movie (or two). What are the Jewish stereotypes Allen draws on to create humor? In what ways do you think these stereotypes influence people's perception of Jews? What do you believe Miya-Jervis thinks about this issue?

4. How do markers of ethnicity affect men and women differently? How are male and female blacks, Hispanics, and Asians perceived differently?

5. Conduct some research into beauty products and procedures directed toward women of color. What sorts of products are available for women? What sorts of plastic surgery are being done? What is the motivation for plastic surgery? What role does the standard of "WASPy white features" play in the beauty industry?

Of Race and Risk

Patricia J. Williams

Many people make their most significant economic decision when they choose a home to live in and arrange financing to purchase it. Very few first-time buyers have the cash to pay outright for a house, so they must rely on banks, on the loan officers there who can help

them buy a house. The process of securing a loan can be forthright:
Banks make loans based on the risk a buyer can reasonably as-
sume. But Patricia J. Williams discovered that getting that loan may
involve unspoken rules that have far more to do with color than
economics. Williams, a professor of law at the Columbia University
Law School, has written articles for The Nation, The New Yorker,
and the Village Voice. *Her books include* The Alchemy of Race and
Rights: Diary of a Law Professor, The Rooster's Egg, *and* On Seeing a Color-Blind Future: The Paradox of Race.

———————— ✦ ————————

Several years ago, at a moment when I was particularly tired of
the unstable lifestyle that academic careers sometimes require, I surprised myself and bought a real house. Because the
house was in a state other than the one where I was living at the
time, I obtained my mortgage by telephone. I am a prudent little
squirrel when it comes to things financial, always tucking away
stores of nuts for the winter, and so I meet the criteria of a quite
good credit risk. My loan was approved almost immediately.

A little while later, the contract came in the mail. Among the
papers the bank forwarded were forms documenting compliance
with the Fair Housing Act, which outlaws racial discrimination in
the housing market. The act monitors lending practices to prevent banks from redlining—redlining being the phenomenon
whereby banks circle certain neighborhoods on the map and re-
fuse to lend in those areas. It is a practice for which the bank
with which I was dealing, unbeknownst to me, had been cited
previously—as well as since. In any event, the act tracks the race
of all banking customers to prevent such discrimination. Unfortunately, and with the creative variability of all illegality, some
banks also use the racial information disclosed on the fair housing forms to engage in precisely the discrimination the law seeks
to prevent.

I should repeat that to this point my entire mortgage transaction had been conducted by telephone. I should also note that I
speak a Received Standard English, regionally marked as North-
eastern perhaps, but not easily identifiable as black. With my
credit history, my job as a law professor and, no doubt, with my
accent, I am not only middle class but apparently match the cultural stereotype of a good white person. It is thus, perhaps, that

the loan officer of the bank, whom I had never met, had checked off the box on the fair housing form indicating that I *was* white. Race shouldn't matter, I suppose, but it seemed to in this case, so I took a deep breath, crossed out "white" and sent the contract back. That will teach them to presume too much, I thought. A done deal, I assumed. But suddenly the transaction came to a screeching halt. The bank wanted more money, more points, a higher rate of interest. Suddenly I found myself facing great resistance and much more debt. To make a long story short, I threatened to sue under the act in question, the bank quickly backed down and I procured the loan on the original terms.

What was interesting about all this was that the reason the   5 bank gave for its newfound recalcitrance was not race, heaven forbid. No, it was all about economics and increased risk: The reason they gave was that property values in that neighborhood were suddenly falling. They wanted more money to buffer themselves against the snappy winds of projected misfortune.

Initially, I was surprised, confused. The house was in a neighborhood that was extremely stable. I am an extremely careful shopper; I had uncovered absolutely nothing to indicate that prices were falling. It took my realtor to make me see the light. "Don't you get it," he sighed. "This is what always happens." And even though I suppose it was a little thick of me, I really hadn't gotten it: For of course, I was the reason the prices were in peril.

The bank's response was driven by demographic data that show that any time black people move into a neighborhood, whites are overwhelmingly likely to move out. In droves. In panic. In concert. Pulling every imaginable resource with them, from school funding to garbage collection to social workers who don't want to work in black neighborhoods. The imagery is awfully catchy, you had to admit: the neighborhood just tipping on over like a terrible accident, whoops! Like a pitcher, I suppose. All that nice fresh wholesome milk spilling out, running away . . . leaving the dark, echoing, up-ended urn of the inner city.

In retrospect, what has remained so fascinating to me about this experience was the way it so exemplified the problems of the new rhetoric of racism. For starters, the new rhetoric of race never mentions race. It wasn't race but risk with which the bank was so concerned.

Second, since financial risk is all about economics, my exclusion got reclassified as just a consideration of class. There's no law against class discrimination, goes the argument, because that would represent a restraint on that basic American freedom, the ability to contract or not. If schools, trains, buses, swimming pools and neighborhoods remain segregated, it's no longer a racial problem if someone who just happens to be white keeps hiking up the price for someone who accidentally and purely by the way happens to be black. Black people end up paying higher prices for the attempt to integrate, even as the integration of oneself threatens to lower the value of one's investment.

10   By this measure of mortgage-worthiness, the ingredient of blackness is cast not just as a social toll but as an actual tax. A fee, an extra contribution at the door, an admission charge for the high costs of handling my dangerous propensities, my inherently unsavory properties. I was not judged based on my independent attributes or financial worth; not even was I judged by statistical profiles of what my group actually does. (For in fact, anxiety-stricken, middle-class black people make grovelingly good cake-baking neighbors when not made to feel defensive by the unfortunate historical strategies of bombs, burnings or abandonment.) Rather, I was being evaluated based on what an abstraction of White Society writ large thinks we—or I—do, and that imagined "doing" was treated and thus established as a self-fulfilling prophecy. It is a dispiriting message: that some in society apparently not only devalue black people but devalue *themselves* and their homes just for having us as part of their landscape.

    "I bet you'll keep your mouth shut the next time they plug you into the computer as white," laughed a friend when he heard my story. It took me aback, this postmodern pressure to "pass," even as it highlighted the intolerable logic of it all. For by these "rational" economic measures, an investment in my property suggests the selling of myself.

For Discussion and Writing

1. Williams says that she was a good credit risk when she applied for a loan by telephone. How can you tell that this is an accurate self-assessment? Why does the author repeat, in the third paragraph, that her loan was arranged almost entirely by phone?

2. Williams writes that "the reason the bank gave for its newfound recalcitrance was not race, heaven forbid." Characterize her tone here. How does Williams show that the bank's decision was, in fact, race-based?

3. The author's realtor says to her, "Don't you get it?" What is it the author didn't grasp at first? Williams is a highly educated lawyer, trained in critical thinking. Why do you think she was slow to "get it," as the realtor says?
4. Closely reread the paragraph beginning "The bank's response was driven by demographic data. . . ." What sort of imagery does the author use to portray the effect of a black person moving into a white neighborhood? What does such figurative language add to the force of her argument?
5. Imagine the beginning of all the author's difficulties. How would you advise Williams if you were her friend, and she asked whether she ought to cross out "white" on the application form? Explain your counsel (you might consider, among other things, whether it helps perpetuate racism or advances fair play).

Freedom from Choice
BRIAN A. COURTNEY

Born in 1973, Brian A. Courtney is a writer in Nashville, Tennessee. Courtney won the Alex Haley Memorial Scholarship while a student at the University of Tennessee. A science and print journalism/ communications major in college, Courtney earned a summer internship at Playboy *magazine. The following essay, first published in* Newsweek *magazine in 1995, written when Courtney was 22 years old, describes his dilemma of choosing a racial identity.*

———————— ✦ ————————

As my friend Denise and I trudged across the University of Tennessee campus to our 9:05 A.M. class, we delivered countless head nods, "Heys" and "How ya' doin's" to other African-Americans we passed along the way. We spoke to people we knew as well as people we didn't know because it's an unwritten rule that black people speak to one another when they pass. But when I stopped to greet and hug one of my female friends, who happens to be white, Denise seemed a little bothered. We continued our walk to class, and Denise expressed concern that I might be coming down with a "fever." "I don't feel sick," I told her. As it turns out, she was referring to "jungle fever," the condition where a black man or woman is attracted to someone of the opposite race.

This encounter has not been an uncommon experience for me. That's why the first twenty-one years of my life have felt like a never-ending tug of war. And quite honestly, I'm not looking forward to being dragged through the mud for the rest of my life. My white friends want me to act one way—white. My African-American friends want me to act another—black. Pleasing them both is nearly impossible and leaves little room to be just me.

The politically correct term for someone with my racial background is "biracial" or "multiracial." My mother is fair-skinned with blond hair and blue eyes. My father is dark-complexioned with prominent African-American features and a head of wooly hair. When you combine the genetic makeup of the two, you get me—golden-brown skin, semi-coarse hair and a whole mess of freckles.

Someone once told me I was lucky to be biracial because I have the best of both worlds. In some ways this is true. I have a huge family that's filled with diversity and is as colorful as a box of Crayolas. My family is more open to whomever I choose to date, whether that person is black, white, biracial, Asian, or whatever. But looking at the big picture, American society makes being biracial feel less like a blessing than a curse.

5   One reason is the American obsession with labeling. We feel the need to label everyone on everything and group them into neatly defined categories. Are you a Republican, a Democrat or an Independent? Are you pro-life or pro-choice? Are you African-American, Caucasian or Native American? Not everyone fits into such classifications. This presents a problem for me and the many biracial people living in the United States. The rest of the population seems more comfortable when we choose to identify with one group. And it pressures us to do so, forcing us to deny half of who we are.

Growing up in the small, predominantly white town of Maryville, Tennessee, I attended William Blount High School. I was one of a handful of minority students—a raisin in a box of cornflakes, so to speak. Almost all of my peers, many of whom I've known since grade school, were white. Over the years, they've commented on how different I am from other black people they know. The implication was that I'm better because I'm only *half* black. Acceptance into their world has meant talking as they talk, dressing as they dress and appreciating the same music. To reduce tension and make everyone feel comfortable, I've reacted by ignoring half of my identity and downplaying my ethnicity.

My experience at UT has been very similar. This time it's my African-American peers exerting pressure to choose. Some African-Americans on campus say I "talk too white." I dress like the boys in white fraternities. I have too many white friends. In other words, I'm not black enough. I'm a white "wanna-be." The other day, an African-American acquaintance told me I dress "bourgie." This means I dress very white—a pastel-colored polo, a pair of navy chinos and hiking boots. Before I came to terms with this kind of remark, a comment like this would have angered me, and I must admit that I was a little offended. But instead of showing my frustration, I let it ride, and I simply said "Thank you." Surprised by this response, she said in disbelief, "You mean you agree?"

On more occasions than I dare to count, black friends have made sweeping derogatory statements about the white race in general. "White people do this, or white people do that." Every time I hear them, I cringe. These comments refer not just to my white friends but to my mother and maternal grandmother as well. Why should I have to shun or hide my white heritage to enhance my ethnicity? Doesn't the fact that I have suffered the same prejudices as every other African-American—and then some—count for something?

I do not blame my African-American or white friends for the problems faced by biracial people in America. I blame society for not acknowledging us as a separate race. I am speaking not only for people who, like myself, are half black and half white, but also for those who are half white and half Asian, half white and half Hispanic, or half white and half whatever. Until American society recognizes us as a distinct group we will continue to be pressured to choose one side of our heritage over the other.

Job applications, survey forms, college-entrance exams and the like ask individuals to check only *one* box for race. For most of my life, I have marked BLACK because my skin color is the first thing people notice. However, I could just as honestly have marked WHITE. Somehow, when I fill out these forms, I think the employers, administrators, researchers, teachers or whoever sees them will have a problem looking at may face and then accepting a big x by the word WHITE. In any case, checking BLACK or WHITE does not truly represent me. Only in recent years have some private universities added the category of BIRACIAL or MULTIRACIAL to their applications. I've heard that a few states now include these categories on government forms.

One of the greatest things parents of biracial children can do is expose them to *both* of their cultures. But what good does this do when in the end society makes us choose? Having a separate category marked BIRACIAL will not magically put an end to the pressure to choose, but it will help people to stop judging us as just black or just white and see us for what we really are—both.

For Discussion and Writing

1. What does it mean to act "black" and to act "white"? From the clues he gives us, what does Courtney seem to mean about acting "black" or "white"? What other observations have you made about what this means? Are there differences of opinion among your classmates about what it means to act as if you are a certain race?

2. Courtney blames society for his struggles because it does not see biracial people as a separate race. He seems to view the solution to his struggles with identity as the creation of another category—a biracial category. What do you think of this solution? Are there other solutions? Are there *any* solutions? Why or why not?

3. Courtney decries the use of labels that neatly categorize people. Analyze how labels work in your own observations and experiences. In what ways are labels useful? In what ways detrimental?

4. When this piece was written in 1995, instructions to indicate only one race on applications and surveys were common. How has that policy changed (in government information forms, job applications, and college and university forms) over the last several years? What are the implications of that change? Do you view this change as positive or negative? Explain.

Reading, Research, and Writing

1. In all the readings from this chapter, writers of color undertake an examination of their personal and ethnic identities. How do they feel about those identities? To what extent are their identities chosen and embraced? To what extent are they assigned by others? Compare and contrast at least three of these pieces to discuss how individuals of different ethnicities view those ethnicities.

2. A question among many ethnic groups is that of assimilation: To what extent do ethnic groups want to adopt the mainstream culture and to what extent do they want to maintain their own cultural traditions? What do you think of the notion of assimilation? How does your own

ethnicity affect your viewpoint? Alternatively, conduct some research into assimilation. How does assimilation occur? Under what circumstances is it resisted? Which groups have assimilated most successfully and which least? Or, choose one ethnic group that interests you and learn about their attitudes toward and patterns of assimilation.

3. The old cliché—appearance is only skin deep—seems to be challenged, at least in part, by the writers included in this section. Drawing on the pieces in this chapter, your own observations and experiences, and further research into such topics as racial profiling and cosmetic surgery, write a paper on the ways in which you explore "appearance." How does the way one looks affect social acceptance, income, treatment by legal institutions, self-image, and so forth? There are attitude surveys and statistical evidence available to help you learn about the role of appearance in success.

4. Conduct some research into ethnicity in the world of games—computer games, board games, and fantasy games—and toys, especially dolls. What racial and ethnic groups do you find represented? How are they represented? Do you find any stereotypes among the characters in games? Write a paper exploring representations of racial and ethnic groups in the world of children's play.

5. Conduct research on interracial dating and marriage. How have interracial relationship patterns changed in the last 25 years? 50 years? 100 years? How have attitudes changed? Are their some race "combinations" that are more "acceptable" than others? As a part of your research, learn about laws that have governed marriage throughout the history of the United States. When did antimiscegenation laws appear? What did they prohibit? When were those laws removed from the books?

CHAPTER 5

Enduring Discrimination: Miles to Go, Promises to Keep

Government profiling also contributed to a wave of popular violence against Arab, South Asian, and Muslim communities. The number of reported U.S. hate crimes against Muslims and Arabs in 2002 increased 1600 percent over the previous year.

The construction of an enemy, through government targeting with media complicity and a popular echo, endangers and dehumanizes millions of Arabs, Asians, and Muslims.

Eleanor Stein

To summarize [the study's findings]: African Americans made up 13.5 percent of the turnpike's population and 15 percent of the speeders. But they represented 35 percent of those pulled over. In stark numbers, blacks were 4.85 times as likely to be stopped as were others.

John Lamberth

There's a lot of talk these days about America becoming a "color-blind" society. Activists, journalists, teachers, and politicians are among the people who advocate such a society, or who assure us that it's here now and we can all relax and enjoy the harmony. Yet our pleasure in the new equality is circumscribed by stories that appear in the news nearly every day. A recent *San Francisco Chronicle* story told of two university students who have been charged with committing hate crimes on campus. A new study shows that white borrowers are routinely offered better terms and rates than people of color. Another study reveals that black job applicants are far less likely to receive work offers than white applicants for the same positions, even though their credentials are as good as or better than those of the white applicants. California voters faced a proposition that would ban race-based data from official records, as if erasing statistical evidence of race in hiring and education would somehow dispel the consciousness of race and lead to a color-blind California (voters did not accept the logic and rejected the proposition). It seems we aren't color-blind just yet, and can't afford to ignore color in the transactions that shape our lives.

But what exactly do people mean by a color-blind society? In its clinical sense, the term *color-blind* signifies a deficit, an unfortunate inability to distinguish part of the color spectrum. In its political sense, the term is offered as a goal or as a utopia to be pursued by practical means. See people not color, one might say. How? See them without skin? See all of them as white? The first option is ludicrous, the second unacceptable. See everyone as essentially the same in matters of law and opportunity? Perhaps the latter comes closest to the ideal sense of the term. Yet correcting historical inequalities has involved something like the opposite of being color-blind. For example, a few decades ago, in the 1960s, organizations like the Alabama Highway Patrol had to be forced to do the right thing, to hire qualified African Americans. Monitoring the progress of that organization's efforts meant reviewers had to be anything but color-blind. How else would anyone know if the police were hiring fairly?

Isn't the blatant favoritism of the Alabama Highway Patrol finally a thing of the past? Yes and no. Take this example from recent events. Investigators examining the hiring practices of Abercrombie and Fitch have claimed that the clothing and outdoor outfitter has maintained a "hire white" policy, and have brought suit against the company. Getting at the truth of the matter requires a decided look at the "color" of the workers.

As the readings in this chapter show, ethnic bias and color prejudice remain facts of American life. In "Driving While Black," John Lamberth argues that statistics show prejudice in law enforcement. He alludes to "DWB," an "offense" otherwise known as "driving while black." Lamberth conducted research that determined black drivers are far more likely than white drivers to be pulled over while driving along a particular stretch of highway in New Jersey. The implication is that this pattern holds true elsewhere in the country. Many African Americans and other people of color have been subjected to discriminatory practices, so one might reasonably ask, "Where is the level field so often invoked by opponents of affirmative action?" Housing is a fundamental human need. Can we really declare that bias is dead if the housing market is plagued by bigotry? Burke Marshall and Nicholas deB. Katzenbach assert in "Not Color Blind: Just Blind" that affirmative action programs do not, as some claim, unfairly favor minorities, and their corrective influence is still needed. In "Blind Spot," Peter Beinart explores the contradiction between privileged white people objecting to affirmative action for students but accepting what Colin Powell called affirmative action for lobbyists who "load our federal tax code with preferences for special interests." Not only is there no such thing as a level playing field, in Beinart's view, but many privileged people work actively to keep advantages flowing their way. Public perception of "otherness" also contributes to persistent discrimination. Eleanor Stein notes in her "Construction of an Enemy" that government policies can work to reinforce negative stereotypes of some Americans. She points out that this was the case with Japanese Americans after the attack on Pearl Harbor, and now Arab Americans find that they are lumped together as suspects in a so-called Islamist conspiracy. Bob Herbert's "Voting While Black" describes discriminatory practices aimed at minority voters. Finally, in a chilling account of modern day slavery in Florida, John Bowe's "Nobodies" depicts a subculture of agricultural workers who live without the law's protection, subject to violence and exploitation by powerful crew organizers who contract with major American corporations to get produce from fields to our tables. Racial and ethnic harmony, these readings suggest, is an ideal, not a guarantee, and certainly not an accomplished fact.

Driving While Black
JOHN LAMBERTH

John Lamberth is a professor emeritus at Temple University. He has studied the psychology of juries and has served as a jury selection consultant in various cases. His article, originally published in the Washington Post *(August 16, 1998), calls attention to disturbing practices of racial profiling in law enforcement. The practice of racial profiling in law enforcement has come under increasing study recently, and experts disagree, sometimes heatedly, about its usefulness. Lamberth focuses in his article on a particular stretch of highway in New Jersey, and he reaches some unsettling conclusions.*

———————————— ✦ ————————————

In 1993, I was contacted by attorneys whose clients had been arrested on the New Jersey Turnpike for possession of drugs. They told me they had come across 25 African American defendants over a three-year period, all arrested on the same stretch of turnpike in Gloucester County, but not a single white defendant. I was asked whether, and how much, this pattern reflected unfair treatment of blacks.

They wanted to know what a professional statistician would make of these numbers. What were the probabilities that this pattern could occur naturally, that is, by chance? Since arrests for drug offenses occurred after traffic stops on the highway, was it possible that so many blacks were arrested because the police were disproportionately stopping them? I decided to try to answer their questions and embarked on one of the most intriguing statistical studies of my career: a census of traffic and traffic violators by race on Interstate 95 in New Jersey. It would require a careful design, teams of researchers with binoculars and a rolling survey.

To relieve your suspense, the answer was that the rate at which blacks were stopped was greatly disproportionate to their numbers on the road and to their propensity to violate traffic laws. Those findings were central to a March 1996 ruling by Judge Robert E. Francis of the Superior Court of New Jersey that the state police were de facto targeting blacks, in violation of their rights under the U.S. and New Jersey constitutions. The judge suppressed the evidence gathered in the stops. New Jersey is now appealing the case.

The New Jersey litigation is part of a broad attack in a number of states, including Maryland, on what has been dubbed the offense of "DWB"—driving while black. While this problem has been familiar anecdotally to African Americans and civil rights advocates for years, there is now evidence that highway patrols are singling out blacks for stops on the illegal and incorrect theory that the practice, known as racial profiling, is the most likely to yield drug arrests. Statistical techniques are proving extremely helpful in proving targeting, just as they have been in proving systemic discrimination in employment.

5   This was not my first contact with the disparate treatment of blacks in the criminal justice system. My academic research over the past 25 years had led me from an interest in small group decision-making to jury selection, jury composition and the application of the death penalty. I became aware that blacks were disproportionately charged with crimes, particularly serious ones; that they were underrepresented on jury panels and thus on juries; and that they were sentenced to death at a much greater rate than their numbers could justify.

As I began the New Jersey study, I knew from experience that any research that questioned police procedures was sensitive. I knew that what I did must stand the test of a court hearing in which every move I made would be challenged by experts.

First, I had to decide what I needed to know. What was the black "population" of the road—that is, how many of the people traveling on the turnpike over a given period of time were African American? This task is a far cry from determining the population of a town, city or state. There are no Census Bureau figures. The population of a roadway changes all day, every day. By sampling the population of the roadway over a given period, I could make an accurate determination of the average number of blacks on the road.

I designed and implemented two surveys. We stationed observers by the side of the road, with the assignment of counting the number of cars and the race of the occupants in randomly selected three-hour blocks of time over a two-week period. The New Jersey Turnpike has four lanes at its southern end, two in each direction. By the side of the road, we placed an observer for each lane, equipped with binoculars to observe and note the number of cars and the race of occupants, along with a person to write down what the observers said. The team observed for an hour and a half, took a 30-minute break while moving to another observation point, and repeated the process.

In total, we conducted more than 21 sessions between 8 A.M. and 8 P.M. from June 11 to June 24, 1993, at four sites between Exits 1 and 3 of the turnpike, among the busiest highway segments in the nation. We counted roughly 43,000 cars, of which 13.5 percent had one or more black occupants. This was consistent with the population figures for the 11 states from which most of the vehicles observed were registered.

For the rolling survey, Fred Last, a public defender, drove at a   10
constant 60 mph (5 mph above the speed limit at the time). He
counted all cars that passed him as violators and all cars he
passed as nonviolators. Speaking into a tape recorder, he also
noted the race of the driver of each car. At the end of each day, he
collated his results and faxed them to me.

Last counted 2,096 cars. More than 98 percent were speeding
and thus subject to being stopped by police. African Americans
made up about 15 percent of those drivers on the turnpike violat-
ing traffic laws. Utilizing data from the New Jersey State Police,
I determined that about 35 percent of those who were stopped on
this part of the turnpike were African Americans.

To summarize: African Americans made up 13.5 percent of
the turnpike's population and 15 percent of the speeders. But they
represented 35 percent of those pulled over. In stark numbers,
blacks were 4.85 times as likely to be stopped as were others.

We did not obtain data on the race of drivers and passengers
searched after being stopped or on the rate at which vehicles were
searched. But we know from police records that 73.2 percent of
those arrested along the turnpike over a 3½-year period by troopers from the area's Moorestown barracks were black—making
them 16.5 times more likely to be arrested than others.

Attorneys for the 25 African Americans who had been arrested
on the turnpike and charged with possessing drugs or guns filed motions to suppress evidence seized when they were stopped, arguing
that police stopped them because of their race. Their motions were
consolidated and heard by Judge Francis between November 1994
and May 1995. My statistical study, bolstered by an analysis of its validity by Joseph B. Kadane, professor of statistics at Carnegie Mellon
University, was the primary exhibit in support of the motions.

But Francis also heard testimony from two former New   15
Jersey troopers who said they had been coached to make race-
based "profile" stops to increase their criminal arrests. And the
judge reviewed police in-service training aids such as videos that
disproportionately portrayed minorities as perpetrators.

The statistical disparities, Francis wrote, are "indeed stark. . . .
Defendants have proven at least a de facto policy on the part of the
State Police . . . of targeting blacks for investigation and arrest."
The judge ordered that the state's evidence be suppressed.

My own work in this field continues. In 1992, Robert L.
Wilkins was riding in a rented car with family members when

Maryland State Police stopped them, ordered them out, and conducted a search for drugs, which were not found. Wilkins happened to be a Harvard Law School trained public defender in Washington. With the support of the Maryland ACLU, he sued the state police, who settled the case with, among other things, an agreement to provide highway-stop data to the organization.

I was asked by the ACLU to evaluate the Maryland data in 1996 and again in 1997. I conducted a rolling survey in Maryland similar to the one I had done before and found a similar result. While 17.5 percent of the traffic violators on I-95 north of Baltimore were African American, 28.8 percent of those stopped and 71.3 percent of those searched by the Maryland State Police were African American. U.S. District Judge Catherine Blake ultimately ruled in 1997 that the ACLU made a "reasonable showing" that Maryland troopers on I-95 were continuing to engage in a "pattern and practice" of racial discrimination. Other legal actions have been filed in Pennsylvania, Florida, Indiana and North Carolina. Police officials everywhere deny racial profiling.

Why, then, are so many more African American motorists stopped than would be expected by their frequency on the road and their violation of the law? It seems clear to me that drugs are the issue.

20   The notion that African Americans and other minorities are more likely than whites to be carrying drugs—a notion that is perpetuated by some police training films—seems to be especially prevalent among the police. They believe that if they are to interdict drugs, then it makes sense to stop minorities, especially young men. State police are rewarded and promoted at least partially on the basis of their "criminal programs," which means the number of arrests they make. Testimony in the New Jersey case pointed out that troopers would be considered deficient if they did not make enough arrests. Since, as Judge Francis found, training points to minorities as likely drug dealers, it makes a certain sort of distorted sense to stop minorities more than whites.

But there is no untainted evidence that minorities are more likely to possess or sell drugs. There is evidence to the contrary. Indirect evidence in statistics from the National Institute of Drug Abuse indicates that 12 percent to 14 percent of those who abuse drugs are African American, a percentage that is proportionate to their numbers in the general population.

More telling are the numbers of those people who are stopped and searched by the Maryland State Police who have drugs. This data, which has been unobtainable from other states, indicates that of those drivers and passengers searched in Maryland, about 28 percent have contraband, whether they are black or white. The same percentage of contraband is found no matter the race. The Maryland data may shed some light on the tendency of some troopers to believe that blacks are somehow more likely to possess contraband. This data shows that for every 1,000 searches by the Maryland State Police, 200 blacks and only 80 non-blacks are arrested. This could lead one to believe that more blacks are breaking the law—until you know that the sample is deeply skewed. Of those searched, 713 were black and only 287 were non-black.

We do not have comparable figures on contraband possession or arrests from New Jersey. But if the traffic along I-95 there is at all similar to I-95 in Maryland—and there is a strong numerical basis to believe it is—it is possible to speculate that black travelers in New Jersey also were no more likely than non-blacks to be carrying contraband.

The fact that a black was 16.5 times more likely than a non-black to be arrested on the New Jersey Turnpike now takes on added meaning. Making only the assumption that was shown accurate in Maryland, it is possible to say even more conclusively that racial profiling is prevalent there and that there is no benefit to police in singling out blacks. More important, even if there were a benefit, it would violate fundamental rights. The constitution does not permit law enforcement authorities to target groups by race.

Fundamental fairness demands that steps be taken to prohibit profiling in theory and in practice. There is legislation pending at the federal level and in at least two states, Rhode Island and Pennsylvania, that would require authorities to keep statistics on this issue. This is crucial legislation and should be passed.

Only when the data are made available and strong steps are taken to monitor and curtail profiling, will we be able to assure minorities, and all of us who care about fundamental rights, that this practice will cease.

For Discussion and Writing

1. What is "DWB"? What does Judge Francis mean when he says New Jersey police were "de facto targeting blacks"? What is the objection to such a practice? What part of the constitution protects one against such a practice?

2. Review the percentages that Lamberth provides. How effective are these numbers in his argument? What else is there in the essay that might persuade readers discrimination played a role in New Jersey traffic control?

3. In what ways were police trained to discriminate? In what ways might such training and the practice of profiling influence arrests? What link can you make between profiling practices, including disproportionate arrests, and the public perception of blacks' involvement in crime?

4. What is the Maryland data that the author refers to, and how does Lamberth link this to his New Jersey research? In what ways are its data misleading?

5. Lamberth points out that about 28 percent of searched drivers have contraband. "The same percentage of contraband is found no matter the race," he reports. What does this fact imply about profiling?

6. How well has the author made his case for ending police profiling? He says that even if racial profiling were a benefit to police, "it would violate fundamental rights." In your view, is the argument basically about rights or about security? Explain.

Not Color Blind: Just Blind

BURKE MARSHALL AND
NICHOLAS DEB. KATZENBACH

Burke Marshall (1922–2003) was an assistant attorney general in charge of civil rights during the Kennedy and Johnson administrations. A former antitrust lawyer, Marshall helped to write the Civil Rights Act of 1964. Nicholas deB. Katzenbach, a former Yale law professor, was an assistant attorney general in the Kennedy administration. He was Lyndon Johnson's attorney general. In this post he helped draft the Voting Rights Act. In 1966, Katzenbach resigned from the post of attorney general after numerous clashes with J. Edgar Hoover over the wiretapping of citizens like Dr. Martin Luther King, Jr. In the essay that follows, published in the New York Times Magazine *(February 22, 1998), the authors take on the more familiar objections to affirmative action programs. Marshall and Katzenbach are not talk show hosts; their informative essay is complex and requires close attention.*

✦

Few African American students are likely to enter the great public law schools of California and Texas in the fall. That is the direct, foreseeable consequence of a California referendum and a Texas federal court decision. So concerned were civil rights groups about the popular and legal doctrine that led to this result that they joined together to deny the U.S. Supreme Court the opportunity to decide an apparently definitive affirmative action case involving teachers in Piscataway Township, New Jersey. Do such events—especially Piscataway—foretell the end of affirmative action, or have we simply lost sight of our long-term vision of a color-blind society?

In 1989, the Piscataway school board, faced with the need to lay off a single teacher, chose to lay off a white while retaining an African American of equal seniority and qualifications. The board gave racial diversity, citing its affirmative action policy, as the sole reason for the choice. Its decision was rejected by a federal judge who found the board in violation of the 1964 Civil Rights Act. That ruling was upheld by a federal appellate court. The school board appealed to the Supreme Court. Late last year, with financial assistance from civil rights groups, the board settled the case and withdrew its appeal.

The settlement has since become a kind of raw shorthand in the national debate about affirmative action because its facts serve to make clear the core of that debate. The seeming baldness of the facts plainly told the civil rights groups' leaders that the case should not be permitted to remain in the Supreme Court, and that it would be prudent to use their funds to avoid its doing so. This may be the first time that money has been used directly to take an important public policy issue off the Court's docket.

All this arose because the case was framed to portray person-to-person competition for a job in which race alone was the decisive factor. This aspect fitted neatly with the notion, widespread among opponents of affirmative action, that it creates a zero-sum game in which there is a loser for every winner and that the game is won and lost on the basis of race. Thus it obscures the larger goal of finding and preserving room for blacks in all aspects—economic, political, educational, social—and at all levels of society.

In addition, the case involved a layoff—the loss of a specific, known job—instead of a positive general decision as to what kind and mix of people are needed in a work force or in a faculty or student body. The facts fitted in not only with some legal learning—that an affirmative action program should not "unnecessarily trammel" the expectations of those not included in the program—but also more importantly with the personalization of the controversy into one in which whites are individually hurt by being deprived of their deserved opportunities, by deliberate and explicit efforts to include blacks.

These aspects of the Piscataway litigation appeared perfect for opponents of affirmative action and a legal land mine for its defenders. The former believed that the facts of the case would lead a majority of the Supreme Court to say, about affirmative action in general, that the case showed its injustices and the malevolent consequences of permitting the use of race as a factor, certainly as a decisive one, in allocating any scarce resources, like jobs or admissions to great universities. Strangely enough, the latter group—the important civil rights organizations and their lawyers as well as the Clinton administration—saw the case in the same way. Thus all concerned either hoped or feared that the Court, when faced with the rejected white teacher, would say: "Enough of this. It has gone on too long already. This is the end of affirmative action for any purpose as far as the law is concerned."

Is affirmative action really the unfair black "preference," or "reverse discrimination," policy that its critics claim and that Piscataway seems to present so starkly? Have we in fact lost sight of the larger goal of integrating blacks into our society? Or have we been so successful in achieving a "color blind" society about which Martin Luther King dreamed that the larger goal need no longer concern us?

Those who oppose affirmative action programs do not make such broad claims. They affirm the goal of an integrated society and do not contend we have yet achieved it. Critics simply argue that it is morally and constitutionally wrong to seek its achievement through race-based programs that give a "preference" to African Americans. Such programs, they maintain, are essentially wrong for the same reasons that it is wrong for whites to discriminate against blacks. It denies "equal opportunity" to whites and is antithetical to awarding jobs or promotions or college admissions on the basis of "merit."

There is no longer any dispute that overt, provable racial bias against blacks in employment or education should be unlawful. The disputed question is whether overt and provable bias is the only form of racial bias with which our society should—or can lawfully—be concerned. Certainly that bias—state supported in the Deep South and rampant throughout the country—was the immediate and most important target of the civil rights laws of the 1960s. Equally, the white majority in this country, despite deep-seated feelings of racial superiority, committed itself to achieving an integrated society. That happened, we believe, for the simple reason that it did not seem possible, then or now, for this country to maintain its democratic principles unless we could achieve Dr. King's dream. Is the elimination of overt bias all we need to do to accomplish that end?

The term "affirmative action" was first officially used in 1961   10
when President Kennedy strengthened an existing executive order prohibiting racial discrimination by government contractors in their employment practices. It was a natural, not a provocative, term to use. In the early '60s, blacks were essentially excluded from every level and every desirable institution of society. In many places they could not enter theaters, restaurants, hotels, or even parts of public libraries, courtrooms, and legislatures. How could that condition possibly have been changed—and the nation as a whole have decided that it should be changed—without taking action affirmatively, positively, deliberately, explicitly to change it?

So it was that there was no real controversy at the national level over the basic idea of acting affirmatively about race, although debate started soon enough, as it should have, over the details of particular steps. But at that time the country saw problems of race as problems to be faced and dealt with as the racial problems they were. The label "affirmative action" became popular perhaps because it suggested that we were at long last dealing with our oldest and most difficult problem. It was applied beyond the Kennedy executive order to a variety of race-based programs, private and public, voluntary as well as legally coerced, that sought to guarantee the employment—or, in the case of educational institutions, the admission—of qualified African Americans. It preceded the Civil Rights Acts of the 1960s and was consciously aimed at racial bias at a time when individuals could not yet sue private employers. But companies' employment of qualified African Americans to insure eligibility for government contracts was measured not individual by individual but by success in achieving reasonable numbers over time.

The technique of setting goals for minority employment is important because of its capacity to deal with all forms of potential bias—overt, concealed, or even inadvertent. Most national corporations have adopted employment goals. They appreciate the economic advantages of expanding and integrating the work force and they understand the need to press hard if the overall goal of inclusion is to be obtained.

The natural inclination of predominantly white male middle managers is to hire and promote one of their own. Most of the time the decision honestly reflects their judgment as to the best candidate without conscious appreciation of how much that judgment may have been conditioned by experience in the largely segregated society we still live in. To hire or promote an African American is often viewed as risky. Will he or she be accepted by fellow workers? A white may be praised for his independence; a like-minded black is seen as not a "team player." If corporations set reasonable hiring and promotion goals and reward management for their achievement, the integration process is speeded up. Public and private policies coincide.

Critics of affirmative action in employment see it not as an effort to create a reasonably integrated work force but as a system for favoring a less-qualified African American over a better-qualified white—a system of "preference" rather than "merit." There are three difficulties with their argument.

15   First, critics seek to reduce what is administered as a flexible system of hiring and promoting numbers of people into a measurement of one individual against another. Affirmative action programs deal with numbers of people at various times and seek to examine flexibly the results in numbers, not whether individual *A* is better than *B*. Such a program does not examine or re-examine each decision or demand precise achievement of numerical goals; it does not require a "quota," like a sales quota. It thus encourages personnel judgments, tolerating individual mistakes whether a white or a black is the victim.

Second, the critics assume that it is possible precisely to define and measure "merit." The best person for one job may not be the best for another, and vice versa; how does one square individual differences, or the "overqualified" candidate, with merit and the requirements of a particular job? Assuming that we are selecting from a pool of candidates who all meet whatever objective criteria are applicable to job performance, selection of the "best qualified" becomes a matter of subjective judgment by the employer—a judgment that involves weighing such intangibles as personality, leadership ability, motivation, dependability, enthusiasm, attitude toward authority. If critics are claiming that affirmative action has resulted in a less-competent work force because of the hiring and promotion of less-qualified blacks, neither evidence nor experience supports that conclusion.

Third, to argue that affirmative action constitutes a "preference" for African Americans is simply to argue that it distorts what would otherwise be a more efficient and fair system. Since the premise of the argument is that affirmative action constitutes a "preference" for blacks, it is fair to assume that proponents believe a "color blind" system would result in fewer blacks being employed. Why? If the pool of qualified applicants is 10 percent African American, then a color-blind system or an affirmative action program would result in about 10 percent black representation in the work force.

Thus, the word "preference" as critics use it is an effort to convert a broad employment effort into a series of individual choices or comparisons, as in Piscataway, with the additional innuendo that the fact of "preference" means a less-qualified African American will always prevail. That is a serious distortion of affirmative action.

Put differently, opponents of affirmative action in employment believe either that today the playing field is level for all races or that, absent overt racial bias, we should act as if it were. By contrast, most African Americans and many whites believe that bias still exists, though not always overtly, and that affirmative action is simply a guarantee that the playing field is not tilted.

Laws forbidding racial discrimination were relatively easy to administer when the bias was overt and widespread. The more that bias goes underground or, worse yet, is unconscious on the part of the decision maker, who believes his decision is uninfluenced by race, the more difficult and controversial that administration becomes. To label and punish unconscious bias as though it wore a hood may well be offensive. Programs of affirmative action avoid that problem while promoting the integrated society we seek. They minimally interfere with discretion in making particular choices and give management a desirable latitude in exercising particular judgments.

The other use of affirmative action most commonly criticized is in college admission. Educational institutions usually create a pool of applicants who meet objective tests designed to determine if the applicant is capable of performing successfully. Tests can reasonably predict first-year performance and do not claim to do more. But selection from the pool is not confined to rank on test scores, and applicants with lower scores are admitted for many reasons. Some applicants are admitted on the basis of judgments about potential and predictions about future performance not unlike those used in employment decisions. A student from a poor school who qualifies may be seen, despite a lower score, as having great motivation and aptitude. In other cases, "merit" is measured by other abilities, like musical or athletic talent. In still others, admissions may be determined by geography, financial ability, relationship to graduates; or relationship to people important in other ways to the institution. And finally, race and national origin may be taken into account and labeled "affirmative action."

If race cannot be taken into account and admission is based on test scores alone, far fewer African Americans will qualify. That was the predictable result in California and Texas, where state institutions were forbidden to take race into account. Again, the word "preference" is unfortunate because critics use it to imply that some kind of racial bias is used to reject better-qualified whites. Most of the students admitted are in fact white, hardly a demonstration of a bias in favor of blacks, and certainly not one that can be equated with past denials of admission to blacks to our best universities.

What proponents of affirmative action in college admissions urge is simply an institutional need for qualified African Americans on the grounds that a diverse student body contributes to educational excellence and to the preparation of students to live in an integrated society. Critics do not question the educational advantage of diversity—though their prescriptions would make its achievement virtually impossible. Further, those African Americans who can qualify for the institutional admissions pool would probably not be as successful as they are without superior motivation and determination—qualities most Americans would associate with merit.

Colleges and professional schools serve as gatekeepers to professional and business careers. If African Americans can successfully do the academic work, they will importantly contribute to the public goal of an integrated society. Studies support the contention that some blacks perform better academically than some whites with better test scores and that African Americans successfully

compete for employment at a comparable level with whites upon graduation. The arguments against this "preference" are similar to those   25
in other affirmative action programs: it is anti-merit and discriminates against whites with higher scores on admissions tests. That argument is not really worth consideration unless one is prepared to argue that all admissions should be measured exclusively by test scores. No one is prepared to go that far. The plea for fairness based on "merit" as measured by test scores appears to be confined to race—a plea that in our society should be regarded with some skepticism.

Affirmative action programs, whether to avoid present bias or to remedy the effects of three centuries of discrimination against African Americans, are race-based. The problems they seek to cure are and always have been race-based. They stem from history—the political, economic, and social domination of blacks by a white majority that regarded blacks as inferior. Undoubtedly there are blacks who are biased against whites and who, given the power to do so, would discriminate against them. Of course, given the power, it would be as morally wrong for them to do so as it has been for whites. But discrimination by blacks against whites is not America's problem. It is not the problem that predominantly white legislatures, businesses, and universities seek to solve through affirmative action programs.

To speak of these white efforts as though they were racially biased against whites and to equate them with the discriminatory practices of the past against African Americans is to steal the rhetoric of civil rights and turn it upside down. For racial bias to be a problem, it must be accompanied by power. Affirmative action programs are race-based not to show preference for one race over another but to resolve that problem. Only if one ignores that purpose and states the matter in Piscataway terms—preferring one individual over another for no reason other than race—does there even appear to be room for argument. If problems of race are to be solved, they must be seen as the race-based problems they are.

It is this aspect of the controversy that recent decisions of the Supreme Court have brought into question. The Equal Protection Clause of the Fourteenth Amendment was designed to insure that former slaves and their descendants were entitled to the same legal protection as white citizens. Like the Thirteenth Amendment abolishing slavery and the Fifteenth guaranteeing the right to vote regardless of race, it was clearly and unequivocally aimed at racial problems—in today's terminology "race based." The Equal Protection Clause has never been viewed as preventing classification of citizens for governmental reasons as long as the legislative classification was "reasonable" in terms of its purpose.

Where that classification involved race, however, the Court determined that it must be given "strict scrutiny." In other words, given our history both before and after the passage of the amendment, the Court understandably thought it wise to regard any racial classifications by overwhelmingly white legislatures with skepticism. When it was satisfied after strict scrutiny that the classification did not have the purpose or effect of discriminating against African Americans or other ethnic minorities, the Court found legislation to be consistent with the amendment. In the context of both our history and that of the amendment, this simply forbade abuse of white political superiority that prejudiced other races or ethnic minorities.

30   More recently, however, a majority has edged toward pronouncing the Constitution "color blind," coming close to holding legislation that uses any racial classification unconstitutional. Reading the Equal Protection Clause to protect whites as well as blacks from racial classification is to focus upon a situation that does not and never has existed in our society. Unfortunately, it casts doubt upon all forms of racial classification, however benign and however focused upon promoting integration. If such a reading is finally adopted by a majority of the Court, it would put a constitutional pall over all governmental affirmative action programs and even put similar private programs in danger of being labeled "discriminatory" against whites and therefore in violation of existing civil rights legislation—perhaps the ultimate stupidity.

The Court has, in short, never accepted as a national priority—in its terms a "compelling state interest"—the necessary race-based efforts, private and public, to include blacks in the institutional framework that constitutes America's economic, political, educational, and social life. Its recent decisions on the distribution of political power through districting outcomes have precluded race as a major factor while permitting incumbency, party affiliations, random geographic features, and boundaries drawn for obsolete historical reasons. Other lines of cases have similar outcomes for university admissions (as against unfair and educationally irrelevant factors like family ties, athletic prowess, and geography) and employment choices. It is very nearly as if this Court has simply mandated that what is the country's historic struggle against racial oppression and racial prejudice cannot be acted upon in a race-conscious way—that the law must view racial problems observable by all as if oppression and prejudice did not exist and had never existed. The Court's majority, in other words, has come very close to saying—and the hope and fear about the Piscataway case was that it would finally say at last—that courts cannot be permitted to see what is plain to everybody else.

For Discussion and Writing

1. What were the basic facts of the Piscataway school board case? Why did the federal judge reject the board's decision? Why did supporters of affirmative action prefer to "take an important public policy issue off the Court's docket"? Both sides in this case "saw the case in the same way." How was that?

2. Marshall and Katzenbach use questions to advance their argument. For example, look at the paragraph that begins, "Is affirmative action really the unfair black 'preference,' or 'reverse discrimination,' policy that its critics claim...?" How do the authors proceed to answer their questions? Pick out several other instances of such leading questions, and discuss their effect on your understanding of the topic. What do such questions contribute to a reader's sense of the reliability and authority of the writers?

3. For the authors, what is the importance of American history in arguments about affirmative action? Why do they point out that the Thirteenth Amendment is clearly race-based?

4. Marshall and Katzenbach write that "the technique of setting goals for minority employment is important because of its capacity to deal with all forms of potential bias—overt, concealed, or even inadvertent." Discuss these forms of bias, distinguishing them from each other. How likely are they to occur today? How might we know that "concealed" discrimination had taken place in a university's admissions, for example?

5. Marshall and Katzenbach present three "difficulties" with the argument that affirmative action is a system that favors "a less-qualified African American over a better-qualified white—a system of 'preference' rather than 'merit.'" Carefully explain each of the difficulties that they lay out.

6. The authors write, "For racial bias to be a problem, it must be accompanied by power." What are the implications of this claim for objections that affirmative action is reverse discrimination? What do they mean when they assert, "If problems of race are to be solved, they must be seen as the race-based problems they are"?

Blind Spot

PETER BEINART

Peter Beinart, a Yale graduate (1993), and winner of both Rhodes and Marshall scholarships, has been editor of the New Republic *since 1999. He has appeared on various news and talk shows, and has written for* Time, The Atlantic Monthly, *and other magazines. In the following article written for the* New Republic *in February 2003, Beinart considers the "color-blindness" of members of the Republican Party in general, pointing out the inconsistencies of some critics of affirmative action who call for a color-blind society.*

──────────── ✦ ────────────

The debate over affirmative action, resuscitated last week by the Bush administration's intervention in the University of Michigan case, is a little like the debate over divestment from Israel. Some people oppose divestment because they claim Ariel Sharon's government hasn't done anything wrong. But the more common anti-divestment argument is that even if Sharon's government has done something wrong, it should not be singled out for censure while other, far worse regimes get off scot-free. Addressing the divestment campaigners in *The New York Times* last October, Thomas Friedman wrote, "You are also hypocrites. . . . How is it that Syria occupies Lebanon for 25 years, chokes the life out of its democracy, and not a single student group calls for divestiture from Syria?"

At the 2000 GOP convention in Philadelphia, Colin Powell hurled essentially the same hypocrisy charge at his fellow Republicans. "We must understand the cynicism that exists in the black community," Powell said. "The kind of cynicism that is created when, for example, some in our party miss no opportunity to roundly and loudly condemn affirmative action that helped a few thousand black kids get an education, but you hardly hear a whimper over affirmative action for lobbyists who load our federal tax code with preferences for special interests." Powell didn't quite say affirmative action was fair; he said it was hypocritical to single out preferences for blacks while leaving other, deeper preferences intact.

At the convention, Powell appealed to Republicans to stop talking about affirmative action in a vacuum as the primary blemish on an otherwise meritocratic and color-blind society. And that remains the GOP's problem today. The next time you hear a Republican denouncing racial preferences at the University of Michigan, test his or her moral consistency with three simple questions.

Have you denounced other identity-based preferences in college admissions? Republicans make a big deal of the fact that under Michigan's numerically based admissions system, black applicants get points just for being black. But students also get points for being from different regions of the country or even different parts of the state. In fact, applicants from Michigan's rural, overwhelmingly white Upper Peninsula get almost as large a preference as blacks—although hailing from a certain region says as little about the content of an applicant's character as does her pigmentation. Geographic preferences may not be as constitutionally vulnerable as racial ones, but surely they are just as unfair. And yet I have never seen a speech by a Republican politician or read a column by a conservative journalist denouncing geographic discrimination.

And, if geographic preferences are as bad as racial preferences, surely parental preferences are worse. At least discrimination in favor of blacks, Hispanics, or kids from rural areas tends to benefit the less privileged—and therefore fosters upward mobility. By contrast, parental discrimination—favoring the children of alumni—generally benefits the wealthy and therefore stifles upward mobility. This kind of affirmative action more often benefits people who vote Republican—it probably got George W. Bush into Yale. Last fall, Democratic presidential candidate John Edwards denounced it as "a birthright out of eighteenth-century British aristocracy." Why have I never heard a Republican politician or a conservative pundit do the same?

Do you believe in color-blindness across the board? Affirmative action opponents might distinguish racial preferences from geographic and parental ones by claiming that, given this country's terrible history, there is something especially toxic about classifying people by race. The problem with that retort is that Republicans and conservatives are perfectly willing to classify people by race when it serves policy goals they like. Many conservative commentators have endorsed some racial profiling of black motorists, given that those drivers are statistically more likely to be transporting drugs, and some racial profiling of black or Hispanic teenagers, given that those teens are more likely to be selling them. And, since September 11, 2001, numerous Republican politicians and conservative pundits have demanded the profiling of Arabs and Muslims on the grounds that they are statistically more likely to be terrorists. Whether such profiling is effective is not the point. After all, Republicans don't primarily criticize affirmative action as ineffective. They criticize it as unjust, as a violation of the sacred principle of color-blindness. Yet, in other contexts—when color-blindness would undermine their security, rather than black kids' upward mobility—Republicans all of a sudden don't deem color-blindness so sacred after all.

There's a third, even more basic, litmus test for Republican critics of affirmative action: Have you denounced the affirmative action in your own party? After all, the 2000 Republican convention was as flagrant an expression of racial preferences as anything taking place in Ann Arbor. Only three Republican governors and four Republican senators received prime-time speaking slots. Instead, the convention's first night featured Paul C. Harris Sr., an obscure African American state legislator from Virginia, and its last featured Abel Maldonado, an obscure Hispanic state legislator from California. Can anyone seriously claim that anything qualified them for the slots besides their race? Or that all the white politicians for whom such a speech would have constituted a major career boost weren't disadvantaged as a result?

Since President Bush took office, Republican reverse discrimination has only intensified. Bush has appointed an African American secretary of education who had never held federal or even state office and a Hispanic secretary of housing and urban development who had never held office above the county level. (When Bush's first choice for secretary of labor bowed out, he selected another nonwhite woman: Can anyone say quota?) In the wake of Trent Lott's downfall, Republican National Chairman Marc Racicot earlier this month vowed to appoint more blacks to positions in the GOP. Given that politically experienced black Republicans are about as common as black college applicants with perfect SAT scores, Racicot has virtually pledged to discriminate against more qualified whites. What Bush and Racicot realize, of course, is that racial preferences can help Republicans appeal to black, and even some white, voters. But, if affirmative action is justified when it helps the political fortunes of the GOP, why isn't it justified when it helps create a racially diverse college campus?

Republicans aren't wrong to espouse merit and color-blindness. They're wrong to espouse merit and color-blindness while ignoring the ways in which they violate those principles themselves. That's what Colin Powell meant more than two years ago in Philadelphia. And, more than two years later, his party still doesn't understand.

For Discussion and Writing

1. What is the hypocrisy that, according to the author, Colin Powell attacked at the 2000 GOP convention? Beinart states Powell didn't "quite say affirmative action was fair." Why might Powell avoid such a claim in his remarks to the convention?
2. What does it mean to "stop talking about affirmative action in a vacuum"? What effect might context have on an audience's view of remarks on this issue? That is, in what ways does discussion in a historical context, for example, differ from discussion "in a vacuum"?
3. The vast majority of American college students are white. Viewed out of context, one might insist this is proof of aptitude and merit. Or, still out of context, one might call it proof of racism. What kinds of questions and information might help to contextualize a discussion of who actually gets into college? Why could such a discussion not be color-blind?
4. Where does Beinart come down finally on the possibility of "color-blindness across the board"? Why does he refer to racial profiling of Arabs and Muslims in an essay about affirmative action?
5. What is meant by the term *color-blind*? Ask different people (differing in age, race, gender, occupation) to explain the term. How do they define the term? Do they refer immediately to affirmative action? Police profiling? A political ideal? Discuss the various ways people understand the term. Discuss whether or not the term has become a cliché, whether its use obscures or clarifies issues.

Construction of an Enemy
ELEANOR STEIN

Eleanor Stein, an administrative law judge with the New York State Public Service Commission, specializes in telecommunications law, which she teaches at Albany Law School. She also teaches a course in women and the law at the State University of New York. She has lectured at the University of Colorado telecommunications program, the National Association of Regulatory Attorneys, the Practicing Law Institute, and bar association events. Her articles have appeared in the Yale Law Journal, *the* New York State Bar Association Journal, *and the* Hofstra Law Review. *In the following online article (http://www.monthlyreview.org/0703stein.htm), Judge Stein considers both the ways in which a people come to be stereotyped as enemies, and the ways that such stereotypes can be resisted.*

—————————— ✦ ——————————

Remember the Nazi technique: "pit race against race, religion against religion, prejudice against prejudice. Divide and conquer!"

President Franklin D. Roosevelt (January 1942)
admonishing Americans not to discriminate against
aliens, weeks before he signed the Japanese exclusion order
(Greg Robinson, *By Order of the President*, 2001)

The aggressive measures instituted by the Bush administration against immigrants and visitors of Muslim faith, or from primarily Muslim Arab and South Asian countries, seem aimed less at their putative foreign targets than at the hearts and minds of our domestic population. Packaged as post-September 11 law enforcement, the new racial profiling has netted few if any prosecutions for terrorist acts, but has done a great deal to demonize Arabs, South Asians, and Muslims, to dehumanize them, and to construct them as the enemy of America in the twenty-first century. Once the state successfully constructs an enemy group, it can justify detentions without charge, military occupation, and other drastic means of waging war against that other, the enemy.

Nativist and xenophobic identification of immigrants with national security threats is a theme coincident with the history of the United States. The Naturalization Act of 1790 prohibited citizenship and civil rights to immigrants of disfavored ethnicity. The Alien and Sedition Acts of 1798 placed restrictions on which ethnicities or nationalities could apply for citizenship, and authorized the president to order the deportation of all immigrants judged dangerous to national security. The "sedition" of concern in 1798 were the ideas of the French Revolution. The Chinese Exclusion (Geary) Act of 1882, in violation of the express terms of a treaty in force between China and the United States, forbade Chinese laborers from entering the United States. The National Origins Act of 1924 established immigration quotas privileging "Nordic" immigrants. The Smith Act of 1940 required registration and fingerprinting of aliens, and added vague classifications of "subversives" and "excludables" to the list of deportable persons. The McCarran-Walter Act of 1952 empowered the Department of Justice to deport immigrants or naturalized citizens engaging in "subversive" activities. The Anti-Terrorism and Effective Death Penalty Act of 1996 granted the executive the authority, based upon secret evidence, to designate any foreign organization a terrorist group and to deport noncitizens as terrorists.

But it was the internment of Japanese Americans during the Second World War that elevated xenophobia into national policy. And it was in the internment cases that the Supreme Court, upholding the internment as a matter of military necessity, wrote the requirement of strict judicial scrutiny of "invidious" distinction into American jurisprudence.

Based upon reports by the military that it had intercepted   5
radio and light signals between offshore locations and the California coast, the evacuation and internment orders forced persons of Japanese descent to leave their homes in specified control areas in California, Arizona, Oregon, and Washington, and move to internment camps. Over 120,000 persons, two-thirds of them U.S.-born citizens, spent the years of the war in such camps.

The internment order was rationalized not only by military necessity—the fear of sabotage and espionage—but also by the military's claim that the normal criminal investigatory work of the Justice Department had been overly slow and inadequate to guarantee U.S. security. The racist hysteria in which the roundups took place was fed by the Hearst press and by California economic interests—such as the White American Nurserymen—in competition with small entrepreneurs of Japanese descent.

Two brave individuals, Fred Korematsu and Gordon Hirabayashi, refused to report for internment and sought to challenge the order in the Federal Courts. In a shameful decision, the U.S. Supreme Court upheld as constitutional this mass internment; included were 80,000 citizens deprived of liberty solely by reason of their ethnic origin. Forty years later, when the two whose refusal to report for internment had led to Supreme Court cases sought (and received) judicial exoneration, it was discovered that the military report, which was the justification for the internment order and the Supreme Court decision, was a complete fabrication. An archival researcher, working in conjunction with a congressional commission appointed to investigate the internment, found the original report. The supposed intercepted radio and light signals, dutifully repeated in the Supreme Court opinion, had never occurred.

The shadow of Manzanar—the California interment camp—looms today over all of the current measures being taken against Arab and Muslim immigrants. These measures can be seen as internment for the twenty-first century—or to coin a more accurate term, externment.

Shortly after September 11, 2001, the "Ashcroft Raids" occured, the secret detention and deportation of up a thousand or more Arab or Muslim men. Some were held for months, even as long as one year, without access to lawyers and in some cases, to families. Ashcroft stated he intended to jail every terrorist he could find, and that net included thousands of Muslim noncitizens. What were the results of this dragnet? Not a single person charged with involvement in the September 11 attacks, and four indicted on charges of support for terrorism, with none of the indictments including any specific violent acts. The Justice Department now admits that at least 766 persons were detained on "special interest" charges after September 11 and held incommunicado; of these, 511 have been deported. The Justice Department claims that among those deported were some who could have been—*but have not been*—charged with terrorism offenses. This in turn has led to reported speculation that one purpose of the mass detention policy was the recruitment of intelligence agents (www.law.com/jsp/article.jsp?id=1052440755868). An additional six thousand were deported for violations of immigration status. Eight thousand were called for interviews on the sole ground that they were recent male immigrants from Arab countries.

10   The USA Patriot Act, enacted within six weeks of September 11, permits the Attorney General to detain noncitizens without a hearing; to bar foreign citizens from entering the United States because of their political opinions; and authorizes deportation based upon support of a disfavored group. None of these restrictions is tied to participation in any terrorist act. On April 29, 2003, the Supreme Court approved mandatory detention of "criminal aliens"

pending deportation—that is, permanent resident aliens convicted of any of a list of crimes who are subject to deportation have no entitlement to a hearing to consider bail for the period they contest or await deportation.

Also coming soon may be Patriot Act II, which modifies the definition of "foreign power" to include all persons, regardless of whether they are affiliated with an international terrorist group, who engage in international terrorism; and defines any person who engages in clandestine intelligence gathering activities for a foreign power as an agent of that power, regardless of whether those activities are federal crimes.

One of the most far-reaching forms of racial profiling is the requirement of the Immigration and Naturalization Service, now merged into the Office of Homeland Security, termed Special Registration. These new rules apply to any male, over the age of sixteen, who is not currently a permanent resident (green card holder), from twenty-five countries: Afghanistan, Algeria, Bahrain, Eritrea, Iran, Iraq, Lebanon, Libya, Morocco, North Korea, Oman, Qatar, Somalia, Sudan, Syria, Tunisia, United Arab Emirates, Yemen, Pakistan, Saudi Arabia, Bangladesh, Egypt, Indonesia, Jordan, and Kuwait. These men were required to register in person at an immigration office during February and March 2003 on a few weeks notice, to be photographed, fingerprinted, and interviewed, in many cases about their political beliefs and associations. More than 125,000 registered; over 2,000 were detained. All must re-register annually and any time they leave the United States. A widespread panic resulted in immigrant communities, and thousands in the New York and New England areas traveled with their families to the Canadian border to seek asylum; however, the United States had closed the border. Hundreds were detained there, their families left without shelter or resources in the bitter New England winter. Local refugee assistance organizations, overwhelmed, were forced to close their doors.

Government profiling also contributed to a wave of popular violence against Arab, South Asian, and Muslim communities. The number of reported U.S. hate crimes against Muslims and Arabs in 2002 increased 1600 percent over the previous year.

The construction of an enemy, through government targeting with media complicity and a popular echo, endangers and dehumanizes millions of Arabs, Asians, and Muslims. Given a dehumanized enemy, bombing its cities and sacking its history was presented on U.S. TV as an extreme sport. The construction of an enemy provides an effective means of control of the domestic population, which visits its fears and frustrations on its Arab and Muslim neighbors. This control is, however, contested. In communities all over the country, towns and cities have passed local government resolutions criticizing and even refusing to enforce the Patriot Act.

15   Fred Korematsu and Gordon Hirabayashi waited forty years for vindication and reparations; and few outside the Japanese-American community, with the notable exception of the Quakers, had opposed internment. Hopefully we are doing better this time.

Interfaith groups are building bridges to Muslim communities. In upstate New York, Women Against War organized a toy drive for children of detainees and deportees to celebrate Eid, the end of Ramadan and, with national civil liberties organizations, recruited attorneys and other volunteers to assist men reporting for Special Registration and their families. And shortly after September 11 the National Asian Pacific American Legal Consortium invited Arab Americans to join them at the National Japanese American Memorial to show solidarity in anticipation of racial profiling. Resistance as ever is based on acts of individual decency, which in these sad times appear as acts of courage. But the liberty interests of all U.S. residents are implicated; if we do not stand by our Muslim neighbors in their registration, detention, and deportation nightmare we will have a yet harder time when these techniques are more widely applied.

For Discussion and Writing

1. Judge Stein begins with an epigraph, quoting President Franklin D. Roosevelt. Discuss the implications of the President's remarks and his subsequent Japanese exclusion order. In what ways, if any, do the events of 9/11 resemble those of December 7, 1941?

2. What does Stein mean by "xenophobic identification of immigrants with national security threats"? She claims that such "identification" is part of our history. She gives many examples of xenophobic acts and policies in America's past. How do such references help to clarify her views about the current treatment of Arabs and Muslims in America?

3. Stein writes of the "construction of an enemy, through government targeting with media complicity and a popular echo." Why does she use the term *construction*? Discuss each of the elements the author identifies in the process of construction, and how these contribute to the making of an enemy.

4. As Stein notes, a new INS Special Registration requirement demands that men over the age of 16 from certain countries register at an immigration office. An annual process, it includes fingerprinting and interviewing. Does Stein present this as a form of racial profiling? How does such a requirement influence public perception of Middle Easterners?

5. Stein closes by noting that Japanese Americans have shown support for Middle Eastern Americans. Why does she include this material? She also states that "if we do not stand by our Muslim neighbors in their registration, detention, and deportation nightmare we will have a yet harder time when these techniques are more widely applied." How does her essay seek to persuade you that this last fear is reasonable?

Voting While Black
BOB HERBERT

Bob Herbert, a columnist for the New York Times, *received his degree in journalism from the State University of New York (Empire State College) in 1988. He has been a national correspondent for NBC from 1991 to 1993, reporting on* The Today Show *and NBC Nightly News. In the following essay, Herbert reports on the actions of Florida police investigating allegations of election fraud. For some observers, their tactics seem aimed at intimidating minority voters.*

◆

The smell of voter suppression coming out of Florida is getting stronger. It turns out that a Florida Department of Law Enforcement investigation, in which state troopers have gone into the homes of elderly black voters in Orlando in a bizarre hunt for evidence of election fraud, is being conducted despite a finding by the department last May "that there was no basis to support the allegations of election fraud."

State officials have said that the investigation, which has already frightened many voters and intimidated elderly volunteers, is in response to allegations of voter fraud involving absentee ballots that came up during the Orlando mayoral election in March. But the department considered that matter closed last spring, according to a letter from the office of Guy Tunnell, the department's commissioner, to Lawson Lamar, the state attorney in Orlando, who would be responsible for any criminal prosecutions.

The letter, dated May 13, said:

> We received your package related to the allegations of voter fraud during the 2004 mayoral election. This dealt with the manner in which absentee ballots were either handled or collected by campaign staffers for Mayor Buddy Dyer. Since this matter involved an elected official, the allegations were forwarded to F.D.L.E.'s Executive Investigations in Tallahassee, Florida.
>
> The documents were reviewed by F.D.L.E., as well as the Florida Division of Elections. It was determined that there was no basis to support the allegations of election fraud concerning these absentee ballots. Since there is no evidence of criminal misconduct involving Mayor Dyer, the Florida Department of Law Enforcement considers this matter closed.

Well, it's not closed. And department officials said yesterday that the letter sent out in May was never meant to indicate that the "entire" investigation was closed. Since the letter went out, state troopers have gone into the homes of 40 or 50 black voters, most of them elderly, in what the department describes as a criminal investigation. Many longtime Florida observers have said the use of state troopers for this type of investigation is extremely unusual, and it has caused a storm of controversy.

5   The officers were armed and in plain clothes. For elderly African-American voters, who remember the terrible torment inflicted on blacks who tried to vote in the South in the 1950's and 60's, the sight of armed police officers coming into their homes to interrogate them about voting is chilling indeed.

One woman, who is in her mid-70's and was visited by two officers in June, said in an affidavit: "After entering my house, they asked me if they could take their jackets off, to which I answered yes. When they removed their jackets, I noticed they were wearing side arms. . . . And I noticed an ankle holster on one of them when they sat down."

Though apprehensive, she answered all of their questions. But for a lot of voters, the emotional response to the investigation has gone beyond apprehension to outright fear.

"These guys are using these intimidating methods to try and get these folks to stay away from the polls in the future," said Eugene Poole, president of the Florida Voters League, which tries to increase black voter participation throughout the state. "And you know what? It's working. One woman said, 'My God, they're going to put us in jail for nothing.' I said, 'That's not true.'" State officials deny that their intent was to intimidate black voters. Mr. Tunnell, who was handpicked by Gov. Jeb Bush to head the Department of Law Enforcement, said in a statement yesterday: "Instead of having them come to the F.D.L.E. office, which may seem quite imposing, our agents felt it would be a more relaxed atmosphere if they visited the witnesses at their homes."

When I asked a spokesman for Mr. Tunnell, Tom Berlinger, about the letter in May indicating that the allegations were without merit, he replied that the intent of the letter had not been made clear by Joyce Dawley, a regional director who drafted and signed the letter for Mr. Tunnell.   10

"The letter was poorly worded," said Mr. Berlinger. He said he spoke to Ms. Dawley about the letter a few weeks ago and she told him, "God, I wish I would have made that more clear." What Ms. Dawley meant to say, said Mr. Berlinger, was that it did not appear that Mayor Dyer himself was criminally involved.

For Discussion and Writing

1. Which state agency in Florida first investigated allegations of vote fraud, and what were its findings?
2. Why, according to Herbert, were the targeted voters in this account especially likely to be frightened by investigators?
3. Compare the first letter's language, claiming no basis for allegations of fraud, with the remarks of Tom Berlinger. What is it that Berlinger says needed clarification?
4. Look into accounts of minority voters in Florida being dropped from the rolls of voters in the 2000 election. In what ways might such actions as dropping minority voters off roles and voter intimidation affect elections?

Nobodies
JOHN BOWE

John Bowe received an M.F.A. from Columbia University's graduate film program in 1996. He co-edited GIG: Americans Talk About Their Jobs, *and is at work on* Slavery Inc., *from which the following piece is taken. Bowe won the 2003 Richard J. Margolis Award, and was also the winner of the J. Anthony Lukas Work-in-Progress Award, the citation for which noted that "John Bowe's work—an examination of slavery throughout the modern world, including the United States—is characterized by a reasoned and painstaking approach to the gathering of his material. . . . His description has no taint of moral superiority." Bowe's account of brutal agribusiness contractors and virtually enslaved workers in Immokalee, Florida, depicts a laboring underclass whose members come largely from Mexico and Central America. As one worker who escaped murderous labor contractors said, "When you're in the kind of situation we were in, you feel like the world has ended."*

---------------- ✦ ----------------

Some forty miles inland from the coastal resorts of Fort Myers Beach and Sanibel Island, the town of Immokalee sits at the bottom of a string of remote agricultural outposts extending through the South Florida interior. The swampy terrain seems an unlikely choice for farmland, but over the past sixty years it has been transformed by canals, pumps, and fertilizer; today, the area is a major source of winter produce sold in the United States.

Three stoplights long, Immokalee (which rhymes with "broccoli" and means "my home" in Seminole) is bordered on the south by the Big Cypress swamp, and surrounded on all other sides by citrus groves and tomato fields. The town's official population is about twenty thousand, but during the growing season, between November and May, it increases to nearly twice that. The town looks more like a work camp than like an American community. Municipal authorities provide little in the way of public services; for several days recently on Main Street, visitors entering town passed a decapitated black dog, left to rot on the median strip across from a new Walgreen's. In 2001, a county sheriff's deputy was sentenced to fourteen years in prison for dealing crack and shaking down local drug dealers.

Forty years ago, Immokalee's population consisted largely of poor whites, African-Americans, and Puerto Ricans. In the eighties, Haitians arrived, and a little later Guatemalans began to trickle in. Today, some Haitians, whites, and African-Americans remain, but the business district is overwhelmingly oriented toward Mexican and Central American migrants.

Between four-thirty and five o'clock every morning, a convoy of crudely painted red and blue school buses arrives at a parking lot on South Third Street, a block from Main Street, to carry workers to the fields. In the afternoon, the buses return, and the sidewalks fill with weary men, many wearing muddy rubber boots, their shirts and pants stained deep green from the juice of tomato leaves. (Ninety per cent of the town's migrant population are men.) In the evening, workers wear tucked-in Western shirts, baseball caps or cowboy hats, and Reebok knockoffs. Some stay home to wash their few items of clothing or cook dinner; those with time left on their phone cards line up in parking lots and on street corners before seemingly innumerable pay phones (a staple of migrant towns) to call Chiapas, Oaxaca, Huehuetenango.

In many parts of the Southeast, agricultural workers are quar-   5
tered in trailer camps miles from town; Immokalee's pickers, as citrus and tomato workers are often called, live in plain sight, densely concentrated between First and Ninth Streets, close to the South Third Street pickup spot. Those who don't live there are forced either to walk a great distance twice a day or to pay extra for a ride to work. As a result, rents near the parking lot are high. The town's largest landlord, a family named Blocker, owns several hundred old shacks and mobile homes, many rusting and mildew-stained, which can rent for upward of two hundred dollars a week, a square-footage rate approaching Manhattan's. (Heat and phone service are not provided.) It isn't unusual for twelve workers to share a trailer.

Immokalee's tomato pickers are paid as little as forty cents per bucket. A filled bucket weighs thirty-two pounds. To earn fifty dollars in a day, an Immokalee picker must harvest two tons of tomatoes, or a hundred and twenty-five buckets.

Orange- and grapefruit-picking pay slightly better, but the hours are longer. To get to the fruit, pickers must climb twelve-to-eighteen-foot-high ladders, propped on soggy soil, then reach deep into thorny branches, thrusting both hands among pesticide-coated leaves before twisting the fruit from its stem and rapidly stuffing it into a shoulder-slung *moral*, or pick sack. (Grove owners post guards in their fields to make sure that the workers do not harm the trees.) A full sack weighs about a hundred pounds; it takes ten sacks—about two thousand oranges—to fill a *baño*, a bin the size of a large wading pool. Each bin earns the worker a *ficha*, or token, redeemable for about seven dollars.

An average worker in a decent field can fill six, seven, maybe eight bins a day. After a rain, though, or in an aging field with overgrown trees, the same picker might work an entire day and fill only three bins.

Migrant workers are usually employed by labor contractors, who provide crews to tend and harvest crops for local farmers, or growers, as they're more commonly known. Contractors oversee workers in groups ranging in size from a dozen to many hundreds, and accompany the workers as they travel with the seasons. They can exert near-absolute control over their workers' lives; besides handling the payroll and deducting taxes, they are frequently the sole source of the workers' food and housing, which, in addition to the ride to and from the fields, they provide for a fee.

About ninety per cent of South Florida's laborers are new each season. Recently arrived pickers are often mystified by American culture, unsure of their rights (or the idea of rights in general), and unlikely to speak English. Workers coming from the highlands of southern Mexico and Guatemala speak dozens of languages, including Zapotecan, Mam, Kanjobal, Tzotzil, and Mixteca, and often cannot communicate with each other. In the post-pastoral fields of industrialized modern agriculture, quaint notions of worker solidarity are unrealistic. A former tomato picker named Francisca Cortes told me that workers begin their mornings in the fields by elbowing one another aside as they scramble for positions close to the collection area, each gradient of productivity worth another quarter, another dollar. Under these circumstances, Cortes said, "It's just a bunch of men and some women. You don't know them. You're not there to say, 'What's your name? How are you? How long have you been here?' There just isn't any time for that."

10   Workers are reluctant to discuss abusive situations with employers, much less with *bolillos*, or white Americans, for fear of losing their jobs and being labelled troublemakers. Those workers without papers live under the constant threat of being seized by *la migra*—the Immigration and Naturalization Service. Some labor contractors use this implicit threat of exposure to keep them in line. Workers often borrow money to travel north from loan sharks back home at interest rates as high as twenty-five percent per month. If they are deported, the loan is foreclosed. Frequently, homes are put up as collateral, so deportation can be a financial calamity for an entire family.

All these factors combine to create, in South Florida, what a Justice Department official calls "ground zero for modern slavery." The area has seen six cases of involuntary servitude successfully prosecuted in the past six years. Describing local migrant-contractor power dynamics, Michael Baron, an agent with the U.S. Border Patrol who knows Florida well, told me, "Most of the time, these workers are housed miles from civilization, with no telephones or cars. They're controllable. There's no escape. If you do escape, what are you gonna do? Run seventeen miles to the nearest town, when you don't even know where it is? And, if you have a brother or a cousin in the group, are you gonna leave them behind? You gonna escape with seventeen people? You'll make tracks like a herd of elephants. Whoever's got you, they'll find you. And heaven help you when they do."

In February of 2001, Adan Ortiz decided to leave his home in the Mexican state of Campeche, on the Yucatán Peninsula, where he lived with his wife and six children in a one-room straw hut, to look for a job in the United States. Since the age of nine, he had worked with a machete and an axe, clearing brush for local ranchers or harvesting sugarcane.

Ortiz gets along in Spanish, but his first language is Mixe, a Mayan language spoken by the Mixe Indians, in southern Mexico. He is short (about five-two) and stocky, with a mustache and soft brown eyes, and looks younger than his thirty-eight years. He has an earnestness about him, and speaks with a studied reserve. When he was asked recently if he had ever owned any land, he almost laughed. "I don't even own the dirt under my fingernails!"

Farmwork in Mexico pays about five or six dollars a day—when it's available. Ortiz considered himself lucky to find work two or three days a week near his home. The only way to bring in more income was to bum around the countryside, looking for work, and there was seldom enough to maintain a family. "People use the term 'provide for' just to refer to a plate of beans and salsa and some tortillas," Ortiz explained. "I think for a family you've got to have milk. Right?"

Ortiz left Mexico with two friends. (The three men are 15 referred to in federal documents only by their initials, and I have changed their names.) None of them had gone to school beyond sixth grade. The youngest, eighteen-year-old Rafael Solis Hernandez, lived in his mother's house with his wife and baby. Mario Sanchez, the father of six children, lived in a house built of cardboard. At forty-three, he had difficulty recalling his birthday. He explained, "It's never been celebrated, so I don't even concern myself with it." To travel north, Sanchez brought what money remained from a crop of peppers he'd managed to grow the year before. Ortiz borrowed twenty-five hundred pesos (about two hundred and fifty dollars) from a man he occasionally worked for, and Hernandez borrowed the money from his mother.

They crossed the border with a large group in early March, in the care of a "coyote," or smuggler, and found themselves in the town of Marana, Arizona. None of them had any money left, but the coyote introduced them to a man they nicknamed El Chaparro (Shorty), who gave them permission to sleep in an abandoned trailer home. Thirty-five of them did so for about a week. Then El Chaparro offered to drive them to a place where they could get jobs picking oranges. Terms were never discussed.

Ortiz, Hernandez, and about a dozen others were packed into El Chaparro's rickety van, and the group set forth, accompanied by a car carrying five more passengers, including Sanchez. The trip lasted three days. El Chaparro stopped once for an hour or two to sleep, but passengers were forbidden to get out, even to relieve themselves. For that purpose, a jug was passed around. When asked whether they ate during this time, Ortiz shrugged, and answered, "We didn't have money."

On March 13th, more than three weeks after leaving home, the men reached their destination: Lake Placid, a low-lying town in the swamps of South Florida, about sixty miles north of Immokalee. The van stopped in front of a Mexican grocery store named La Guadalupana, and the passengers were ordered to stay put while El Chaparro got out and talked to two labor contractors, who were later identified to the migrants by their nicknames, Nino and El Diablo.

El Diablo, whose real name is Ramiro Ramos, is a short, solidly built man with close-cropped, graying hair, an impassive manner, and bloodshot eyes. Born in Guanajuato, Mexico, he arrived in this country as an orange picker in the early eighties. He became a *tigre*, or super-picker, whose output was legendary. By the end of the decade, he had worked his way up to contracting. He developed a reputation as the kind of boss who seemed friendly at first, a man "who'd give you your first meal free," a former employee recalled, but who became menacing if angered. He also had a history of threatening his workers with violence.

Ramos had married a Mexican-American named Alicia Barajas, whose family runs several sizable labor-contracting operations. "You have to be careful with the Barajases," Baron said. "Their name comes up a lot in law enforcement."

Ramiro Ramos, his brother, Juan Ramos (Nino), and a loose 20 network of cousins and in-laws employed thousands of migrant workers, from South Florida to North Carolina. Records from one of their companies, R & A Harvesting, indicate that between 2000 and 2002 it employed several hundred workers.

Ortiz recalls that when he and his friends first met the new bosses "Señor Nino asked if we had someone to pay El Chaparro for our ride." Ortiz says that Nino shoved a phone in his face, knowing, of course, that the new arrivals had no one to call. Then, according to Ortiz, Nino said, "Well, O.K., we'll pay for you." The workers saw Nino write out a check to El Chaparro. They were told that the bosses had paid a thousand dollars for each of them.

Nino has the same short, solid build as his brother but comes across as less threatening. His belly protrudes over his belt, and his hair, regardless of grooming, consistently looks windblown. (One of his acquaintances told me, "Nino always looks like he's just come from a party.") Nino didn't make anyone sign a contract. Instead, he simply warned his new recruits, "You'll have to pay us back. And the work is very hard." Nino then added a final detail, according to Ortiz: "He told us that if anyone took off before paying he'd beat the fuck out of us. He didn't say it like he was joking." At that point, seeking another job wasn't an option. As Ortiz explained, "I couldn't have gone elsewhere. I owed the money to them. If I refused, what was I going to do?"

El Diablo took the new arrivals to their lodgings, a former bar known as La Piñita, which had been converted into a filthy, crowded, dormitory-style barracks where workers slept six to a room on stained bare mattresses on the floor. While the men were being shown to their places, Hernandez, a soccer fan, noticed a small television set in one room. When he asked if he could perhaps arrange to have a set for his room as well, he recalled, El Diablo said angrily, "If you keep up with this kind of attitude, I'll pump you full of lead."

Ortiz, Hernandez, and Sanchez spent the next month working for the Ramoses, eight to twelve hours a day, six or seven days a week. Every Friday after work, Nino or El Diablo would pull up to the groves or in front of La Guadalupana (which was owned by Alicia Barajas) in a Ford F-250 pickup truck, holding a large sack full of money. After charging workers a check-cashing fee, the brothers then garnished for rent, food, work equipment, the ride from Arizona, and daily transportation to and from the fields. Whatever remained was usually spent on food at La Guadalupana. The three friends and their fellow-laborers barely broke even.

They were also under constant surveillance. La Piñita was only a few yards away from Highway 27, which runs through the citrus belt west of Lake Okeechobee. One day, when Hernandez and another worker tried to telephone their wives from a nearby Kash n' Karry convenience store, El Diablo pulled up behind them, asked whom they were calling, and pointedly offered them a ride home. When the Ramos brothers weren't around, workers were watched by relatives and supervisors carrying cell phones who lived in the barracks and patrolled the surrounding area. Ortiz recalled being told by one supervisor, "If you want to leave, go ahead. But I'll call the bosses, and they'll feed you to the alligators." The supervisor pointed to a lake behind La Piñita and said, "They haven't eaten for awhile." For the newcomers, life in the United States wasn't quite what they had expected. Sanchez later recalled, "All of a sudden, you realize you're completely in their pockets."

25   There are more than a million migrant workers living in the United States, about half of them illegally. They plant, tend, and harvest most agricultural commodities, including oranges, grapefruits, cherries, peaches, apples, watermelons, tomatoes, onions, eggplant, peppers, squash, cucumbers, mushrooms, cotton, tobacco, and Christmas trees.

As in other sectors of the food economy, the production and distribution of South Florida's tomato crop has become increasingly concentrated. A handful of private firms like Six L's Packing Company, Gargiulo, Inc., and Pacific Tomato Growers supply millions of pounds of tomatoes, either directly or indirectly, to supermarkets and corporations such as Taco Bell, Wendy's, Burger King, McDonald's, and Carnival Cruise Lines.

Ownership and distribution is even more tightly controlled in the citrus industry. Lykes Brothers is a billion-dollar conglomerate with holdings in insurance, real estate, and cattle as well as citrus. Larger still is Consolidated Citrus, which owns fifty-five thousand acres in Florida alone. A majority of the state's crop, in the form of either fruit, juice, or concentrate, goes to three final buyers: Cargill, a fifty-one-billion-dollar commodities giant and one of the largest privately owned companies in the world, with operations in fifty-nine countries; Tropicana, which is owned by Pepsico; and Minute Maid, owned by Coca-Cola. These companies are quick to point out that they don't actually own the groves or harvest the fruit themselves. They merely employ supervisors who test for quality and sugar content, coördinate prices on world commodities markets, and, ultimately, control the harvest.

In the past two decades, according to the United States Department of Labor, farm receipts from fruit and vegetable sales have nearly doubled. Between 1989 and 1998, however, wages paid to farmworkers declined, dropping from $6.89 to $6.18 per hour. The national median annual income for farmworkers is $7,500. A University of Florida survey found that the average income for Immokalee farmworkers is even lower—in 1998, just $6,574.

According to the Department of Justice, the number of prosecutions of human-trafficking cases throughout the country has tripled in the past three years; there are currently a hundred and twenty-five investigations of such cases under way. Typically, these cases take years to pursue, and convictions with meaningful sentences are difficult to obtain. An often insuperable obstacle is the agricultural workers' mistrust of enforcement agents. Michael Baron, of the Border Patrol, says, "Workers see us and think we're here to pick them up and deport them. They don't give us the time of day." Prosecutors cite an additional hurdle: witnesses travelling from state to state without telephones are difficult to reach, much less schedule for depositions and trials.

For this reason, the Justice Department has been relying on an advocacy group called the Coalition of Immokalee Workers. The coalition has been instrumental in five of South Florida's slavery prosecutions, uncovering and investigating abusive employers, locating transient witnesses, and encouraging them to overcome their fears of testifying against former captors. While other farmworkers'-rights organizations offer health care or legal representation, the coalition holds weekly meetings, conducts weekend "leadership trainings," makes outreach trips throughout the southeastern states, stages hunger strikes, and has launched a boycott of Taco Bell, in an effort to raise wages for tomato pickers working in what it calls "sweatshop-like conditions."

30

The organization has more than two thousand members. (It costs five dollars to join.) Most members move on after a year or two in Immokalee to other cities and states, but enough of them stay in touch to create a network that keeps the group informed about working conditions throughout the country.

Lucas Benitez, a twenty-seven-year-old former tomato picker from Mexico with silver teeth (the signature of Central American dentistry), explains the coalition's focus on worker awareness. "If you want true change, it won't come from Washington, or from the lawyers," he says. "It will come from the people in the field." Benitez, one of the coalition's seven elected representatives, sat in his office with his feet up on his desk. Despite his youth and a playful attitude, he is a powerful speaker. "If you win a case or get a judgment, the problems of slavery, of abuses, still remain," he said. "If you change people's consciousness, the people them-selves take care of it." When asked about the government's role, he shrugged. "Who cares what happens to a bunch of *pelagatos*— a bunch of nobodies?"

The group's headquarters is a dilapidated storefront on South Third Street, next to the pickup spot where the workers congregate each morning. The paint is peeling off the walls and the carpet is ripped and threadbare. The principal furnishings include a lumpy old couch, two desks, a few dozen metal folding chairs, and a large papier-mâché replica of the Statue of Liberty, holding a tomato bucket. The walls are adorned with photographs of protest marches, cartoons depicting labor relations between bosses and workers, and newspaper articles in Spanish, English, and Creole. Migrant workers stream through all day and into the evening, buy-ing tortillas, Jarritos soft drinks, and mole-sauce mix at the coali-tion's co-op grocery store. The place has a feel somewhere between a college social club and Third World political-party branch office.

The group's representatives come from Haiti, Mexico, Guatemala, and the United States. They are paid two hundred and seventy-seven dollars a week—slightly more than a farm-worker earning minimum wage for a forty-hour week. They live in trailers and shacks, and work seven days a week, and their con-versations seldom stray from the subject of workers' rights. There is a familial esprit de corps among the leadership, but it's not hard to offend them.

35   Greg Asbed and Laura Germino, a couple now in their late thirties, who met at Brown University, helped start the coalition,

in the mid-nineties, while working for Florida Rural Legal Services. Germino is an intense, graceful woman whose family has been in Florida for six generations. She drives a silver 1970 Malibu—her "muscle car," as she calls it—but she wouldn't seem out of place at a country club. Asbed is a handsome, athletic man with stubbled cheeks who favors old T-shirts and worn jeans; he spends three months a year harvesting watermelons with other coalition members.

Before coming to Florida, Germino volunteered with the Peace Corps in Burkina Faso, and Asbed worked for a community-development organization in rural Haiti. Asbed says that, even after working in Haiti, he was appalled to learn what went on in South Florida. "I mean, it's this hidden aspect of life in the country that you wouldn't expect existed," he said. "Until you actually hook up with it and get an in-depth, insider's tour of the world, it's incredible. You don't know what's out there." The couple was inspired by local Haitian, Mexican, and Central American activists who were beginning to organize workers, and, after launching a general strike of more than three thousand migrants, the coalition began to hold regular meetings.

Both Germino and Asbed are reluctant to discuss their own lives. When I asked Germino whether her upbringing had anything to do with her choices, she said only, "I was raised to think that people should be treated justly and that you're supposed to live free and that every human being should be treated as such. I mean, those are pretty basic." She laughed. "Everybody should at least have that kind of consciousness!" When I pressed for more, she answered abruptly, laughing again, but with finality, "This has nothing to do with your story! Don't make me be the story. The workers are the heroes!"

According to Germino, modern slavery exists not because today's workers are immigrants or because some of them don't have papers but because agriculture has always managed to side-step the labor rules that are imposed upon other industries. When the federal minimum-wage law was enacted, in 1938, farmworkers were excluded from its provisions, and remained so for nearly thirty years. Even today, farmworkers, unlike other hourly workers, are denied the right to overtime pay. In many states, they're excluded from workers' compensation and unemployment benefits. Farmworkers receive no medical insurance or sick leave, and are denied the right to organize. Germino said, "There's no other industry in America where employers have as much power over their employees."

Five of South Florida's six recent slavery cases involve workers picking tomatoes or citrus. Taco Bell buys millions of pounds of tomatoes each year through local packing companies. According to Jonathan Blum, vice-president for public relations of YUM, the parent of Taco Bell, the company does not divulge the names of its suppliers, and has refused requests from the coalition for help in negotiating with local growers for better pay and conditions. "It's a labor dispute between a company that's unrelated to Taco Bell and its workers," Blum told me. "We don't believe it's our place to get involved in another company's labor dispute involving its employees." As for the relation between slavery in South Florida and his company's chalupas, Blum said, "My gosh, I'm sorry, it's heinous, but I don't think it has anything to do with us."

40   Citrus-industry representatives similarly maintain that because they don't own or operate the groves the problem of slavery is not their responsibility. A spokesperson for Tropicana, one of whose largest suppliers employed the Ramoses, assured me, "We do our very best to make sure our growers operate at the highest ethical standards. If labor abuses came to our attention, we would terminate our contract with that grower." When I asked her if that had ever occurred, she checked and reported back that, as it happened, no contract had ever been terminated.

The State Department estimates that every year smugglers bring into this country illegally some fifty thousand women and children, either involuntarily or under false pretenses. In 2000, the department, alarmed by the increase in human trafficking, worked with allies in Congress to pass the Trafficking Victims Protection Act. Essentially, it proposed a federal felony charge for involuntary servitude, updating the Thirteenth Amendment's prohibition of slavery to take into account the forms of debt peonage and psychological coercion that characterize modern slavery. Early drafts of the bill provided a prison sentence for any person who profits, "knowing, or having reason to know," that a worker will be subject to involuntary servitude. According to people involved in the process, by the time the bill left Congress the provisions regarding "knowing, or having reason to know" had been stripped, largely at the insistence of Senator Orrin Hatch, of Utah, who threatened to hold up the bill in committee indefinitely. As a result, the penalties for involuntary servitude apply virtually only to labor contractors—the lowest rung of employers in the long chain that brings produce from the field to the table.

In one of the most vicious operations uncovered thus far by the coalition, Miguel Flores, of La Belle, Florida, and Sebastian Gomez, of Immokalee, were arrested seven years ago on charges of extortion and slavery. Flores, a contractor, controlled hundreds of workers in agricultural camps between Florida and North Carolina, and charged his laborers exorbitant prices for food, insuring continued indebtedness. Workers were forced to work six days a week, netting at most fifteen dollars a day. According to one Flores victim, female camp residents were raped, and gunfire was often used by guards to keep order. Flores warned his workers that if they ever spoke about their experiences he would cut out their tongues. The coalition, however, located a dozen witnesses, and, working with Michael Baron and other officials, encouraged them to testify. Flores and Gomez are now spending fifteen years in a federal prison.

In April of 1998, Rogerio Cadena and fifteen others, including several relatives, were charged with smuggling twenty women and girls, some as young as fourteen, into the United States from Mexico with promises of jobs in housekeeping, landscaping, and child care. The women were made to pay a smuggling fee of more than two thousand dollars each and held in sexual slavery in trailer-home brothels in South Florida and the Carolinas.

Federal officials said the brothels' clients were usually agricultural workers, who were charged twenty dollars by the brothel operators, or *ticketeros*. The women were required to perform between fifteen and twenty-five sexual acts per day, and received three dollars for each one. The women were told that they would be free to go once they paid off their debts, but those debts never seemed to decrease. "At the end of the night, I turned in the condom wrappers," one woman testified in a Senate hearing. "Each wrapper represented a supposed deduction from my smuggling fee. We tried to keep our own records, but the bosses destroyed them. We were never sure what we owed."

Beatings and threats of reprisals against their families in Mexico were used to keep the women in line. Several who attempted to escape were hunted down and returned to the brothels, and were punished with rape and further confinement. Victims who became pregnant were forced to have abortions and to return to work within weeks; the cost of the abortion was added to their debt. Although six of Cadena's accomplices pleaded guilty in the case, nine others managed to run away and slip back across the border. The victims were worried about the risks of testifying until Julia Gabriel, a witness in the Flores case who later became a coalition member, met with them and urged them to stand up for themselves.

According to Leon Rodriguez, a former prosecutor with the Justice Department's Civil Rights Division who helped prosecute the Flores case, the number of women in sexual-slavery rings around the country is not in the hundreds but in the thousands. "You can't just look at these as isolated labor violations or sex crimes," he said. "What you get with agriculture is a pattern of exploitation that can be understood only as a system of human-rights abuses."

The Coalition of Immokalee Workers initially learned about the Ramoses' slavery operation through its worker network. Germino recalled, "We had this one woman who sells cassettes out of her van, a peddler. She came into the office out of the blue and said, 'You guys really need to go look at what's going on up there in Lake Placid.' This is like in '99 or something. She left a number. Eventually, we called her, but her number was out of order. Then we heard something from a van driver." *Servicios de transporte* serve the migrant community throughout the country; tickets are sold primarily through grocery and drygoods stores that cater to workers. According to Germino, the van driver, a coalition member, told her, "They've got some deal going on up there in Lake Placid, where it's pretty out of control. They're buying and selling people, and people aren't free to leave."

In May of 2000, an Immokalee *servicio* owner named Jose Martinez was called to make a pickup at El Mercadito, a Mexican store on Highway 27 in Lake Placid. There was nothing unusual about the call; the citrus season was ending, and pickers were heading north to work elsewhere. At approximately 11:30 P.M., however, while Martinez's drivers and four vanloads of workers were preparing to leave, two pickup trucks pulled up. Six or seven armed men jumped out and began to attack the drivers. While one group of attackers held the forty or so passengers at gunpoint and smashed the vans' windows, others demanded to know who the boss was. When they found Martinez, several attackers surrounded him and pistol-whipped him with a Llama .38, splitting his forehead open. When Martinez tried to call 911 on his cell phone, his assailants kicked the phone from his hand and continued beating him until he collapsed in the dust, unconscious, his face and shirt covered with blood. During the melee, the passengers fled. One of them called the police. Another called the coalition.

Germino and Benitez arrived around midnight. At least three of the attackers had managed to escape, but police had arrested Juan and Ramiro Ramos, along with a cousin, Jose Luis Ramos, who had a gun. Germino recalls that one of the cops at the crime scene shook his head, saying, "It's the same guys who did this three years ago. Only last time they killed the guy."

The coalition learned that Ramiro Ramos had been questioned by the Highland County sheriff's office about the 1997 murder of Ariosto Roblero, a van driver who had been shot in the head, execution style, next to his vehicle, in circumstances strikingly similar to the attack on Martinez. A subsequent search of Ramos's house by federal agents and local police had produced an arsenal of weapons not normally associated with labor management, including a Savage 7-mm. rifle, an AK-47, a semi-automatic rifle, a Browning 9-mm. semi-automatic pistol, and a Remington 700 7-mm. mag. rifle. In the end, however, no charges were brought, and the murder of Roblero was never solved.

To the coalition, the attacks on van drivers were a strong indication of involuntary servitude. "These incidents are like a canary in a coal mine," Germino said. "Cutting off people's escape routes is the same as locking them behind a fence or holding guns to their heads. There's no difference." Local prosecutors were less alarmed. A state assault charge against the Ramoses was plea-bargained to a year's probation and restitution for Martinez's damaged vans and cell phone.

When the coalition presented its suspicions about the Ramoses to the Justice Department's Civil Rights Division, however, the initial response was tepid. According to a Justice Department official, the case was hampered partly by procedural issues: since the state had already charged the Ramoses with assault, investigation and prosecution by the Feds could raise double-jeopardy issues. A case simply couldn't be built yet—especially since there were no witnesses.

To find out more about the Ramoses' operation, a nineteen-year-old Guatemalan coalition member named Romeo Ramirez volunteered to go undercover. He approached the Ramoses, asked for a job, and worked for them, observing firsthand the conditions in the fields and at La Piñita, where Mario Sanchez, Adan Ortiz, and Rafael Solis Hernandez were being held against their will.

What Ramirez reported confirmed the rumors of involuntary servitude, and on Palm Sunday, 2001, several coalition members visited the workers at La Piñita and asked about their situation: Did they know that in America even debtors can work anywhere they wish? Were they free to come and go as they pleased? Open conversation was impossible, because of the guards, but a worker whispered to Germino, "We're not free here. We can't go anywhere we want because we're not free to leave." Germino slipped him a card with the coalition's phone number.

55   The following Saturday, Hernandez sneaked out of the barracks to the Kash n' Karry and called the coalition. An escape plan was set for later that evening. Around midday, though, Nino showed up at La Piñita in a rage. A worker had escaped the night before. Nino swore and shouted at the remaining workers that if anyone else left he would hunt them down and kill them.

For the three friends, it was too late to change their plan. Ortiz recalled his feelings about entrusting his safety to the strangers who had promised to help him. "We were shivering," he said. "We were shaking. Because we thought maybe they are his people, too, and they might kill us. But then we thought, Oh, well. If we're going to die anyway, better to die trying to escape." As a final precaution, Ortiz tucked a pair of scissors into his boots. Then the three men went into the yard outside the barracks, trying to act as if they were simply passing the time.

Around sunset, a white Mercury Grand Marquis with tinted windows pulled off Highway 27, a short distance from La Piñita. Lucas Benitez emerged and raised the hood, as if checking an overheated radiator. From the balcony of a nearby hotel, Asbed and Germino signalled that the coast was clear.

Ortiz, Sanchez, and Hernandez sat on a railroad tie at the camp's edge, near the highway, debating what they were about to do. Then, leaving all their belongings, including their Mexican documents, behind, they walked slowly toward the roadside. As they neared the Grand Marquis, they suddenly began sprinting, and jumped into the back seat as Benitez slammed the hood closed, got behind the wheel, and gunned the car down the road.

The passengers kept their heads out of view until they were twenty miles away.

Now that witnesses were available, the government finally became involved. Two days after the escape, F.B.I. agents interviewed the freed workers. The Ramoses, along with their cousin Jose Luis, were arrested and eventually charged with conspiracy, extortion, and possession of firearms.

The Ramos trial took place in the U.S. District Court for the 60 Southern District of Florida, in Fort Pierce, a hundred miles up the coast from Miami, and lasted three weeks. Of the three attorneys defending the Ramoses, the lead strategist was Joaquin Perez, a handsome Miami Cuban in his fifties with thoughtful eyes, a full head of lightly gelled black hair, and a flair for stylish suits. Perez, who has represented Carlos Castano, the head of the Colombian paramilitaries, spends most of his time defending high-level drug cases. He told me that he wouldn't make as much money representing Ramiro Ramos as he normally made, but he found the case engaging anyway. "I mean, slavery—it's exciting, right? It's sort of sensational."

Perez's defense argument was simple: Florida agriculture is an unsavory world. Why should the Ramoses be the only ones on the stand? What about the companies that hired them? The case would never even have come to trial, he said, if not for the Feds' need to seem proactive, the coalition's desire to make a name for itself, and the pickers' desperation for working papers, which they would receive in return for testifying.

The prosecution presented testimony from Department of Labor and Social Security Administration employees confirming that, of six hundred and eighty Social Security numbers used by the Ramoses for payroll, only ten were legitimate. Jose Martinez, the van-service owner, described being pistol-whipped by the Ramoses the night of the van attack—use of a deadly weapon and interference with interstate commerce. Ortiz, Hernandez, and Sanchez testified that they had been held and forced to work against their will.

Toward the end of the defense's case, Perez called Jack Mendiburo to the stand. Mendiburo, a tall, stalwart man, is the safety, labor, and environmental-compliance manager for Consolidated Citrus, one of Tropicana's largest suppliers. The Ramoses had worked for the company for years.

Perez asked Mendiburo to describe how pickers were paid. Mendiburo explained that checks were made out to the workers themselves, but only after passing through an account held by the Ramoses. The Ramoses, however, were legally and technically unable to access the account. Nevertheless, Mendiburo emphasized that his company was not the employer of the pickers. When Perez asked to what extent the company felt responsible for the workers, Mendiburo answered that Consolidated was reluctant even to use terms like "co-employer" when referring to its relationship with orange pickers. "It would bring to our company certain dynamics that we do not want."

65   In a sidebar, the defense approached the bench and asked the judge, K. Michael Moore, to dismiss the charges, on the ground that the prosecution of the Ramoses was selective and arbitrary. Perez asked, "Do you not think for one moment, you know, that the growers don't know what's going on? . . . Everyone knows that somebody has to buffer them."

The Judge answered, "That's the way the whole system works. I'm not defending it. You come up with proof of that, and maybe you can talk to the U.S. Attorney's office about it and expose the whole system for what it's about."

After a day and a half of deliberation, the jury found the Ramoses guilty. On November 20th, Juan and Ramiro were sentenced to twelve years; their cousin Jose Luis was sentenced to ten. At the sentencing, Judge Moore, without excusing the Ramoses' actions, gently admonished the prosecutors not to devote the lion's share of their resources to the "occasional case that we see from time to time that this case represents" but, rather, to recognize that "others at a higher level of the fruit picking industry seem complicit in one way or another with how these activities occur."

Since leaving the Ramoses' employ, Ortiz, Hernandez, and Sanchez have worked in Georgia, South Carolina, Missouri, Indiana, and Kentucky. Today, they live together in Florida, in a working-class neighborhood lined with palm trees and live oaks, sharing a tidy one-bedroom apartment with no phone. Inside the doorway are several pairs of cowboy boots, polished and standing in a row. A lime-green stuffed dog sits on top of the TV, between the rabbit ears. In the corner are a set of keyboards and a guitar. On the stove are pots and pans filled with Mexican, Chinese, and Italian food, the result of a foray into international cuisine.

Ortiz, Hernandez, and Sanchez work in a furniture warehouse. (They received papers allowing them to work in the United States for at least another year in exchange for coöperating with the Ramos prosecution.) Ortiz says that he likes his job. He has learned to drive a forklift, which he enjoys, and his bosses never tell him to run or hurry up. "I work like a normal person, and they treat me like a normal person." He works from two in the afternoon until eleven or midnight, and is earning enough to call home frequently and send money to his family to buy food and medicine for his son, who has leukemia.

Hanging from a mirror is a commemorative I.D. pass that Ortiz wore at a recent march with the Coalition of Immokalee Workers. He's been to several protests, including a recent road trip to Taco Bell headquarters, in Irvine, California. "I get to talk to people who've been through what we went through," he said of the coalition marchers. "You know, thank God. Because if they hadn't done anything we wouldn't be free right now, and we wouldn't be here." Ortiz, Sanchez, and Hernandez hope to become more involved with the coalition, but how they'll do so depends on money and work opportunities. Most likely, they'll follow the summer watermelon harvest through Florida, Georgia, and Missouri, then return to Florida.

The men are reluctant to talk about the Ramoses, fearing that it might be taken as a provocation. Hernandez said, "You know, I'm a pretty cocky guy. I like to joke around a lot. But I'm scared. I'm still having nightmares about guys coming after me with machetes and stuff."

Ortiz said, "When you're in the kind of situation we were in, you feel like the world has ended. And once you're back here on the outside—it's hard to explain. We feel a little strange still, because when you get out of something like this you feel a little nervous, a little mixed up. Everything's different now. Just imagine if you were reborn. That's what it's like."

For Discussion and Writing

1. Bowe notes that tomato pickers are paid "as little as forty cents per bucket," and calculates that to earn fifty dollars a day a "picker must harvest two tons of tomatoes, or a hundred and twenty-five buckets." The author also gives concrete details about picking oranges and grapefruits. In what ways are such figures and details effective in this essay?

2. "All these factors combine to create, in South Florida, what a Justice Department official calls 'ground zero for modern slavery.'" What are the major factors referred to? How do they work together to create "ground zero"?

3. Bowe reports that the labor contractor Nino "didn't make anyone sign a contract." What kept the workers on the job? On payday, what deductions were made from a worker's paycheck? Check figures for current poverty-level income in the United States. How do these figures compare with agricultural workers' salaries?

4. What specific link does Bowe make between modern slavery and labor rules in America? What links does he make between workers and corporations like MinuteMaid and Pepsico? How would you characterize his tone in making such links? That is, does he sound judgmental, angry, free of affect?

5. One lawyer defending a client accused of crimes in connection with labor contracting said the growers know what's going on, the everyone knows "somebody has to buffer them." What is his point? Whom did Judge Moore seem to refer to when he noted that "others at a higher level" were complicit in crimes against workers?

6. What do you make of the fact that most of the workers come from Mexico and Central America? What links this fact with their exploitation? Who else might do the actual picking of oranges, tomatoes, and other crops?

Reading, Research, and Writing

1. Former President Gerald Ford wrote, in an August 1999 op-ed *New York Times* piece, "Of all the triumphs that have marked this as America's century—breathtaking advances in science and technology, the democratization of wealth and dispersal of political power in ways hardly imaginable in 1899—none is more inspiring, if incomplete, than our pursuit of racial justice." He was defending this pursuit in the context of the recent affirmative action dispute at the University of Michigan. Research this case and survey media responses of all sorts to the controversy (see, e.g., Greg Winter, "After Ruling, 3 Universities Maintain Diversity in Admissions" April 13, 2003 *New York Times*). Determine the essential features of the Michigan admissions process in 2003 as well, like the fact that the school uses almost a dozen factors in admitting students. Find out what these are. Try to decide whether and how U.M.'s affirmative action program served the "pursuit of racial justice."

2. John Bowe writes about immigrant workers who suffer outside the protection of the law. They are generally outside the sympathy of many

Americans as well, even though these same Americans often benefit from their cheap labor. Do some research into the odyssey of such workers as they seek employment in our midst. Also, look into the writing and behavior of anti-immigrant groups. In particular, read about Operation Ranch Rescue and its efforts to police our border with Mexico. What fears drive these unofficial "police"? Who are they? When have they clashed with actual officials? Write a paper that explores the world of "illegals" and the responses to them.

3. Some observers of our culture suggest that racism is largely a thing of the past, that racial tensions have all but vanished. Write a paper that assesses this claim. You might begin by designing a survey that asks fellow students about their views on race in America. You can then research under the heading of "hate crimes and race," and gather a dozen or so stories from the press. You can do this on LexisNexis as well as through Google. Analyze the stories, paying attention to the racial composition of victims and their assailants, the level of violence, and apparent motives behind the crimes. What do such incidents suggest about race in America? Are there certain organizations teaching young people about race, and what are these people teaching? Who, if anyone, is working to combat racism and hate crimes? What tactics do these people use? If you need ideas in this regard, visit http://www.splcenter.org or the PBS site at http://www.pbs.org/niot/. These and similar sites offer ideas you can evaluate.

4. Hate crimes against Arab Americans rose sharply after 9/11. Look into assaults against Muslims and Middle Eastern Americans in general in the last several years, and examine media portrayal of Arabs and Arab Americans. Search online and in your library's databases for articles about violence against Middle Eastern Americans after 9/11. Write an essay that explores the relationship between violence and stereotypes. Be wary of simply linking these causally. The key word here is "explore."

5. In the recent book *White-Washing Race: The Myth of a Color-Blind Society*, by Michael Brown et al., the authors refer to some studies that show recent and continuing discrimination in hiring practices throughout our culture. Employers, they report, often prefer to hire whites because they simply assume black workers are less qualified, and that customers just prefer white employees. Do a little research on discrimination in hiring practices. Look for an example that especially interests you, such as the lawsuit against Abercrombie and Fitch that alleges the retailer tried to "hire white," to maintain a certain "look" that is, in fact, white. In your writing, explore the ways that subtle or covert discrimination works in a particular part of our culture such as housing, employment, or health care.

Algranati, Melissa. "Being an Other," from *Becoming American, Becoming Ethnic College Students Explore their Roots*, edited by Thomas Dublin.

Angelou, Maya. "Graduation," from *I Know Why the Caged Bird Sings* by Maya Angelou. Copyright © 1969 and renewed 1997 by Maya Angelou. Used by permission of Random House, Inc.

Begley, Sharon. "Three is Not Enough," from *Newsweek* (Feb. 13, 1995). Copyright © Newsweek Inc. All rights reserved. Reprinted by permission.

Beinart, Peter. "Blind Spot," reprinted by permission of *The New Republic*. Copyright © 2003, The New Republic, LLC.

Bowe, John. "Nobodies," reprinted by permission of author.

Chapa, Julie. "The Don Juan Syndrome," reprinted by permission from Hispanic Publishing Group.

Chow, Claire S. "Ethnicity and Identity: Creating a Sense of Self," from *Leaving Deep Water* by Claire S. Chow. Copyright © 1998 by Claire S. Chow. Used by permission of Dutton, a division of Penguin Group (USA) Inc.

Churchill, Ward. "Crimes Against Humanity," reprinted with permission of the author.

Cofer, Judith Ortiz. "The Myth of the Latin Woman: I Just Met a Girl Named Maria," from *The Latin Deli: Prose and Poetry* by Judith Ortiz Cofer (University of Georgia Press, 1993). Reprinted by permission.

Courtney, Brian A. "Freedom From Choice" (1995), reprinted by permission of author.

DeMott, Benjamin. "Put on a Happy Face: Masking the Differences Between Black and White," from Harper's Magazine. Copyright © 1995 by *Harper's Magazine* (Sept. 1995). All rights reserved. Reproduced from the September issue by special permission.

Herbert, Bob. "Voting While Black," from the *New York Times* (Aug. 20, 2004). Reprinted by permission of the New York Times.

Hongo, Garrett. "Fraternity," from *Volcano: A Memoir of Hawaii* by Garrett Hongo. Copyright © 1995 by Garrett Hongo. Used by permission of Alfred A. Knopf, a division of Random House, Inc.

hooks, bell. "Baby," from *Bone Black* by bell hooks (pages 22–24). Copyright © 1996 by Gloria Watkins. Reprinted by permission of Henry Holt and Company, LLC.

Houston, Jeanne Wakatsuki. "Living in Two Cultures," from *Beyond Manzanar* by Jeanne Wakatsuki Houston. Permission granted by author.

Lamberth, John. "Driving While Black," reprinted by permission of author.

Le, C. N. "The Model Minority Image," reprinted by permission of author.

Marshall, Burke, and Nicholas deB. Katzenbach. "Not Color Blind: Just Blind," from the *New York Times*. Reprinted by permission.

Miya-Jervis, Lisa. "My Jewish Nose," from *Body Outlaws: Rewriting the Rules of Beauty and Body Image*, edited by Ophira Edut. Copyright © 1998, 2000, 2003 by Lisa Jervis. Reprinted by permission of Seal Press.

Mukherjee, Bharati. "American Dreamer," originally published in *Mother Jones*. Copyright © 1997 by Bharati Mukherjee. Reprinted by permission of author.

Muwakkil, Salim. "Real Minority, Media Majority," from *In These Times* (Jun. 28, 1998). Reprinted by permission of In These Times.

Nga, Tiana Thi Thanh. "Long March from Wong to Woo: Asians in Hollywood," from *Cineaste Magazine* (Dec. 1995). Copyright 1995 by *Cineaste Magazine*. Reproduced with permission of the author via Copyright Clearance Center.

Noda, Keysaya E. "Growing Up Asian in America," from *Making Waves*, by Asian Women United of California. Published by Beacon Press. Reprinted by permission of author.

Sawaquat, Lewis (Johnson). "For My Indian Daughter," reprinted by permission of author.

Shaheen, Jack. "Hollywood Targets Arab and Muslim Americans Since Sept. 11," reprinted by permission of the author.

Soto, Gary. "Like Mexicans," from *The Effects of Knut Hamsun on a Fresno Boy: Recollections and Short Essays* by Gary Soto. Copyright © 1983, 1988, 2000 by Gary Soto. Reprinted by permission of Persea Books Inc. (New York).

Stein, Eleanor. "Construction of an Enemy," reprinted by permission of Monthly Review Foundation. Copyright © 2003 by MR Press.

Tan, Amy. "Mother's English," originally presented as a speech at the California Association of Teachers of English, 1990 Conference. Copyright © 1990 by Amy Tan. Reprinted by permission of the author and the Sandra Dijkstra Literary Agency.